"Smith tackles one of the most significant causes of damaged souls in many churches: the lack of transparency and how to overcome it. He brings a pastor's heart and wisdom to bear using Scriptures and scholarship to help us uncover the excuses we use to avoid being vulnerable. And he provides practical help on how to foster a spirit of loving acceptance within the Christian community. This is how to apply Gospel grace through humility. This is Biblical transparency."

Brian Godawa—Hollywood screenwriter, *To End All Wars*; best-selling fiction author, *Chronicles of the Nephilim*; and author of the classic cultural text *Hollywood Worldviews*

"*Transparency* addresses a universal human virtue that everybody cares about but nobody talks about—except to complain at its absence. Yet transparency lies at the heart of the gospel and remains one of the most pertinent indicators of church health. Smith handles the topic with remarkable thoroughness, piercing insight, sage counsel, and, especially, appropriate transparency."

Peter Krol, President of DiscipleMakers campus ministry and author of the Knowable Word blog and the book *Knowable Word: Helping Ordinary People Learn to Study the Bible*

"A timely book on a topic that is vital to the emotional and spiritual health of each believer—and of the church overall. Smith does a masterful job of unmasking the reasons why Christians tend to avoid transparency in the church. He then offers a vision for transparency as it should be between believers. I plan to recommend this book to clients and use it as a focus of study in my adult Sunday school class."

David Rising, Ed.D.—Licensed Psychologist

"A remarkable five-star book. It draws together the wisdom of a vast array of writers and teachers from a Biblical worldview on the many facets of transparency. Smith's generous use of Scriptural examples adds to his drawing from so many wise teachers. For myself, I found it a great encouragement, and as a psychotherapist, a resource I would like many of my counselees to benefit from. A marvelous resource for individual edification and a tremendous resource for group study."

Timothy A. Bryant, Ph.D.—Licensed Marriage and Family Therapist

KYLE & BRIAN —

THOUGHT YOU MIGHT ENJOY THIS, EVEN THOUGH I KNOW YOU DON'T HAVE A PROBLEM W/ THIS! WE VALUE OUR LONG FRIENDSHIP!

Joe

TRANSPARENCY

A Cure for Hypocrisy in the Modern Church

Joseph W. Smith III

FIRST EDITION

Cover design by Patrick Newman
Author photo by Cassie Blair

Library of Congress Cataloging-In-Publication Data has been applied for.
ISBN: 1721849106
ISBN-13: 978 1721849109

for my sons,

who helped me understand

the importance of this issue

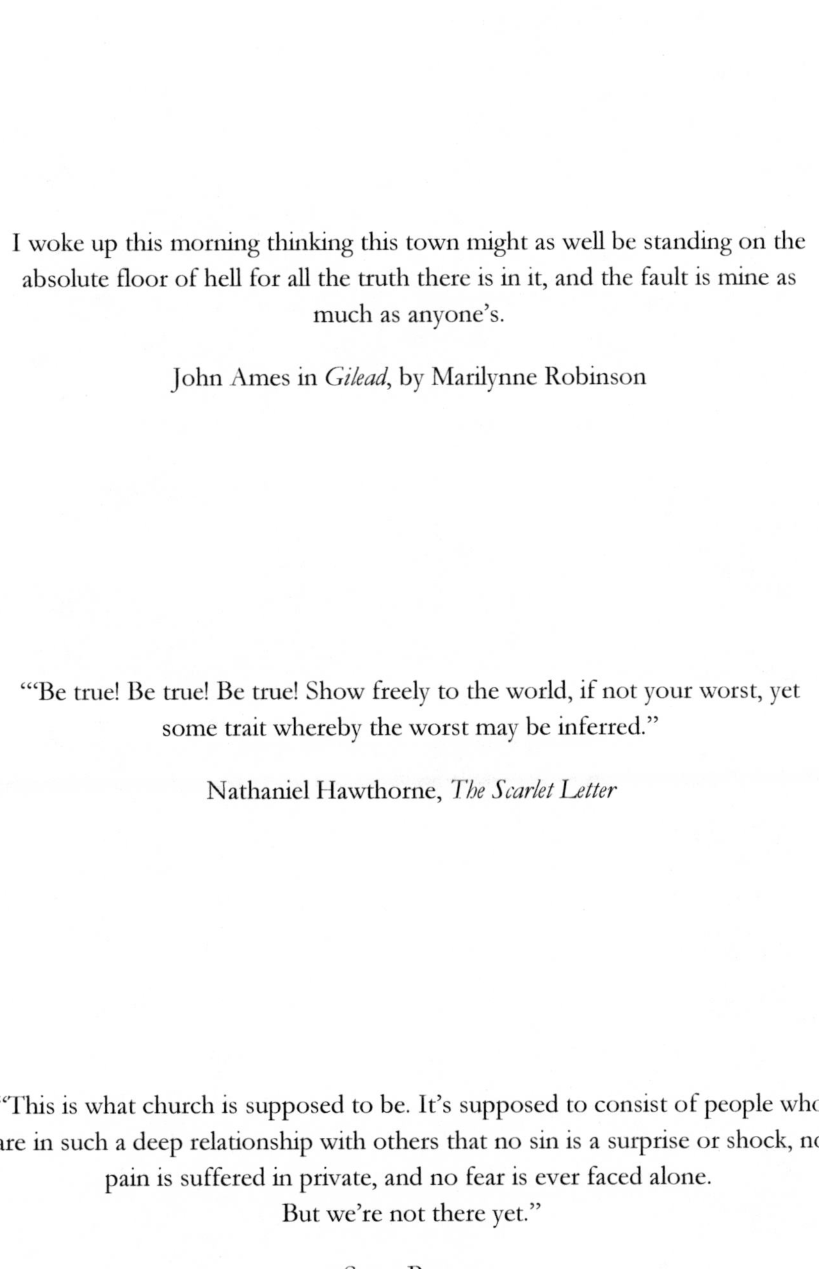

I woke up this morning thinking this town might as well be standing on the absolute floor of hell for all the truth there is in it, and the fault is mine as much as anyone's.

John Ames in *Gilead*, by Marilynne Robinson

"'Be true! Be true! Be true! Show freely to the world, if not your worst, yet some trait whereby the worst may be inferred."

Nathaniel Hawthorne, *The Scarlet Letter*

"This is what church is supposed to be. It's supposed to consist of people who are in such a deep relationship with others that no sin is a surprise or shock, no pain is suffered in private, and no fear is ever faced alone.
But we're not there yet."

Steve Brown

CONTENTS

INTRODUCTION

"If We Say We Have No Sin"

The Situation As It Is

In the mid-1980s, I was part of a tiny lunchtime Bible study in Manhattan—a mere four souls who had met through a random encounter on the subway. At one memorable session, only two of us had managed to get away from work. After we'd finished discussing our Scripture passage for the day, Ken said to me, very hesitantly, "Can I ask you a question? Why is it that you three guys seem to have it so together spiritually? I mean, I feel like I'm the only one who struggles all the time. . . ."

Somewhat taken aback, I responded, "I thought it was *you* three who had it all together!"

Imagine our feelings at that moment—a blend of surprise, chagrin, and relief, undergirded with quiet joy at having stumbled onto what can only be described as true fellowship. And yet . . . don't you find that these moments of blissful communion are rare in church life?

Indeed, as I was preparing this book, a Christian coworker asked what it was about. I answered, "Transparency—especially in church. You know, being open about our struggles and sins—not turning on the 'church button' and pretending everything is OK when it isn't.'"

"Oh," he said. "So it's a work of fiction!"

Whenever I recount this quip, its pointed humor is apparent even to those with little interest in church or the Bible. Everyone seems to know that the evangelical world has a little problem with honesty. And in truth, that is hardly a "little" problem.

In case you still need convincing, here's a more telling anecdote:

Some time ago, my wife and I learned that a local Christian woman was struggling with loneliness and a perceived inability to fit in. We asked her out to dinner in hopes of at least making a connection and understanding where she was at. Since we did not know her well, we avoided personal questions during the meal; we just wanted to get to know her, and try to open up lines of communication. After a pleasant dinner and plenty of chit-chat, I asked if there was anything in her life we could be praying about. She swiftly answered, "No!"—with a palpable note of panic that told us this question was, quite simply, off limits.

A short time later, she attempted suicide.

I don't mean to suggest that an answer from her, and subsequent prayers on our part, would have made all her unhappiness vanish; but it certainly couldn't have hurt! Yet among fellow churchgoers, we consistently refuse to open up about our deepest pains, sins, weaknesses, and struggles; and—like my wife and me at that meal—we don't do much courageous probing in that direction either. Perhaps this young lady would have been more willing to share if my wife and I had at least tried to ask about some of the deeper things going on in her life—or if we had discussed more of our own struggles and distresses. It's a vicious cycle: No one asks because no one tells; and no one tells because no one asks. So we all skulk around thinking, "I must be the only one who's such a mess; and if that's the case, there's no way on earth I'm going to tell anyone the truth."

Dietrich Bonhoeffer pinpoints the problem in his book *Life Together*: "The pious fellowship permits no one to be a sinner. So everybody must conceal his sin from himself and from the fellowship. . . . The final breakthrough to fellowship does not occur, because, though they have fellowship with one another as believers and as devout people, they do not have fellowship as the undevout, as sinners."[1]

If the church is going to function as a true community, as a family—as a healthy, interdependent body of the sort Paul describes in 1 Corinthians 12—then we simply must take off the mask, drop the act, and let others see what's really going on in our lives. We must have "fellowship as sinners." Only then will move toward fuller sanctification, real intimacy, and the glory of God—who longs for us to love and depend upon one another in Christ.

OPENNESS IN THREE PARTS

As I began to feel more and more convicted about the lack of transparency in church life—about how widespread this problem is, and how imperative it is to fix it—I decided to teach an adult Sunday school class on the topic. With the help of my thoughtful fellow-believers in that weekly class, I began to formulate a three-part approach—the same structure that is now reflected in the book you are holding.

The first thing to consider would be why we aren't transparent: fears about what others will think; the desire to come across as cool, polished, and perfect; and the deep-seated sense of self-preservation—along with various cultural influences. School, for instance—with its long-lasting mandate to fit in . . . or else! And of course the media, whose onslaught of idealized images and stories makes us want to conceal ourselves beneath a similarly shallow patina.

Part Two lays out the *reasons* to cultivate transparency: the proper functioning of Christ's body, in which every part needs and works with every other part—even the "weaker" and "unpresentable" ones! (1 Cor. 12:21-26); the greater power to conquer sin that comes when we confess to others and seek their support; the biblical need to be ever aware of our weakness and helplessness; the genuine intimacy that is fostered when others know us deeply; and the blessed restfulness of no longer having to pretend.

Part Three puts the rubber to the road, showing first how to move toward transparency by accepting what God says about us: that we really are desperately sinful, and that he loves us anyway—with an undying affection. This final section then lays out what transparency actually looks like, citing dozens of Bible passages that urge confession while also examining the many Bible figures who demonstrate openness—people like Moses, David, Job, Peter, Paul, Jesus, and even God himself. This section finishes with material on how to exhort and challenge others, on how to praise and encourage them in a biblically open manner, and on how to respond with Christ-like love when fellow-believers are transparent with us.

By the time I finished my considerable research for these transparency classes, I realized that: A) I had still not found a single book that covered all this material; and B) I had more than enough notes to write one of my own. Such a book would condense the best of what we had covered: hundreds of Bible passages; numerous insights from folks who attended those sessions; and copious research in works by such authors as Ed Welch, Larry Crabb, and Brene Brown

Other writers have diagnosed this problem as well.

In *TrueFaced*, Bill Thrall, Bruce McNicol, and John Lynch offer this telling diagnosis:

> We believe that if others could spend a moment inside us they would be disgusted by what they discover. We're appalled because we have already discovered it. And we are deeply afraid that they will discover the truth about us. So we pretend to be someone we are not. . . . We hide, position, strive, perfect our self-effort, and polish our image. . . . We look very impressive—we have learned to package our techniques well—but our self-effort keeps us self-centered & immature. . . . We are all performers, but

> because of sin we've lost confidence that we will always please our audience, and so we put on a mask. As an unintended result, no one, not even the people I love, ever get to see my true face.[2]

In her insightful book *Extravagant Grace*, Barbara Duguid writes, "Few people, and perhaps especially few pastors, are willing or able to open up their lives and hearts for public exposure and scrutiny. Most of us prefer to hide our sin and weakness instead of revealing ourselves and experiencing shame and humiliation. As a result, our churches have become places where we perform well for others and speak far more about our victories than our struggles. In consequence, many Christians wrestle with the agony of sinful failure in isolation and desperation."[3]

And as Henry Cloud notes, "It is interesting to compare a legalistic church with a good AA group. In the church, it is culturally unacceptable to have problems; that is being called sinful. In the AA group, it is culturally unacceptable to be perfect; that is called denial. In one setting people look better but get worse, and in the other, they look worse but get better."[4] So I ask you: Which kind of setting should the church be?

John's first letter points us to the answer: "If we say we have no sin, we deceive ourselves, and the truth is not in us. If we confess our sins, he is faithful and just to forgive us our sins and to cleanse us from all unrighteousness. If we say we have not sinned, we make him a liar, and his word is not in us" (1 John 1:8-10). Indeed, this famed passage is best read not in isolation—as it usually is—but rather in the context of John's earlier comments in verses 6 and 7: "If we say we have fellowship with him while we walk in darkness, we lie and do not practice the truth. But if we walk in the light, as he is in the light, we have fellowship with one another. . . ." In other words, genuine fellowship depends on genuine openness—on leaving the "darkness" and "walking in the light," which is then explained by the apostle's insistence in verses 8-10 that we give up pretense and frankly confess our sins. *This* is how we achieve biblical "fellowship with one another": by walking in the light of transparent honesty about our sins.

DEPENDING ON OTHERS

By now, you've probably noticed my fondness for quoting other writers—a tendency you will also find elsewhere in the book; I hope this can be seen not as laziness on my part, but rather as an admission of my own weakness and inadequacy—as transparency, if you will. Though I feel a throbbing urgency to promulgate this message, I have no degree in counseling or psychology, and I have often looked to others for expertise and guidance. The strengths I do bring to the project include a fair personal penchant for openness, along with 25 years of work as an officer in a small church—during which time I have seen everything from gossip, burglary, and premarital sex to addiction, arson, adultery, and murder.

In my experience, it has often been all but impossible for church leaders to work appropriately with people ensnared in such sins, because a thick cloak of shame and opacity keeps getting in the way. We may even be aware of dire sin in the lives of our members, yet somehow still cannot get those involved to actually talk about it with us. At times, it's been clear that if there had been openness at an earlier stage, these problems might have been intercepted long before they became so intractable and explosive. In one memorable case, the session was paying one of its regular visits to a church family and sensed much unspoken trouble in their lives; yet despite some pointed probing on our part, we simply could not get them to tell us what was going on. Before long, such catastrophic disaster broke out in that family that I cannot even describe it to you here, for fear of perpetuating their shame and heartbreak.

Another more recent crisis involved a suicide attempt by the husband and father in one of our church's families. Yet in spite of the glaring need in this case, it has been difficult to even broach the suicide attempt with him, to get permission to talk about it publicly, or to convince the suffering and embarrassed man to return to church. As the elders struggled to help this precious family, his spouse told us frankly, "We always assumed we weren't the kind of family this happened to—you know, this only happens to 'other people.'" The fact is, we are *all* the kind of people this happens to. If we think we aren't, we may be feeding the very mindset that leads to suicide: *No one else struggles like I do; I have to keep performing at this level; if others seem to admire me a lot, why do I feel so alone? I'm such a hypocrite!*

I'll wager nearly every reader can relate to one of those statements. And just to flesh this out further, let me ask another question: Have you ever arrived at church feeling so miserable—so depressed, such a failure, such an absolute *train wreck*—that it was all you could do not to fly out the door, rush straight home, and dive back into bed? My own long experience in church life suggests that this is not unusual—and that the subconscious thinking process goes something like this: "I just can't face these people again and put on a smile when I'm completely falling apart inside."

What is going on here? Shouldn't church be the very place we can come when we feel this way? Shouldn't it be a refuge from the performance-based atmosphere that pervades so much of our daily lives? I remember praying together with my fellow church-leaders as we prepared to meet with the grieving husband and family discussed above. In the memorable words of one elder, we begged God to bring us all to the point where the church felt more like a hospital, rather than just one more option for entertainment and social life. Ironically, it seems like much of our so-called "fellowship" is undercut by an urgent desire to *prevent* those around us from finding out what's really going on in our lives; at times, we have an even harder time opening up in church than we do with coworkers and friends.

As James says in another context, "My brothers, these things ought not to be so" (3:10). If anything, church should be the one place where we can let down our guard, drop out of the exhausting rat race, and connect on a deep and enduring level with others who share the same struggles—the same sins, traumas, fears, weaknesses, and needs.

If I could presume a bit further on your patience, I'd like to conclude this introduction with one final excerpt—from the only book I found with my topic in its title. Published in 1979 and long out of print, it's called *The Trauma of Transparency*. Author J. Grant Howard imagines the following spiritual dynamic:

"God says: 'Talk to Me and to each other, openly and honestly, and you will find wisdom and peace.' The church often says: 'Listen to the pastor and the Sunday School teacher and you will find wisdom and peace.' People are looking for instant insight and short cuts to serenity. Peace without openness. Wisdom without honesty. Fellowship without intimacy. There isn't any."[5]

Every sane Christian wants true fellowship—love, support, intimacy, community. Ironically, we think we can get this by *covering up* our sins so that people will love us more. But—like the Apostle John in his first letter—Howard is insisting that the opposite is true. *There is no peace, fellowship, or intimacy without openness.* If you want those things, you are going to have to open up to others. That is why I wrote this book, and that is why you should read it.

OPEN FOR DISCUSSION

1. Have you ever felt like everybody else had it all together, and you were the only one with such extreme struggles, temptations, and sins? Do you sometimes feel this way at church? What effect does this have on your interactions with fellow Christians?

2. Have you ever tried to draw someone else out in terms of *their* struggles? What kind of response did you get?

3. Have you ever sensed that someone was holding back from sharing with you their weaknesses and sins? What did that feel like?

4. What do you think Bonhoeffer means when he says that we "do not have fellowship as the undevout, as sinners"? Is he right? Is this something we *should* have?

5. For us in the 21st century, is church more like a hospital for recovery, or a venue for entertainment and socializing? Which should it be, and why?

6. What might it feel like in church if we were more open with one another about our sins and struggles?

7. In preparation for the next five chapters in Part One, discuss *why* we seem to have such a hard time opening up to one another. What are some of the personal and cultural factors that contribute to this?

Part One

WHY WE AREN'T TRANSPARENT

CHAPTER ONE

"Great Fear of the Multitude"

Worrying About What Others Think

How much time do you spend worrying about what other people think of you?

How much of your daily energy goes into pondering what someone else said—how he or she responded to your Facebook post—or even the way they looked at you—as you try to determine whether there was something negative or critical in the interaction? How often do you beat around the bush, *not* saying what you really feel, just because you fear giving offense and having someone else upset with you?

If you're like me, honest answers to these questions can be embarrassing.

As Christians, we are supposed to focus principally on God's love—and on his high standards of holiness that make other people's opinions seem relatively unimportant. Sadly, most of us are better at this in theory than in reality. Instead, our lives continue to manifest all the awful symptoms of excessive man-fearing: anxiety, posturing, lying, exaggerating, back-pedaling, people-pleasing, reading too much into what someone says, despair or even panic over criticism or insults. . . . Need I say more?

Let's face it: We all worry far too much what other people think, and this is the main reason we find it hard to be transparent.

On the most basic level, we fear that if we show others what we're really like—our temptations, our idols, our emotional ups and downs, our failure to put God first, and the many other sins that flow from this—then they simply won't like us anymore. They may even be appalled and draw away. In a startling but little-known Bible verse that could serve as the keystone for this chapter, Job alludes to the fear of rejection that makes us want to cover over our sins. Insisting that he did not fall prey to this temptation, the famed sufferer nonetheless suggests that the tendency is both powerful and widespread. Job says he has not "concealed my transgressions as others do by hiding my iniquity in my bosom, because I stood in great fear of the multitude, and the contempt of families terrified me, so that I kept silence . . ." (Job 31:33-34).

The fact is that most of us "keep silence" about our sins because we have a seemingly bottomless need to be liked and admired by as many folks as possible—preferably everyone in our circle of acquaintance. As writer and counselor Ed Welch puts it, "People are our cherished idols. We worship them, hoping they will take care of us, hoping they will give us what we feel we need"—as though they could somehow take the place of God himself, and bestow upon us the blessing and benediction we so badly want in our lives.[1]

And we believe that we can receive this blessing from other people *only* if we come across as virtually perfect in their eyes. So we work not merely to look good, but also to hide our blemishes, mistakes, weaknesses, and sins. And there goes transparency—replaced instead by an exhausting battle to put up a good front, lest anyone should discover what we're really like inside.

One key problem here is that this desire is indeed "bottomless": It's the famous "God-shaped hole" we're trying to fill; and as such, this need can be met only by what is infinite, eternal, and unchanging—not by something fluid and capricious like other people's feelings. If you pursue this treacherous path to self-fulfillment, you will never find final satisfaction.

Indeed, as Donald Miller points out, most of us are seeking to impress people, when what we actually need is love—not just shallow esteem or veneration. Miller, who made a splash with his 2003 book *Blue Like Jazz*, suggests that we have confused admiration—which is fleeting, often superficial, and generally not very nourishing or satisfying—for the deep, long-lasting love that is what we really desire at the deepest level.[2] And sadly, you cannot foster love by constantly striving to prove what an amazing person you are. People may look up to you in that case—for a while anyway—but such relationships lack true connection, empathy, closeness; they are worldly and soulless. As we shall see in our later study of intimacy (Chapter Eight), an authentic emotional bond can actually be nurtured *only* in the context of sharing our most desperate needs and failures; without this, we will never be sure the person actually loves us for who we are—that they will go on loving us even when we aren't especially cool or admirable. A love that hinges on being impressive is not love, and it will not sustain you through a life of sin and struggle.

CONTROL ISSUES

Yet another problem with striving so hard to please and impress is that we cannot really control what other people think of us. In fact, our desperation for esteem flips this on its head, so that others wind up controlling us instead. In his appropriately titled book *When People Are Big and God Is Small*, Ed Welch encourages us to self-diagnose just how much we are controlled by the fear of others: Did you ever tell "little white lies" or "cover-ups" where you are not technically lying but just stretching the truth? These, Welch says, are "usually ways to make ourselves look better before other people"—and they also indicate control: The desperate and perhaps unspoken desire for others' good opinion has caused us to sin by mishandling the truth. In the same way, if others make you angry, depressed, or drive you nuts, "they are probably the controlling center of your life." Indeed, even if you avoid people, you are still controlled by them. Even hermits, after all, are still dominated by the fear of man! "What's the greater risk?" asks another writer. "Letting go of what people think or letting go of how I feel, what I believe, and who I am?"[3]

When we yield control to others, we become what they want us to be, rather than who we really are. Again, transparency goes out the window—along with authenticity. And probably peace of mind as well. As a famous comedian once said, "I don't know the key to success, but the key to failure is trying to please everybody."

SHAME ON US

In examining our apparently ubiquitous efforts to look great before others, several writers identify *shame* as an important factor. One such author is Brene Brown, who puts it this way in her aptly titled book *I Thought It Was Just Me*: "Shame often prevents us from presenting our real selves to the people around us—it sabotages our efforts to be authentic. How can we be genuine when we are desperately trying to manage and control how others perceive us? How can we be honest with people about our beliefs and, at the same time, tell them what we think they want to hear?"

Like Welch, Brown urges us to scrutinize our own motivations by finding what she calls "shame triggers." To do so, you simply complete these statements:

> "I want to be perceived as ______________________________ and ______________________________. I do NOT want to be perceived as ______________________________ and ______________________________."[4]

Now ask yourself this: Do the items you put in the first two blanks reflect the actual truth about you, or is this just what you want people to think? Similarly, looking at the items in the second set of blanks: Do these perhaps—just perhaps—point to some aspect of your *real* personality? Maybe one you don't want others to know about? If so, your "shame triggers" are working only to cover up the real you and serving largely to prevent transparency. Going back to Miller's insight: Do you want people to love the real you, or the fake one? If your answer is the latter, you are going to spend a lot of time feeling tired and alone.

THE BIBLE TELLS ME "NO"

Proverbs 29:25 calls the fear of man "a snare," and the rest of Scripture proves that we modern-day believers aren't alone in our struggle with this problem. King Saul got caught in it when he spared the Amalekites rather than killing them as God commanded. Saul's reason for this lapse? "I feared the people and obeyed their voice" (1 Sam. 15:24). While not directly linked to a lack of transparency, this surely shows a sinful anxiety about what others think—like those Christ condemned because "they loved the glory that comes from man more than the glory that comes from God" (John 12:43; see also 5:44).

Peter is another Bible figure who had a long battle with the fear of man. After Christ's arrest, the apostle repeatedly denied even knowing his master—twice to a mere servant girl and a third time by invoking curses on himself (Mark 14:66-71). Christ, of course, later forgave Peter for this sin, tenderly restoring him to a position of leadership among the disciples (John 21:15-19); yet even later in life Peter still seemed far too worried about others' opinions—withdrawing from his usual fellowship with the Gentiles upon the arrival of legalistic Jews who would've frowned on such fraternizing. In the words of his fellow apostle Paul, Peter was "fearing the circumcision party," and Paul publicly condemned this "hypocrisy" because it "was not in step with the truth of the gospel" (Gal. 2:11-14).

It's well worth noting, however, that Peter may eventually have put this fear to rest—as indicated by these telling verses in a letter that likely postdates his contretemps with Paul: "Now who is there to harm you if you are zealous for what is good? But even if you should suffer for righteousness' sake, you will be blessed. Have no fear of them, nor be troubled, but in your hearts honor Christ the Lord as holy . . ." (1 Peter 3:13-15).[5]

In any case, Paul was in a solid position to expose Peter's pretense, because he himself was never unduly influenced by what others thought. Just a few verses before his passage lambasting Peter, Paul asks rhetorically, "Am I now seeking the approval of man, or of God? Or am I trying to please man? If I were still trying to please man, I would not be a servant of Christ" (Gal. 1:10). The implication here is that service to Christ almost automatically requires us to stop pursuing the approval of other people. As Paul told the Corinthian church that had belittled his ministry, "With me it is a very small thing that I should be judged by you or by any human court" (1 Cor. 4:3); this helpful verse affirms that Paul did not *entirely* disregard others' judgments of him; for him, it was "a thing"—but a very small one!

And Paul had certainly experienced his share of shame in the world. The Corinthian disparagement of his gifts is something most of us would take quite personally. Of him, they said that "his bodily presence is weak, and his speech is of no account" (2 Cor. 10:10); and the list of abuses and ignominies to which he'd been subjected is staggering: a stoning, three beatings with rods, and five separate sets of 39 lashes each—plus a host of dangers and difficulties including starvation, sleeplessness, exposure, and three different shipwrecks (2 Cor. 11:23-28). The great apostle sums this up in a passages that highlights the public nature of the shame he and his colleagues bore: "I think that God has exhibited us apostles as last of all, . . . like the scum of the world, the refuse of all things" (1 Cor. 4:9-12).

Yet in Philippians, Paul can declare his confident disregard and even contempt for this type of worldly shame. As Ed Welch puts it, "He said that worldly shame has lost its power. It's dead. It's stupid. It might sting a bit here and there, but in Christ we have immunity to worldly rejection."[6] Unlike us, Paul was neither rattled nor unstrung by the shame that had beset him—by the public abuse and imprisonment; by the forfeiture of his considerable status as a Pharisee; by the contempt others showed toward him and his ministry. All this was unimportant, powerless, rubbish—not worth worrying about in comparison to knowing Christ and being "found in him" (3:7-10).

And of course, in his experience of "worldly rejection," Paul was merely following in the footsteps of his lord and savior. Next time you're feeling embarrassed or angry that someone disagreed with your latest Facebook post, consider the rejection and contempt that was heaped upon Christ throughout his ministry: dismissed by the entire religious establishment of his own day (Luke 9:22); accused of being a drunkard and a glutton (Matt. 11:19)—and of having a demon (John 8:48, 52); forsaken by his disciples when he was arrested (Mark 14:50), and then—far worse—by the Father himself as he hung on the cross, soiled and besmirched with the sins of the whole world (Mark 15:34). And let's not forget the public horror of crucifixion—one of the most ignominious forms of execution ever conceived. No wonder the writer of Hebrews reminds us of the "reproach" Christ bore in this desolate locale that was "outside the camp" (13:13). And yet even while being mocked and taunted on the cross, Jesus thought of his detractors rather than himself; he was more concerned about their shame than he was about his own.[7]

Indeed, the writer of Hebrews confirms the attitude taken by our Lord, "who for the joy that was set before him endured the cross, despising the shame . . ." (Heb. 12:2).

> *Despise* in this context can be translated as "to look down upon," "to be unconcerned about," or "to give no mind to." . . . Jesus absorbed the shame of the world and despised it by never being controlled by it. Jesus looked down on shame. He attributed no worth or influence to it; he treated it as an outcast. Shame never distracted him from his mission. It was simply not an issue. With the Son of God, certain of his connection with the Father, shame for the first time in history had lost its power.[8]

A key factor in this attitude toward shame is the phrase "certain of his connection with the Father." If we too could confidently grasp the fullness of our relationship with God, and live out of the joyful assurance it provides, then the opinions and detractions of others would bother us a lot less.

THE GLORY AND THE GOSPEL

Paradoxically, this healing connection with God is two-pronged; it involves not only basking in the peace we have with our heavenly father, but also a recognition of his power and glory, which is infinitely greater—and frankly *scarier*—than any person or power we will ever meet in this world. Jesus himself expressed this quite starkly: "Do not fear those who kill the body but cannot kill the soul. Rather fear him who can destroy both soul and body in hell" (Matt. 10:28; see also Luke 12:4-5). This well-known verse pinpoints not only the problem, but also the solution: Proper fear of God drives out the fear of man.

"In the fear of the Lord one has strong confidence," says the writer of Proverbs (14:26); in other words, "a vital and appropriate fear of God invariably delivers us from ungodly inhibitions and paralyzing fears."[9] Citing Isaiah's life-changing personal encounter with a God who is "holy, holy, holy" (Isa. 6:1-7), Ed Welch asserts that "when you spend time in the throne room of God, it puts things in perspective. The opinions of others are less important, and even our opinions of ourselves seem less important."[10] Consider, for example, how Moses' fear of the Egyptians and Jacob's fear of his wronged older brother were both cured by encounters with a holy and overpowering God (Exodus 3; Genesis 32).

Among other things, putting God front and center will help quench the ridiculous tendency we have to be more concerned about shame than we are about the sin itself.[11] If, for example, you had a loud, nasty, public quarrel with another churchgoer right in the sanctuary after worship, wouldn't you be more concerned that others had *seen* your fight than you were about the sinfulness of the fight itself? If your spouse catches you in a lie, aren't you more bummed about being caught than about the fact that you lied? As Christians serving a holy Lord, how can we feel worse about the loss of face than we do about actually breaking God's law?

Rather than worrying so much about how others react to our sins, our main concern should be the offense against God; we must emulate King David, who, after sins of adultery and murder that obviously affected those around him, could nonetheless tell God, "Against you, you only, have I sinned and done what is evil in your sight . . ." (Ps. 51:4).

As Welch says in *Shame Interrupted*, the worst deception of shame "is its insistence that our problem is with the judgments of people more than the judgment of God. . . . Our problem is not the judgments of people. Our true problem is before God. Once we are secure in that relationship, disdain from mere humans loses its sting."[12]

The simple fact is that we urgently need to believe what God says about us:

First, we are "desperately sick": "None is righteous, no, not one. . . . All have sinned and fall short of the glory of God" (Jer. 17:9; Rom. 3:10, 23). If we really believed this, deep in our hearts, and could fully understand how we have offended and rebelled against an infinitely holy God, we would have far less trouble admitting this rebellion and failure to mere fellow-sinners.

Second, we need to believe that these sins have been erased, expunged, canceled out—cast into a pit of oblivion through the sacrifice of Christ (Rom. 3:23-25; see also Ps. 103:12 and Col. 2:14). As a result, we now stand before God as holy children, fully accepted by a loving father who will never criticize or belittle us the way others often do (see Col. 1:22; Rom. 8:1). "Once shame has been addressed in your relationship with God, it won't constantly attack you in your human relationships."[13]

I myself have always been a hopeless people-pleaser. I can hardly stand to have someone else express irritation, anger, or even disagreement with me—and the knowledge that this disapproval is lurking in the background can make it almost impossible for me to concentrate on my regular daily tasks. Only recently have I begun to experience some success in allowing this icy discomfort to melt under the blazing light of God's steadfast and unquenchable love. When someone else is upset with me, I simply ask myself how that can bother me when the only One whose opinion matters has already given assurance of his intimate and undying affection: "He will rejoice over you with gladness; he will quiet you by his love; he will exult over you with loud singing" (Zeph. 3:17). During those times when I manage some comprehension of this overwhelming love, I can almost *welcome* the scorn of the world—for it drives me to the arms of the one who will never judge, reproach, or condemn. There is incredible rest and peace to be found here, even in the midst of the conflicts, disagreements, and misunderstandings that plague our merely human relationships. Others may misunderstand me, criticize me, hate me—but God never does!

Of course, as we navigate through these ideas, we are straying from our key topic here—why we *aren't* transparent—and starting to flesh out the "how to" of Part Three in this book. And indeed, this simple notion of *believing the gospel* is so vital that I will later devote an entire chapter to it. But I just could not finish out this crucial first salvo on transparency without at least pointing us in the right direction—the glory of God's good news, in which we are loved with such fullness, grace, and permanence that the world's valuation starts to look like a mere plastic trinket beside a necklace of 24-carat gold and diamonds.

It seems to me that we've become a nation of hypersensitive victims, so touchy and so easily offended that we not only fear to speak the truth about ourselves—but also, we likewise fear to hear it from others, or to speak frankly about what we see in their lives. We spend countless hours with e-mails, texts, and social media pussyfooting around some important issue just so others don't think we've been the least bit critical about them—because they fear our rejection, and we fear theirs.

Brothers and sisters, we must allow God to set us free from these fears. Only by coming face to face with the infinite, transcendent love and holiness of God will we be able to risk transparency. For "perfect love casts out fear" (1 John 4:18).

OPEN FOR DISCUSSION

1. Start by filling in the blanks in Brene Brown's self-assessment under the subhead "Shame on Us" above. Why do you suppose you desire to be viewed (or not viewed) in this way?

2. Are you afraid of what people think about you? What exactly is it that you fear? In other words, what will actually *happen* if someone else thinks poorly of you?

3. Why are you afraid of that happening? Be honest: Would that really be such a catastrophe? Or might God use it to do something worthwhile in your life?

4. Describe a time when "fear of man" affected what you said or did. How might you have handled it differently?

5. Have we become a nation of oversensitive victims who are touchy and easily offended? Can you cite examples of this from your own experience?

6. Describe a proper attitude toward God. What does it mean to "fear" him, and what does it mean to actually believe in his love for us through Christ?

7. How can this sort of reverence and faith help drive out the fear of man?

CHAPTER TWO

"White-Washed Tombs"

Perfectionism

Merriam-Webster's Collegiate Dictionary defines "perfection" as "freedom from fault or defect," and "the quality or state of being saintly."

That's a good thing.

"Perfectionism," on the other hand, is defined as "a disposition to regard anything short of perfection as unacceptable."[1]

That is not a good thing.

Researcher Brene Brown expands a bit on *Webster*'s definition: Perfectionism is "the belief that if we live perfect, look perfect, and act perfect, we can minimize or avoid the pain of blame, judgment, and shame." From a biblical standpoint, perfectionism is downright deadly; for it does not merely attempt to avoid rejection, but also, it upends the gospel by seeking a self-worth based on some measurable, artificial goal. Perfectionism places our identity in deeds rather than in Christ. As Brown insists, it's a "debilitating belief system: I am what I accomplish and how well I accomplish it."[2]

Like legalism—best viewed as a psychological partner-in-crime on this issue—perfectionism takes the broad, convicting, and impossibly difficult mandates of Christian conduct and reduces them to a few simple, superficial things we actually *can* achieve. This then leaves us feeling better about ourselves—even though, in the words of Christ, we may well have "neglected the weightier matters of the law." Rather than concerning ourselves with such issues as "justice and mercy and faithfulness," we worry about how our outfit looks, about checking off items on a to-do list, about faultless attendance at work or school, a well-manicured lawn, a glowing report card, a flawless casserole. Such things can be worthy in their place, since even Jesus credited the Pharisees for a few minor things that they "ought to have done"; yet he also condemned them as "white-washed tombs, which outwardly appear beautiful, but within are full of dead people's bones and all uncleanness" (Matt. 23:23-28).

Deep in his heart, the perfectionist knows he can never wholly fulfill the law of God; so he substitutes his own easier code, thereby reducing, blocking, or even replacing the majestic commandments to love God and neighbor, and to do so with abandon—commandments whose very impossibility drives us to Christ. Thus, the perfectionist can—in the scathing words of Christ—"outwardly appear beautiful" and "righteous," when in fact he may be far more hypocritical and lawless than even those who don't have any external appearance of perfection. Concerning this replacement of God's standard with a human one, Christ was blisteringly sarcastic: "You have a fine way of rejecting the commandment of God in order to establish your tradition!" (Mark 7:9).

Paul understood the grave spiritual danger of substituting outward accomplishments for genuine reliance on Christ. In Philippians 3:4-6, he recounts his own considerable human qualifications, including ritual circumcision, membership in the tribe of Benjamin, and law-keeping so zealous that the apostle at one point calls himself "blameless." But in subsequent verses, Paul rejects these merely external achievements as "rubbish" compared with knowing Jesus and being "found in him, not having a righteousness of my own that comes from the law, but that which comes through faith in Christ . . ." (Phil. 3:7-9). Paul is saying that if his peerless credentials become ends in themselves, serving as a basis for smug self-righteousness and complacency, then they actually count as a "loss."[3] Truly, whatever eclipses our fellowship with Christ and our entire dependence on him—no matter how lovely, admirable, or worthwhile in itself—must be rejected as a liability, not an asset. This includes perfection.

Perfectionism is dangerous not merely for the false impression it gives to others, but for the delusion it foments in our own hearts that we have somehow fully attained righteousness—and that we have done so on our own, without any apparent need for Christ. In this way, even those aspects of our lives that seem to be good can actually distance us from God, and blind us to our sin.

As we saw in the introduction, Scripture is insistent on this matter: "If we say we have no sin, we deceive ourselves, and the truth is not in us." Note well John's use of the present tense here, which indicates ongoing sin in every Christian's life; furthermore, by using "we," the aged and saintly apostle includes even himself among those who must confess their sins and thereby "walk in the light" (1 John 1:6-9).[4]

There is no such thing as perfection in this life, and those who think they've reached it are not being transparent with others, with themselves, or with God.

THE "TWENTY-TON SHIELD"

If the fear of man is a snare—as we saw in Chapter One—then perfectionism is an even more insidious trap. For those who struggle with these psychological shackles, I commend Brene Brown's *The Gifts of Imperfection* (Hazelden, 2010). In this slim but exceptionally helpful volume, Brown lays out several reasons why perfectionism is truly a hopeless endeavor.

In one sense, the perfectionistic mindset is all about perception; "we want to be perceived as perfect." Yet this is unrealistic and elusive, since we cannot control the way others perceive us; many of those "others" are struggling with the same thing, and they're liable to see right through our artifice anyway. In my own life, as I juggle and dance to convince others that I have it altogether—that everyone should like and admire me because I have no major flaws—it has often become painfully apparent that I'm not fooling anyone.

Except maybe myself.

On a more basic level, "Perfectionism is self-destructive simply because there is no such thing as perfect. Perfection is an unattainable goal."[5] It's almost laughable for the perfectionist to substitute his or her own "easier" standard of righteousness—let's say, a well-dressed child or a spotless kitchen—because even these simple goals are impossible to keep at all times. And when they are, perfectionists still know that sanctification consists of much more than merely arranging bookshelves in precise alphabetical order. Deep in their hearts, they know they aren't perfect in any real sense. So the perfectionist strives for flawlessness in his or her life, but inevitably finds it out of reach. And then, feelings of guilt, hypocrisy, and failure set in, along with a concomitant desire to hide. In this way, the quest for perfection backfires: Rather than eliminating our sense of inadequacy, perfectionism can actually make it worse.

Those who insist on being perfect are in for a life of perpetual disappointment.

Research shows that perfectionism actually impedes success. In fact, it can often lead to depression, anxiety, substance-abuse, addiction, and paralysis. "Perfectionism is a twenty-ton shield that we lug around thinking it will protect us when, in fact, it's the thing that's really preventing us from taking flight."[6] For me personally, its most pernicious effect has been a tendency to constrict or narrow my life. I will often work hard to avoid risks; steer clear of messy relationships; keep a firm stranglehold on my time and resources; avoid endeavors where I don't have much control over how things will turn out—because all of these things might allow some of that dreaded imperfection into my life! In so doing, I miss out on experiences that can be among life's most rewarding, even if they are sometimes accompanied by risk, pain, and failure. A "perfect" life like mine is necessarily going to be a small one—for if I insist on avoiding failure, I'm likely to miss out on success as well.

As I see it now in retrospect, this tendency toward constriction has affected others around me as well. Neither of my children is currently following Christ, and while there are no doubt many factors involved in this, one key contributor may have been my staunch refusal to ask messy questions as they were getting older. During their years of adolescence, I could sense that they were having doubts and questions, and perhaps even that they were continuing to attend church and to tolerate family devotions only from a dutiful sense of pleasing Mom and Dad. I should have been asking about their true feelings, allowing them to debate and struggle, walking with them into areas of discomfort, anger, and rebellion. But that was outside the bounds of my flawless little life. And so instead, I lazily allowed us to go on looking like a "perfect" church family—the result being that now we are not. Because in fact, we never were.

Taking this a step further, I'm sure my children were able to sense this subconscious commitment to avoid "mess," which made them in turn less willing to share; in fact, they may have felt that I would like or love them less if I knew what they were really struggling with. For as Brown points out, one corollary to a perfectionistic mindset is this: When you work too hard to sidestep imperfections in yourself—to pretend they aren't there—then you won't be able to accept them in others, either.[7]

May Christ forgive us if our perfectionistic attitudes are forcing others to feel that they cannot be honest with us.

THE PERFECT SOLUTION

Like so much else in the Christian life, getting unshackled from perfectionism starts with Scripture.

Jesus himself illuminates the proper perspective in the Matthew 23 passage we examined above: He condemns contemporary religious leaders for their reductionistic approach to the faith. Straining unclean bugs from their food and tithing tiny garden crops such as mint and dill, they meanwhile neglect "the weightier matters of the law" (vs. 23). In other words, they are majoring in minors. True, the minors can be important ("these you ought to have done," Christ tells them in vs. 24)—yet they cannot become *more* important. They certainly cannot—as seems to have been the case here—simply replace such major issues such as "justice and mercy and faithfulness" (vs. 23). Perfectionists don't like these issues because they are bigger, messier, hard to attain, and impossible to measure; unlike washing the car or trimming the bushes, you can never be "done" with these and sit back admiring your flawless work. But God wants us to get our hands dirty—and in some sense, to keep them that way. One of my favorite verses is a lesser-known adage from Proverbs 14: "Where there are no oxen, the manger is clean, but abundant crops come by the strength of the ox" (vs. 4). Translation: Some things are big and messy, but you can't live a truly productive life without a little dirt. This trade-off is simply a no-brainer.

The habitual perfectionist is going to have to start meditating on some of these big, messy things—things like justice, kindness, and walking humbly with God (Mic. 6:8); like loving God will all your heart, soul, mind, and body—and loving your neighbor as yourself (Luke 10:27); like dying daily to yourself, taking up the cross, and following Christ (Matt. 16:24-25; Luke 9:23-24). But if you're a perfectionist like me, you react to these commands with near panic, feeling like you have to do them perfectly—just like everything else in your life.

In this case, our first challenge is to consider the infinitely precious blood of Christ, and commit to believing that it covers our daily failures in these areas just as it covers all the past sins committed before we even became Christians. Go ahead: Boldly strive, struggle, and fail: fail to be kind, even though you tried; fail to walk humbly, fail to love God with all your heart, fail to love others as yourself. You can work diligently and still fail at these things because there is "now no condemnation for those who are in Christ Jesus" (Rom. 8:1).

The second and perhaps even tougher challenge involves the Greek word that is so often translated as "perfect" throughout the New Testament.

In such passages as Romans 12:2, Philippians 3:12, and James 1:4, the word "perfect"—appearing in the English Standard Version—literally means "having reached its end, complete."[8] In many other places, this Greek term—*teleios* or *teleioo*—is rendered by the word "mature," as in "grown up" or "adult." In Ephesians 4:13, for example, the church works to produce "mature manhood" in its members (see also 1 Cor. 2:6, 14:20, and Col. 1:28). Or take the famous passage from Hebrews 5 and 6, where "solid food is for the mature" and believers are urged to "go on to maturity" by advancing beyond teachings aimed at children (5:13-6:1); in all these passages, this same Greek term clearly means something other than the impeccable spotlessness implied by the English word "perfect." Even the very convicting words of Matthew 5:48 ("be perfect, as your heavenly Father is perfect") do not imply a state of absolute sinlessness, but rather, they urge us not to be satisfied with the sort of half-baked, merely external righteousness of Pharisees or unbelievers—the kind of thing that is elsewhere condemned in the very same passage. No, what Christ speaks of here is something beyond mere moral perfection: "a life totally integrated to the will of God and thus reflecting his character." (Anyone who thinks this verse might mandate total sinlessness should recall that a mere 12 verses later, Christ prescribes a prayer requesting forgiveness for sins; see Matt. 6:12.)[9]

Greek scholar Reinier Schippers explains that in such contexts, this "perfect" term "applies to the man who has reached maturity, the grown man who has come of age. . . ." The New Testament "does not speak of an ideal ethical perfection which is to be realized by degrees"; rather, it describes "the undivided wholeness of a person in his behaviour" (see

James 1:4 and Matthew 19:21).[10] Our arrival at this state is assured by the grace and faithfulness of God (see, for instance, Phil. 1:6, 1 Thess. 5:23-24, Rom. 8:29-30, and especially Heb. 10:14). But . . . the ongoing struggle is an admission that we are not there yet. Perhaps the ability to hold these ideas in tension is part of what it means to be "mature."

Consider Philippians 3, where Paul firmly asserts that he is not perfect (v. 12), but then later uses the same word to describe his present state—"mature," in verse 15. As J. Grant Howard observes, this very contrast between perfection and imperfection—the notion that he isn't there yet—is what actually enables Paul to grow in sanctification and thus move *toward* perfection.[11]

In other words, the antidote to perfectionism is not to abandon all desire for excellence. It is rather to set out on a journey to maturity. It should focus not on some cushy external state we'll soon reach, basking in self-satisfaction and the admiration of others. Rather, it is a process of perpetually getting better, predicated on never quite being all the way there.

Admittedly, it is difficult to imagine striving for improvement while simultaneously accepting imperfection in daily life. Perfectionists like me, who prefer to think in clear-cut categories, will have an especially difficult time with this notion: Can I really "always strive but never arrive"?

And the perplexity is only sharpened when we consider that true perfection *is* urgently required in many areas of human endeavor. Clearly, we both want and expect perfection from our dentists, our pharmacists, our surgeons, our commercial airline pilots, our nuclear power-plants—perhaps even our plumbers and mechanics. If a neurosurgeon is stressing out because the laser will induce paralysis if it's two millimeters off, no one is going to tell her or him to quit majoring in minors.

How do we resolve this?

I think the answer has something to do with humility. If the surgeon or the nuclear physicist thinks he or she has somehow arrived at perfection—that it is attainable as a permanent and perpetual state—then that person is, ironically, much less likely to be actually perfect. He's arrived, he can let his guard down—and there's an open door for the fatal mistake. By contrast, the man or woman who sees work as a quest for perfection, as an unending struggle to get it just right—the one who perhaps even fears that she or he might not get it right because perfection is so elusive—*that* is the person more likely to do the very best job. It's stressful, yes—but remember, the perfectionist is seeking an *end* to stress by arriving at a place where no failure, flaw, or disappointment is possible. The one who, on the other hand, proceeds with a God-given knowledge that he or she has failed in the past, and that failure is always an option—*that* is the person worthy of our trust: the person who pays scrupulously minute attention to even the smallest detail, because he knows that he's missed it in the past and could very well miss it again. He gets close to perfection because he frankly acknowledges his many flaws, mistakes, and weaknesses.

In the words of an oft-quoted saying: "Don't let perfection get in the way of excellence."

OPEN FOR DISCUSSION

1. Re-read the definitions of "perfectionism" at the beginning of this chapter. Are these accurate? Or is there something you want to add or change?

2. Would you describe yourself as a perfectionist? If so, how does this impact your daily life? What are some of the negative effects of trying too hard to be perfect all the time?

3. Describe a time in your life when you majorly failed—perhaps even in some public way that everyone could see. What did that feel like? How did you get past it?

4. What evidence is there that life in this world can never be perfect?

5. Considering your answers to questions 3 and 4, are there benefits to admitting failure and accepting imperfection?

6. If we need to stop "majoring in minors," then what *are* the "major" issues that we need to focus on? And if that is the case, why do we so often focus on the smaller issues? What is the solution to this imbalanced approach to serving Christ?

7. How can we resolve the tension between avoiding legalistic perfectionism (which is a bad thing) and striving to do our very best (a good thing)?

CHAPTER THREE

"Let Each One Test His Own Work"

Rivalry and Blame-Shifting

Shortly after becoming a Christian way back in the 1980s, I discovered the Old Testament book of Ecclesiastes, with its many bold statements that often seem even bolder in the New American Standard translation I loved and still rely on. One proverb stood out with special force: "I have seen that every labor and every skill which is done is the result of rivalry between a man and his neighbor" (4:4).

While the NASB is virtually the only translation to use the word "rivalry" here, even a substitution of the more common "envy" or "jealousy" still makes this a rather shocking assertion: Absolutely *everything* we do is motivated by some innate sense of competition with the rest of humanity. And doesn't this explain so much of our daily lives? Think of the constant one-upmanship and jostling for superiority; the gossip, slander, and criticism that seek to lift us up by putting others down; and, of course, the desperate need to conceal our weakness and sin, lest we yield whatever elusive high ground we seem to have gained through all our "labor and skill." Sometimes it feels all but impossible to establish any sense of identity or stability without pinpointing someone else as inferior. And often, that "someone else" is an entire group of people, in which case we may have entered the realm of racism, bigotry, or—sadly—politics. Put this together with social media, and you've got some ugly by-products indeed.

This sort of ugliness shows up clearly in the parable contrasting one Pharisee's prayer with that of a tax collector—a parable which Jesus aimed at those "who treated others with contempt." Here the Pharisee, one of the scrupulously self-righteous religious leaders in Christ's time, brazenly raises himself up by putting down the man beside him. Using the word "I" no less than five times, he thanks God that he is not like others, "or even like this tax collector"—who demonstrates a far more humble attitude in pleading for God's mercy. In the original Greek that is rendered "be merciful to me, a sinner!", the tax collector actually says "*the* sinner"—as though the poor man were seemingly unaware that anyone else (including the nearby Pharisee, for instance) could possibly be worse than he (Luke 18:9-14).[1]

Even Christ's disciples fell prey to this pharisaical jockeying for superiority. As Mark's gospel indicates, James and John once asked Jesus to seat them at his right and left hand in glory (10:35-37)—foolishly reversing their master's advice about taking the lowest seat at the table rather than "the place of honor" (Luke 14:8-11). Worse yet, both Mark and Luke recount incidents in which the disciples argued over who was greatest among them—prompting some embarrassment when Christ asked about their discussion, gently rebuking them with an admonition to adopt the lowly attitude of a servant or child (Luke 9:46-48; Mark 9:33-37).

Taking a cue from the disciples' rivalry, Dietrich Bonhoeffer insists that "no Christian community ever comes together without this thought immediately emerging as a seed of discord. . . . From the first moment when a man meets another person he is looking for a strategic position he can assume and hold over against that person. . . . It is the struggle of the natural man for self-justification. He finds it only in comparing himself with others, in condemning and judging others."[2]

The application to transparency is obvious: The insidious quest to be better, greater, and more admired—this merely exacerbates an innate tendency to cloak our many flaws and sins. It creates a vested interest in *not* letting other people see what I am really like. If they do, they might lord it over me; or worse, I might somehow lose face before a judging world, forced to admit that I am "*the*" sinner—the one who belongs at the lowest place, who must not be exalted or honored over anyone else. This vested interest, working to keep others from seeing my sins, likewise can prevent *me* from seeing my own sins as well. And when it does, transparency is impossible; I become a self-righteous Pharisee, smugly certain that I'm doing just fine, and that everybody else is the problem.

REJOICING IN THE TRUTH

Fortunately, several New Testament passages provide a solution to this dangerous mindset. In 2 Corinthians, for example, Paul inveighs against those who "measure themselves by one another and compare themselves with one another," saying they are "without understanding." He adds that he and his coworkers "will boast only with regard to the area of influence God assigned to us"—wisely suggesting that we focus on our own tasks and responsibilities, rather than looking around at others all the time (10:12-13). 1 Corinthians makes the same point: Struggling to ensure that "none of you may be puffed up in favor of one another," Paul admonishes his critics to wait until the Lord comes, when "each one will receive his commendation from God." Again, this keeps the spotlight on what is happening between God and each individual, rather than making futile, uninformed, and *unloving* comparisons. In this passage, Paul then goes on to remind his hearers that any merit or goodness they have is a gift from God, and no fit reason for feeling superior: "What do you have that you did not receive? If then you received it, why do you boast as if you did not receive it?" (4:5-7).

Likewise, in Galatians, Paul again urges us to focus on our own weaknesses rather than those of others—even when we are in the process of dealing directly with the specific sins of a fellow-believer: "Brothers, if anyone is caught is any transgression, you who are spiritual should restore him in a spirit of gentleness. Keep watch on yourself, lest you too be tempted." Indeed, after spending only one sentence on our interaction with the other person in this case, Paul then devotes another five sentences to self-examination, concluding with this strident mandate for humility: "If anyone thinks he is something, when he is nothing, he deceives himself. But let each one test his own work, and then his reason to boast will be in himself alone and not in his neighbor. For each will have to bear his own load" (6:1-5). Again we find the apostle urging us to focus on our own responsibilities—and our own weaknesses—rather than foolishly looking down on others.

Writer and pastor Tim Keller is helpful in this area, offering a somewhat different key to resolving the rivalry and competition that characterize so much social interaction. His little booklet *The Freedom of Self-Forgetfulness* paints a well-nigh blissful portrait of what it might be like to free ourselves from jealousy toward others: "Wouldn't you like to be the skater who wins the silver, and yet is thrilled about those three triple jumps that the gold medal winner did? To love it the way you love a sunrise? Just to love the fact that it was done? For it not to matter whether it was their success or your success. Not to care if they did it or you did it. You are as happy that they did it as if you had done it yourself—because you are just so happy to see it."[3] Keller admonishes us to make real the love that is so famously defined in 1 Corinthians: It is a love that "does not envy or boast," that "does not rejoice at wrongdoing, but rejoices with the truth" (1 Cor. 13:4-6)—even if that joy-inducing truth and righteousness are found outside ourselves.

We need to start thinking about others' success the way we think about our children. No parent in his right mind would be *jealous* over the achievements and successes of his own kids. Rather, we look upon them with a 1 Corinthian 13 type of love—with frank enjoyment, gratitude, and even pride; with appreciation for what God has done in their lives; with true joy for the good thing in and of itself—rather than concern about the fact that we don't have it or didn't do it. If we could bring this type of selflessness to *all* our relationships, our fellowship here on earth would begin to look more like it will in heaven—where the fact that some others have greater rewards for their earthly work will serve only to increase the widespread joy among a loving body of selfless worshipers.

POINTING THE FINGER

Blame-shifting is one especially insidious form of focusing on others' faults rather than one's own; like rivalry, it is forcefully illuminated in some key passages from Scripture.

Let's start with what is surely the gravest sin ever to befall the human race—namely, Adam and Eve's transgression in the garden. Though Adam himself had clearly been charged not to eat from the tree of the knowledge of good and evil (Gen. 2:16-17), here is his explanation for why he broke God's commandment: "The woman whom you gave to be with me, she gave me the fruit of the tree, and I ate." With the finger now pointing at her, Eve then explains, "The serpent deceived me, and I ate" (Gen. 3:12-13). Adam blames the woman, and she in turn blames the snake. By implication, Adam also suggests God is partly to blame for giving him Eve in the first place (it was "the woman whom you gave to be with me").

In Chapter One, we examined an obscure verse where Job asserts that he has not concealed his sins "as others do" (Job 31:33). Tellingly, that final phrase can also be translated "as Adam did"—pointing to Genesis 3 as a prototype for hiding one's sin. From that moment on, humanity begins to fashion a façade—a fig leaf, as it were—working to conceal transgression, shame, and failure from ourselves, from one another, and from God. And we generally do it not only by clumsily covering up, but also by pointing the finger at someone else. J. Grant Howard calls this "hiding and hurling"—and he suggests that it is the default human response to guilt and sin.[4]

Aaron also tries to squirm his way out of blame—for forging a golden idol in Exodus 32. Aaron's brother, Moses, had been on Mt. Sinai receiving detailed covenant promises and commands, and during this delay the Israelites became impatient; so Aaron told them to gather up all the gold they had, "and he received the gold from their hand and fashioned it with a graving tool and made a golden calf." Then he also built an altar, and they worshiped this false god with offerings and a celebratory feast (Ex. 32:1-6). Later confronted by his angry brother, Aaron responds, "You know the people, that they are set on evil. For they said to me, 'Make us gods who shall go before us.' . . . So I said to them, 'Let any who have gold take it off.' So they gave it to me, and I threw it into the fire, and out came this calf!" (Ex. 32:21-24).

Scripture's account of this incident in the early part of Chapter 32 devotes a single verse to the actions of the people (vs. 1) and four to those of Aaron (vss. 2-6); in all four, Aaron himself is the active agent. When it comes time to discuss this with Moses, however, Aaron pretty much reverses the ratio by focusing almost entirely on the people. And then, when his narrative reaches the actual construction of the calf, Aaron simply departs from the original account: He portrays himself as uninvolved—the calf just came out all by itself! In other words, Aaron downplays his own role by implicating "the people" more heavily than himself, and then by citing some sort of bizarre providence by which the calf simply popped out with no human assistance whatsoever. So too, when we are forced to recount our sins, "we conveniently leave out the details that might put us in a bad light. And to the extent that we admit that we did anything wrong at all, we want to tell our side of the story, so people will know that what we did wasn't as bad as it looked."[5]

Ed Welch posits that our modern-day culture of pandemic victimization has exacerbated this self-deluding tendency. "It is always the other person's fault. You are responsible for my actions. . . . We are saying that other people control our behavior." He goes on to assert that this too classifies itself as the same "fear of man" we examined in Chapter One. "If we are chronic victims, we are shifting the locus of control from ourselves to others."[6]

So ask yourself if you also have this tendency to place the blame for sin elsewhere—perhaps on your circumstances, your family, your church; on politicians, parents, genetics, or some other convenient scapegoat that prevents you from being transparent with yourself and others about where the responsibility actually lies.

And if you find such a tendency in yourself, contrast it with the attitude of truly repentant sinners in Scripture: figures like the tax collector, calling himself the "the sinner!" (Luke 18:13); figures like the prodigal son, telling his father plainly, "I have sinned against heaven and before you. I am no longer worthy to be called your son" (Luke 15:18-19); or like King David, who tells God, in the wake of adultery and murder, "Against you, you only, have I sinned and done what is evil in your sight" (Ps. 51:4).

"The only hope for any of us is in a perfectly honest manliness to claim our sins. 'I did it, I did it,' let me say of all my wickedness. Let me refuse to listen for one moment to any voice which would make my sins less mine. It is the only honest and the only hopeful way, the only way to know and be ourselves."[7]

OPEN FOR DISCUSSION

1. Do you see evidence of rivalry in your own experience? Do you sometimes feel like you are competing with others—with friends, or perhaps with your spouse? If you are willing, discuss one specific example and how you think it affected (or still affects) the relationship.

2. Why do we have so much rivalry with others? What exactly are we trying to achieve? Whatever that thing is that we seek through rivalry—is it really worth achieving?

3. How does such rivalry contradict the gospel ethic to love God and others with complete abandon?

4. How can we fight and overcome this tendency toward rivalry?

5. Do you see evidence of blame-shifting in your own experience? Are you willing to discuss a specific time you blamed someone or

something when in fact it was your own fault? How much of the blame actually lay with you, rather than that other person or circumstance?

6. What are some negative effects of shifting blame in this manner?

7. Why do you think it is so hard to take responsibility for our sins in a frank and open manner? How do we get past this?

CHAPTER FOUR

"He Who Is in the World"

School and Cool

The popular "Cathy" comic strip once recounted an episode in which its twenty-something protagonist was invited to a high school reunion. "This is your chance," ran the invitation, "to have 600 ex-classmates stare at you and see whether you got fat and/or wound up with a loser. . . . In one fun-filled evening, we will re-create every insecurity you've spent the last 10 years trying to overcome. See you there! (Or else we'll *really* talk!)" Having read this missive aloud to a friend, Cathy remarks, "Nice to see they haven't lost the old school spirit."[1]

Like so many other "Cathy" episodes, this is funny because it's so easy to relate to; even as adults, we can all too easily recall the pain, shame, and social ostracism experienced during our teen years—and many of us are still trying to climb out from under the leaden weight of those feelings.

I think this is yet another reason we tend to hide our weaknesses, mistakes, and sins. To put it frankly, the lingering traumas from middle and high school leave us pathologically sensitive—terrified of being excluded, rejected, or left out. Those years taught us that we can pay a massive price for being different, uncool, or "less than." We don't ever want to go through *that* again! So forget about any kind of sharing or honesty that might resuscitate those ghastly memories and experiences.

Tell the truth: Can't you easily think of at least one episode from that awkward teen period when you felt so thoroughly excluded, so alone and detested by peers, that it still makes you squirm in discomfort, even after these many years? I have a friend who is 83, and she still gets a little choked up over how badly she was treated by two girlfriends roughly 70 years ago.

In my own case, I recently found on Facebook the name of a guy who had beaten me up several times in high school. Handsome, cool, strong, and popular, this upper-classman was everything I wasn't—and his ability to direct mass contempt toward me was even more painful than the blows he inflicted with feet and fists. Now, as I stared at the screen and re-experienced some of that shame, I was shocked to discover a strong desire to contact him. Where on earth did *that* come from? Perhaps I just want to see if he still hates me; perhaps I'd feel better if he didn't. Perhaps I'm trying to patch a hole, to salve an open wound, to find some of the acceptance I wanted so badly more than four decades ago. Successful, happy, and blessed with more pals than a guy could hope for, I still felt a need to undo at least some of the damage he inflicted.

(For the record, this old nemesis of mine did not have his own Facebook account, and I never did work up the courage to contact him through our mutual online friend.)

We've all heard studies showing that most of our personalities are set in place by age six—but experiences from early adolescence certainly seem to stick just as deep. Shame researcher Brene Brown tells us that in one of her studies, 85 percent of the men and women were able to recall a school incident so shaming that "it changed how they thought of themselves as learners." She also points out that during those dreaded school years, most of us learned the hard way how crucial it is to be liked, to fit in, and to meet the expectations of others.

> The lessons were often taught by shame; sometimes overtly, other times covertly. Regardless of how they happened, we can all recall experiences of feeling rejected, diminished and ridiculed. Eventually, we learned to fear these feelings. We learned how to change our behaviors, thinking and feelings to avoid feeling shame. In the process, we changed who we were and, in many instances, who we are now. . . . Being real, genuine or sincere can feel secondary to fitting in.[2]

So ask yourself how often you trim or edit "the real you" in order to fit in better with a given social group. As we shall explore more thoroughly in Chapter Seven—which addresses intimacy—this constant need to fit in is actually counterproductive. What we want is *belonging*—a sense of community and connection with other individuals; if the person who's "fitting in" is not the true you, then you still don't really belong, and you still won't feel connected.[3] Instead, you'll continue posing and putting up a front. As you did in school, you'll spend lots of time and energy worrying about your place in this group instead of resting in the sort genuine bond we all need.

Just try to recall how much peace and companionship you felt in seventh-grade study hall, or the high school locker room. Why on earth would you still want to live that way?

JOINED AT THE HIP

As many of us nonetheless persist in striving to fit in, Brown asserts that we often do so by trying to seem "cool" and somehow "above it all": "We hustle for our worthiness by slipping on the emotional and behavioral straitjacket of cool and posturing as the tragically hip and the terminally 'better than.'" She adds that trying to be cool has become "one of the most rampant forms of cynicism. *Whatever. Totally lame. So uncool. Who gives a s---?* Among some folks it's almost as if enthusiasm and engagement have become a sign of gullibility. Being too excited or invested makes you *lame*. . . . How did being perceived as cool become a driving value and what was the cost of pretending that things didn't matter?"[4]

There is something truly insidious going on in post-modern culture—something so subtle, deep-seated, and unconscious that it is very difficult to identify and describe. Somehow, when we interact with people, we like to employ a sort of knowing, jocular, world-weary sarcasm that suggests we're just too slick and cool to ever be hurt, rattled, shocked, upset, or even joyful and appreciative. We act as though the world as a whole is *supposed* to disappoint us, that we are somehow above it all, and we're just going to tough it out without ever allowing ourselves to seem seriously fazed. This attitude is so pronounced that we sometimes even pretend to be mildly bemused by the things that hurt or scare us most.

And it's not just composure we feign; no, what we also want is for everyone to know that we can handle it. Any of it. All of it. The common declaration "No problem" is a glaring emblem of this—often said at the very time when there is in fact a substantial problem. Think of it as the Bruce Willis approach to hardship: We proceed with a wink, a smirk, or a bemused groan, as if to say, "That's life," and we will move right along because we're completely in control. It's a 21st-century brand of stoicism that's somehow too hip to even admire itself for being stoic. We're so cool that nothing is cool.

And that's not cool.

I notice this in myself because, as a long-time high school teacher, it helps with discipline if nothing ever upsets me—if I remain thoroughly composed in the face of classroom chaos. Of course, a calm and level-headed approach can be invaluable in maintaining some order among jostling, hyperactive teens. The problem is that if I come across as someone who's never been hurt, who never loses his cool, never fails, never struggles, someone who's always on top of the situation—well, this is good for discipline, but perhaps not so good for morale, for a sense of true community and transparency in the classroom.

Many of these kids struggle horribly with a variety of devastating issues—bullying, abusive parents, peer pressure, academic failure, and rapidly changing bodies that simply won't cooperate with "cool"; at the risk of looking weak and admitting my many needs and failures, it might actually help my students to know that even adults are struggling, that none of us should have to cram it all down inside and pretend to cruise along on the slick, polished surface of life, looking imperturbably calm just like all the cool kids who supposedly don't have any problems.

Now apply this to church as well. Don't we spend too much of our precious fellowship time joking, chatting, and perhaps even posturing as cool, till it seems like it's in downright bad taste to mention hurts, passions, worries, temptations, and the devilish personal idols we can't seem to get free from? Indeed, as Christians, we know that idolatry is always a problem—that is, caring so much about something in this world that it begins to affect our devotion to God. But we cannot then react by caring too little, or not caring at all. Cynicism, stoicism, and being "tragically hip" do not represent a Biblical approach to life. This attitude merely subjugates and represses some of the most serious issues in our hearts—and, as we have already seen so often in this book, it also persuades others that they're all alone: If everybody else is so unflappably cool and capable, there must be something wrong with anyone who's got serious ongoing issues.

Brown links this attitude to what she calls "numbing"—a desire to *not* feel anything, and to be "above it all." She further posits convincingly that the epidemic of substance abuse we are now seeing in our culture stems partly from a widespread need to anesthetize ourselves to various issues too painful to deal with or even admit in public.[5] We actually need artificial and sometimes very dangerous help to blot out or suppress the fears, sins, wounds, and worries that everyone is too hip to confess.

Sometimes, being "cool" carries a very high price.

"I SAW IT ON TV"—OR, MAYBE NOT

For young people especially, this perennial struggle to be cool is exacerbated by the glamorous and highly polished iconography of modern pop culture: TV shows filled with beautiful faces and bodies; carefully edited and airbrushed photos on glossy magazine covers; popular big-budget action movies in which slickly clad superheroes whiz about vanquishing colossal threats to mankind and/or Planet Earth; music videos in which the latest hunk or lovely lady cavorts in fabulously expensive garb, surrounded by adoring and similarly clad members of the opposite sex.

As Brown puts it, contemporary media makes flawlessness look eminently achievable by flooding us with images that are literally edited for perfection. Looking at such images, we feel hopelessly defeated—because we are "comparing our lives, our marriages, our families, and our communities to unattainable, media-driven visions of perfection, or we're holding up our reality against our own fictional account of how great someone else has it."[6]

By now, most folks recognize the damaging effect of all this, especially on shy, fragile, or self-conscious teens. Indeed, at this particular cultural moment, it might even be objected that glitziness is less of a problem, since reality TV has taken such a prominent spot in our hearts and viewing habits. After all, don't these shows tend to emphasize all the warts, problems, and occasional sleaziness of actual people in their everyday lives? Yet in the words of my friend Niel Bech, who has worked in media for years: "When you see a reality show, it isn't."

Even these supposedly "real" and "unedited" programs are very carefully staged, rehearsed, and often re-filmed repeatedly to get exactly the desired effect. Sure, this effect sometimes makes the subject look *worse* than we do—but that then only serves to feed the fatal sense of superiority we condemned in Chapter Three; and in any case, it's still not "reality"!

In fact, pop culture has a parallel effect that is in some ways even more damaging than our initial sense that "I can never look that good." To be specific, glamorous shows like *Baywatch*, *Pretty Little Liars*, and *Gilmore Girls*; exciting shows like *Game of Thrones* and *The Walking Dead*; less glamorous "reality" TV along the lines of *Duck Dynasty* and *Hoarders*—all these convey to us, perhaps unconsciously, what Brown calls "fear of the ordinary": the sense that our humdrum lives just aren't spicy enough. We are made to feel that the run-of-the-mill, day-to-day routine is somehow insufficient—that we're missing out on all the cool, thrilling stuff that's happening on some sunlit beach, in some far-off fantasy land, in a world of high-powered detectives, or even in the down-and-dirty "reality" of some other person's volatile and supposedly more authentic life. Could it be that one further reason for our lack of transparency is a desire to make our own lives look a bit less ordinary, and more like those of the "cool" people—even if those folks, now that we're older, have moved out of the middle-school cafeteria and onto screens and magazines?

In this way, says Brown, we miss out on the rich and challenging diversity of real life—which, however "ordinary" it may seem, is actually far more satisfying than some media-driven vision of the way things are supposed to look and feel. "Our culture is quick to dismiss quiet, ordinary, hardworking men and women. In many instances, we equate *ordinary* with *boring* or, even more dangerous, *ordinary* has become synonymous with *meaningless*." Indeed, Brown insists that she learned the most about "the value of the ordinary" from interviewing people who had suffered terrible trauma, such as the loss of a child: "The memories that they held most sacred were the ordinary, everyday moments."[7] I too am convinced that on our deathbeds, it will be hardest to say goodbye not to the "big" events—awards, promotions, glorious vacations in Hawaii or the Alps—but to the priceless fabric of daily life we fail to appreciate while we pine away wishing things were more glamorous. Granted, all this doesn't have too much to do with transparency—except that in yearning for our lives to resemble the media, we abandon the restful acceptance of plain old authenticity.

THE "DISNEY DELUSION"

Related to all this is the way media approaches problem-solving.

During any given detective show, we proceed to the solution of a complicated crime in roughly 40 minutes of screen time; sit-coms can sometimes resolve a problem in 20. That, of course, is your 60- or 30-minute program minus credits and commercials. Speaking of which, during that brief prime-time window, we watch countless ads which also purport to resolve a wide array of life's difficulties. From mundane hassles like bad breath, body odor, and erectile dysfunction to more major issues like loneliness and financial insolvency, these little vignettes present swift and apparently effortless solutions in a time frame of 15, 30, or 60 seconds. Middle-agers like me have been ingesting a steady diet of these speedy solutions for five decades or more. Clearly, this is going to have a cumulative effect on our ability to admit that most difficulties in life cannot be dismissed with that kind of ease, convenience, and celerity.

On a similar note, Barbara Duguid, in her fine work *Extravagant Grace*, takes aim at what she calls "the Disney Delusion": Thanks to films like *Mulan*, *Cinderella,* and *The Little Mermaid*, "We Americans in particular live in a culture that teaches us from our youngest days in preschool that simply believing something makes it true, and that no one can stop us from reaching our dreams."[8] We would like to keep telling kids—in the words of 2016's *Finding Dory*—that "you can do whatever you put your mind to"; but there's no question that this is not literally true. Kids can't fly to the moon, buy up every single toy at Wal-Mart, or suddenly turn into the long-lost princess of some gorgeous and magical utopia. The notion that such dreams can readily be achieved (often in the space of an 85-minute movie!) could well make it harder, not easier, for them to face the fact that even simple personal problems like overeating and temper tantrums can take years to overcome—and that, in some cases, they will never be entirely eradicated in this life.

VICTORY IN WEAKNESS

The connection to transparency is important, if not immediately obvious: We have been carefully trained by media to believe that life-long problems should generally be subject to quick and simple solutions—and that if you have to spend months, years, or an entire lifetime working against certain temptations and sins, there must be something wrong with you. Yet the very things Scripture enjoins (love, faithfulness, kindness, humility)—and those things it forbids (lust, greed, malice, envy)—these are just the sort of deep-seated issues that take a lifetime to address. Think of those sins you most despise in your own life, the ones you desperately want to get free from. Aren't these the very sins you have to keep confessing over and over again? And don't you need at least one true friend who can come alongside with assurance of forgiveness, grace, and divine aid when you've committed that sin for the 491st time? How can we enlist help and support from the church as a whole, or even a few close Christians friends, if the entire culture is geared to making us feel that our worst problems can be solved with a little hard work and just the right commercial product—or saddest of all, that they can be dreamed right out of existence just because we want to be this or that very different kind of person?

To look at it another way, the contemporary church often seems saddled with a vision of "victorious Christian living" that is badly at odds with what we see in the ministry of the Apostle Paul and his letters to first-century congregations. Both Corinthian letters indicate, for instance, that Paul's work had been undermined because he was not apparently glamorous enough for some of his converts ("his bodily presence is weak, and his speech of no account"—2 Cor. 10:10). Paul, however, is perfectly content to be ordinary—for God has chosen what is "low and despised in the world" in order to "shame the strong, . . . so that no human being might boast in the presence of God" (1 Cor. 1:27-29).

These principles will certainly help us with the first of the media-generated problems we've discussed—that is, with not feeling quite as "polished" and "cool" as all those folks we see in pop culture. As Paul might put it if he were alive today, God prefers to work through people who are not really all that cool.

But what of media's implicit assertion that most of our problems can easily solved?

In his book *Why Do Christians Shoot Their Wounded?*, Dwight Carlson points to such Bible passages as 1 Thessalonians 5, where the church is full of folks who are "idle," "faint-hearted," and "weak"; he rightly observes that in this very passage, Paul commands us to be "patient" with such deep-seated personal issues. "Note that the verse gives no indication that these deficiencies will be resolved in a week, a month or a year. In many instances both the strong and the weak need to accept the reality of lifelong deficiencies, or else we fail to 'be patient with all men'"[9] (see 1 Thess. 5:14).

Paul himself surely demonstrates such patience in his Corinthian letters, where he continues to call those in Corinth "saints" and "the church of God" (2 Cor. 1:1); he compliments their "zeal," "generosity," and "readiness" (2 Cor. 9), despite the fact that the church was plagued by rampant division (1 Cor. 3), incest (1 Cor. 5), lawsuits (1 Cor. 6:1-8), and drunkenness during the Lord's supper (1 Cor. 11:21)—along with members resorting to prostitutes (1 Cor. 6:12-20) and attending pagan worship (1 Cor. 8). In spite of all this, in the very same letter that cites all these disasters, Paul can "give thanks to my God always for you because of the grace of God that was given you in Christ Jesus, that in every way you were enriched in him in all speech and knowledge, . . . so that you are not lacking in any spiritual gift . . ." (1 Cor. 1:4-7).

The 29 chapters in these two precious letters—which actually represent only part of the Corinthian correspondence, since some of it has been lost—clearly show that Paul was in it for the long haul; he is able to see God mightily at work in this precious flock, even though he had no Disney-like delusions about the terrible sins that continued to beset them. Victorious Christian living emerges not by denying sin and wishing it away, but by believing the words of the Apostle John: "He who is in you is greater than he who is in the world" (1 John 4:4).

Christ is not only greater than the world, but also sovereign over the Accuser, who daily assaults us with doubts and self-recrimination. So He will continue to work in and through your life—even if you the world rejects you; even if you're still smarting from the cruelties of American adolescence; even if you feel inadequate, uncool, ordinary, "less than"; even if your problems won't go away; even if you can't ever seem to "be all that you can be"; even if you're still battling with the same lifelong doubts and sins you first saw when you were converted many years ago.

And even if you admit all this to others.

OPEN FOR DISCUSSION

1. Recall an incident of shaming, bullying, ostracism, or rejection from your teen years. What did it feel like? Do you still suffer with a sense of injury from such incidents? Why do these hurts seem to last so long?

2. Is that sense of injury continuing to affect your daily life in any way? How can you get beyond this?

3. Re-read the material about our complex modern guise of cool, calm, capable, and tragically hip (under the subhead "Joined at the Hip" above). Do you feel this accurately describes the way some people act today? Does it ever seem to infect your own thinking? In what ways is it harmful or counterproductive?

4. Describe the "Disney delusion." Can you think of examples in modern pop culture? What are some positive aspects of encouraging kids to believe in their dreams? What are some negatives?

5. Consider your most persistent and frustrating sin-struggles. Why is it that these seem so hard to get control of? How do you deal with

it when you find yourself falling into the same sin over and over again?

6. Cite some passages or examples from the Bible in which God worked through sin or sinful people.

CHAPTER FIVE

"More Highly Than He Ought To Think"

Self-Preservation

When I began my adult Sunday school series on transparency, I asked the class to cite some factors that impede transparency. One of their first answers was "pride," which can be defined as "conceit" or "inordinate self-esteem"; synonyms include "arrogance," "disdain," and "insolence."[1] Scripture, however, sees pride principally as a rejection of God's prerogative and authority; such rebellious pride is a refusal to submit to God, to depend on him, to be subject to him—all the while bestowing upon oneself the honor and authority that is properly due to God alone.[2] For this reason, in this final chapter on why we don't open up with each other, I will concentrate not so much on pride per se, but on its root: our abominable narcissism. Not only does this highlight the true nature of pride, but also, it will emphasize the perilously positive view our culture takes on "self."

After all, we have a host of common terms featuring the word "self": "self-help," "self-starting," "self-actualization," "self-service," "self-expression," "self-reliance"—and of course, the ever-admirable "self-made man." And except for the universally reviled "selfish" and "self-centered," most "self-" compounds that come readily to mind have a positive connotation in this day and age.

But for the Christian, whose starting point is the failure of self, and whose entire life is to be lived in a state of utter dependence on Christ, most of these "self" concepts run counter to Scripture. At this point, I do not wish to present a treatise on biblical self-denial, which falls more properly in Part Three of this book—how to be transparent (see Chapter Twelve). However, I would like to point out here the danger of two driving forces in current culture, both of which make transparency difficult—namely, self-sufficiency and self-esteem.

THE MYTH OF SELF-SUFFICIENCY

In the previous chapter, we examined the modern-day attitude in which we pose as cool and capable, never fazed by crazy circumstances, always just a little "above" whatever life may throw at us. Calling this "the myth that we all have life figured out," Ed Welch writes: "We spend too much time concealing our neediness. We need to stop hiding. Being needy is our basic condition."[3]

In a recent blog entry, pastor, author, and speaker Paul David Tripp expands on this problem:

> It's hard to admit your need for help. It's hard to admit that there are things you don't know and don't understand. It's hard to admit that there are things that you can't do. It's hard to reach out and cry out for help.
>
> It's hard to confess to weakness and ignorance. It's hard to have to depend on another for what you think you should be able to supply for yourself. It's hard to talk about what you don't know and what you can't do. It's hard to admit to poor judgment and wrong responses. It's hard to receive correction and to confess to sin.

Asking why we have so much trouble in these areas, Tripp points to "two very seductive lies"—autonomy and self-sufficiency:

> Autonomy tells me that I'm an independent being with the right to do what I want to do, when, where, and how I want to do it. . . . Every time you defend yourself against the correction of another or tell someone not to tell you what to do, you buy into this lie.
>
> Self-sufficiency . . . tells me I have everything within myself to be what I'm supposed to be and to do what I'm supposed to do. . . Each time you resist reaching out for help or each time you act as if you're okay when, in fact, you're not, you've bought into this lie.[4]

Since "independence" and "the pursuit of happiness" are built right into America's founding documents, it's not hard to see why these ideas so thoroughly infect even the evangelical community, leading not only to a general refusal to lean on others by being transparent, but also to the jaw-dropping abandonment of church we are seeing in this cultural moment.

As a long-term officer in a denomination that emphasizes the authority of Scripture and of the local church, I can readily attest to the number of Christians nowadays for whom autonomy is simply part of their hard-wiring. Time and again, I have watched genuine believers make a public vow of submission to Christ—and to the elders of the local church; but later, when push comes to shove and they are being advised or exhorted by the session, they are resolutely committed to heeding their own counsel.

One man refused to return to his wife, whom he had abandoned, thereafter moving to the other side of the country. Another was a convert from Islam who, later fearing militant Islam, had wound up recanting his faith in a letter to his Iranian family. A wife and mother persisted in her conviction that she no longer needed to attend church.

All this in spite of the fact that in every one of these cases, the entire session was unanimously counseling a different course of action.

In these and so many other instances, self-determination tends to trump submission, often with tragic results for the precious unity of Christ's body—and for the one who will not listen. Among the above cases, the man who left his wife is now about to marry an unbeliever. The Islamic convert eventually murdered his own daughter and died in jail.

Autonomy has the appealing ring of freedom; but sometimes it comes at a great price.

IT'S NOT GOOD TO BE ALONE

Even for the many willing souls who have learned to yield their self-direction, it can still be hard to forsake "self-reliance"—our annoying and unbiblical penchant for trying to solve our own problems without help from others. To put it simply, if we want to be seen as competent, capable, and in control, then we will not regularly ask others to pray for us.[5] In this case, we neglect one of the church's most vital resources—a resource, incidentally, which the Apostle Paul was eager to use. Indeed, this giant among men urgently requests prayer for himself and his ministry no less than eight times in his letters. In this way, he affirms not only his neediness—his *lack* of self-sufficiency—but also the vital role other disciples and converts could play in his ministry. In 2 Corinthians, for example, Paul tells his hearers, "You also must help us by prayer, so that many will give thanks on our behalf for the blessing granted us through the prayers of many" (2 Cor. 1:11). What a joy and encouragement for Paul's followers to know of his need for their help and prayer (they "must," he insists)—and to know of their active participation in this work that was turning the Mediterranean world upside down.

We are designed to be needy; as Henry Cloud and John Townsend put it, any so-called "self-sufficient" Christian who claims he doesn't need others is like someone afflicted with anorexia, slowly starving to death while stoutly insisting that she or he simply isn't hungry.[6]

Thus Tripp concludes his blog entry by affirming the Christian's need for community: "We were designed to live in worshipful community with God and humble community with people. We were never constructed to live all by ourselves." As proof, Tripp cites Adam and Eve, pointing out that even in a perfect world before the fall, "they were still needy because they were not created to live life on their own."[7] Ever notice the number of times God says something was "good" in Genesis 1? But in the next chapter, when he sees that Adam is all by himself, he says by contrast that this is "not good"—the first time that phrase is used in Scripture (Gen. 2:18).

Even in paradise, it's not good to be alone.

"THE TROUBLE WITH SELF-ESTEEM"

At the moment, there are more than 2,000 books available on self-esteem, not to mention thousands more papers and studies—all promoting an improved self-image as the key to personal success and a healthy society. One study even goes so far as to tie terrorism to "feelings of worthlessness" on the part of individual hijackers and suicide bombers.

This information is taken from "The Trouble with Self-Esteem," a 2002 *New York Times Magazine* piece by psychologist Lauren Slater.[8] Citing America's long-standing entrepreneurial spirit, as well as our fixation with "self-improvement," plus Ralph Waldo Emerson's famed 19th-century essay "Self-Reliance," Slater calls self-esteem "a quasi-religion" in this country—"woven into a tradition that both defines and confines us as Americans." She adds pointedly, "If we were to deconstruct self-esteem, to question its value, we would be, in a sense, questioning who we are, nationally and individually."

Yet Slater cites studies showing very little connection between low self-esteem and failure in school or life. "There is absolutely no evidence that low self-esteem is particularly harmful," says researcher Nicholas Emler in her piece. "It's not at all a cause of poor academic performance; people with low self-esteem seem to do just as well in life as people with high self-esteem. In fact, they may do better, because they often try harder." To take it further, the problem with—for instance—men who are antisocial, racist, or violent, is *not* low self-esteem, but quite the contrary: In Emler's words, "they don't feel bad enough about themselves."

THE BLIND LEADING THE BLIND

For Christians, it goes without saying that an emphasis on high self-esteem runs counter to what the Bible says about our minds and hearts. Both the Old Testament and the New give a dire diagnosis of man's innate, ongoing sinfulness. In Matthew 15, for example, Jesus affirms that "out of the heart come evil thoughts, murder, adultery, sexual immorality, theft, false witness, slander" (Matt. 15:19), while Paul tells the Ephesians that before being saved by Christ, they were "dead" in their "trespasses and sins," and were "by nature children of wrath" (2:1-3). Confirming our inability to extricate ourselves from this state, Proverbs 20 asks rhetorically, "Who can say, 'I have made my heart pure; I am clean from my sin'?" (20:9); and Ecclesiastes bluntly avers, "Surely there is not a righteous man on earth who does good and never sins" (7:20).

Indeed, from the moment of our birth, we are—as one 17th-century document puts it— "wholly defiled in all the parts and faculties of soul and body." To put it another way, human beings are "utterly indisposed, disabled, and made opposite to all good, and wholly inclined to do all evil. . . ." Worse yet, this drastic state of sin, this corruption of our nature, continues to manifest itself even in "those that are regenerated."[9] In other words, we continue to battle this in-born sinfulness even after we have committed our lives to serving Christ—as we see plainly in the struggles Paul describes so poignantly in Romans 7: Speaking of "the law of sin that dwells in my members," Paul laments, "I do not do the good I want, but the evil I do not want is what I keep on doing" (vv. 19-23).

With such overwhelming Biblical evidence—not to mention the many Old Testament narratives detailing man's obstinate wickedness and idolatry—why would we Christians want to deny our own sinfulness by jumping on the self-esteem bandwagon, thereby deluding ourselves into thinking that we're better than we really are, and that don't need to worry about getting help or working at sanctification?

Yet this is precisely the trap we often fall into when interacting with fellow believers—and perhaps even when examining ourselves in the privacy of our own devotions. If I go into church pretending I am anything other than a desperate sinner saved by grace, I am only perpetuating a secular self-help gospel in which—to quote a famous title—"I'm OK, you're OK." And I never need to face the inky blackness in my soul—the "law of sin that dwells in my members," that makes life an unending battle against narcissism and idolatry, and that requires me to call out urgently for help rather than act as though everything in my heart and soul is perfectly fine.

What's especially damaging about the sin-denying self-esteem movement is that, as we maintain a vested interest in *not* seeing our own problems, we then simply fail to address those issues; instead of moving toward God, we remain muddled, sinful, stuck, blind—forever mired in a state of "I'm OK" that is, of course, not OK. And thus, ironically, this insistence on "self-worth," allegedly designed to secure happiness and success, actually backfires: For deep inside, we surely know the unhappy truth about ourselves; and worse, having wished it away, we fail to see and act on the need for improvement—thereby making us even more unhappy.

In "The Trouble with Self-Esteem," Slater quotes therapist David Reynolds: "The most miserable people I know have been self-focused." And she goes on to insist that rather than wandering in the murky wasteland of deluded self-approval, we must develop an accurate and objective understanding or ourselves—in order to become the kind of people we truly want to be. "We must first know both where we flail and stumble, and where we are truly strong, before we can make disciplined alterations."

Not surprisingly, that appropriate self-analysis is also commended by the Apostle Paul. In one of the key Bible verses on self-image, Paul shows us that suitable self-assessment does *not* necessarily imply thinking poorly of oneself, but rather thinking with prudence and level-headed sanity: "For by the grace given to me I say to everyone among you not to think of himself more highly than he ought to think, but to think with sober judgment, each according to the measure of faith that God has assigned" (Rom. 12:3).

Indeed, as we shall see in the next chapter, a long-term tendency to think poorly of oneself—to overemphasize one's flaws and obsess over failures—is just an alternate brand of narcissism. It's navel-gazing wrapped in a mantle of sham humility. No—the solution to self-focus is amply apparent in the title of Tim Keller's helpful booklet *The Freedom of Self-Forgetfulness.* It's likewise apparent in this famous C. S. Lewis passage on pride, reminding us that the truly humble person is not focused on either his successes *or* his failures:

> Do not imagine that if you meet a really humble man he will be what most people call "humble" nowadays: he will not be a sort of greasy, smarmy person, who is always telling you that, of course, he is nobody. Probably all you will think about him is that he seemed a cheerful, intelligent chap who took a real interest in what *you* said to *him.* If you do dislike him it will be because you feel a little envious of anyone who seems to enjoy life so easily. He will not be thinking about humility: he will not be thinking about himself at all.[10]

Self-sufficiency is a myth, and self-esteem an illusion. Christians need God and others. If we think differently, well—that's just one more roadblock on the path to transparency.

OPEN FOR DISCUSSION

1. Do you think our culture has a "myth of self-sufficiency"? If so, what does this look like, and how does our culture perpetuate it?

2. Has this "myth" made its way into the church? Has it made its way into your own life? What effect does it have on the body of Christ?

3. Cite some Bible passages suggesting that "self-sufficiency" is scripturally untenable.

4. How would you describe the "self-esteem" movement? Have you seen evidence of this in your own community (i.e., school, work, social life, personal life)?

5. Do you think the self-esteem movement has penetrated the evangelical church community? If so, how—and what effect does this have on believers and the body of Christ?

6. Is *some* self-esteem necessary? If so, how much? And how do we know when we have crossed the line into inordinate focus on self-worth?

7. What is the biblical response to the self-esteem movement?

8. As we prepare for the next five chapters in Part Two, discuss some compelling reasons *why* we should be transparent.

Part Two

WHY WE SHOULD BE TRANSPARENT

CHAPTER SIX

"Let Us Cleanse Ourselves"

Sanctification

Anyone who has studied Scripture with an open mind for even a few months should recognize that God wants us to excel in personal holiness. As Jesus Christ puts it, "You therefore must be perfect, as your heavenly Father is perfect" (Matt. 5:48).

A handful of similar verses will serve to drive this point home:

"Unless your righteousness exceeds that of the scribes and Pharisees, you will never enter the kingdom of Heaven" (Matt. 5:20).

"Let us cleanse ourselves from every defilement of body and spirit, bringing holiness to completion in the fear of God" (2 Cor. 7:1).

"In your struggle against sin you have not yet resisted to the point of shedding your blood. . . . Strive for peace with everyone, and for the holiness without which no one will see the Lord" (Heb. 12:4, 12).

Clearly, every effort of body and mind must be ceaselessly exerted as we work toward that righteousness which God requires of his people.

Given this indisputable truth, the point of our current chapter is simple: We cannot run this race alone. Sharing your weaknesses, struggles, and sins with fellow-believers is absolutely imperative for steady growth in sanctification. It will help you identify sins in your own life, and it will also help you put them to death.

KNOW THYSELF

Nathaniel Hawthorne's *The Scarlet Letter* may be the greatest novel ever written on the effects of hiding your sin from others.

In this 1850 classic, a major character has been covering up a terrible transgression for years—and it is slowing killing him. As this revered civic leader prepares to give the most important speech of his career, he's convinced that his reputation is about to soar, despite the fact that he's been deceiving everyone in town—while also allowing a kind-hearted single mother to bear the entire weight of shame for their shared sin. Reflecting on this delusion about who he really is, the narrator remarks, "No man for any considerable period can wear one face to himself and another to the multitude, without finally getting bewildered as to which may be the true."[1]

The poor man had spent so much time deceiving others that even he himself can no longer tell who he really is. If you lie to other people about who you are, then you may wind up fooling yourself worst of all. To put it more positively, you must be honest with others in order to fully understand yourself.

"It has become a psychological truism," writes John Powell, "that I will understand only as much of myself as I have been willing to communicate to another." In his material on this phenomenon—found in the aptly titled *Why Am I Afraid to Tell You Who I Am?*—Powell cites physician and counselor Paul Tournier: "No one can develop freely in this world and find a full life without feeling understood by at least one person. . . . He who would see himself clearly must open up to a confidant freely chosen and worthy of such trust." And this cannot be a one-shot deal—a sort of "confess it all at once and get it out of the way." Rather, since our battles, our wounds, our hopes, and even our identities often change, sharing one's deepest self with at least one other person should be, as it were, a lifestyle choice, an ongoing process—one we are committed to over the whole course of a relationship.[2]

Along the same lines, both Powell and Tournier reject the idea that careful introspection is a valid alternative to sharing with others; while some self-analysis is invariably important, nonetheless, lengthy and intensive introspection cannot, by itself, really yield the truth about your own hearts and minds. "Self-examination is an exhausting undertaking," writes Tournier. "The mind becomes so engrossed in it that it loses its normal capacity for relationship with the world and with God. Locked in a narrow round of endless and sterile self-analysis, the person becomes shrunk and deformed, while false problems multiply *ad infinitum*. . . . A person can confide all of his secrets to the docile pages of his personal diary, but he can know himself and experience the fullness of life only in the meeting with another person."[3]

"The heart is deceitful above all things, and desperately sick," says Jeremiah. "Who can understand it?" (17:9). Because of our untrustworthy hearts, we will find it all but impossible to gain a true understanding of ourselves without help—help from Scripture, from the Holy Spirit, and yes, from other people. Just as an athlete needs coaches to point out his errors; just as a writer sends his work around to friends for feedback; just as a new mother will pore over books and ask everyone she knows for advice—so we also, if truly serious about sanctification, will enlist aid by sharing our struggles and seeing if other people can perhaps point out things about ourselves that we're unable to see.

That's what friends are for.

PAY THE PRICE

The Scripture passages quoted at the beginning of this chapter make it abundantly clear that Christians are in the sanctification business. Admittedly, this is hard work. Like much of the rest of the process, openness about sin and weakness is never easy. "Transparency is traumatic. Open communication is like getting an immunization shot. It hurts, but it helps. If you are looking for painless ways to grow toward each other and toward maturity, call off the search. In God's sovereign plan, a certain amount of discomfort is built into the growing process."[4]

Yet even if the price of sanctification includes the hard work of confessing to others, then we ought gladly to fork over the facts, taking advantage of this precious resource for becoming more Christ-like. If we won't commit to this hard work, it could mean that we aren't really interested in transformation and holiness.

After all, if you made a firm and unwavering commitment to confess your sins to others, would this not serve as a deterrent in temptation—if you knew for a fact that you had to confess this sin to a certain person afterwards?

In my own life, I have struggled with pornography since adolescence, and it continued to plague me through my early years as a married Christian. I finally became so convicted about the adulterous nature of this sin that I actually signed a written pact with my wife, promising that I would immediately confess to her any and all such transgressions. I still have this somewhat bedraggled piece of paper, now nearly 25 years old. It has not been foolproof, of course; but for readers who struggle similarly—who know how deep-seated this drug-like addiction can be, and how hard it is to quit—I assure you that knowing I'd have to confess at once has made a huge difference in my ability to turn away from temptation. In recent years, as porn has become so perilously widespread and so instantly available through the Internet, this commitment has been especially precious and helpful.

In his majestic *Christian Directory*, the great Puritan scholar Richard Baxter suggests that this habit of confession to others is one indicator of true repentance. That is, you can tell how willing you are to repent by how willing you are to share your sin and struggle someone else.[5] I may tell God over and over again that I'm sorry for a certain sin; I may ask repeatedly for his forgiveness, and for his help as I promise not to do it again; but . . . if I am not also willing to confess that sin to someone else and enlist help—then just how genuine is my repentance?

Dietrich Bonhoeffer has a similarly convicting question: Why do we generally find it easier to confess to God than we do to our brother, who is a fellow sinner like us? If we find this to be the case, then "we must ask ourselves whether we have not often been deceiving ourselves with our confession of sin to God, whether we have not rather been confessing our sins to ourselves and also granting ourselves absolution. And is not the reason perhaps for our countless relapses and the feebleness of our Christian obedience to be found precisely in the fact that we are living on self-forgiveness and not a real forgiveness? Self-forgiveness can never lead to a breach with sin. . . ." Only by confessing directly to a sister or brother can we be sure that our confession is thorough and final. Only then can we break the cycle of self-deception and bring our sin out into the light—where it can be exposed and dealt with once and for all.[6]

IT BREAKS THE POWER OF REIGNING SIN

Confessing sin to others actually helps loosen its stranglehold in our lives. In some mysterious fashion, the very secrecy of sin and shame helps give them power over us—perhaps because the solitude itself only exacerbates our sense of helplessness.

"Shame is tackled best in the context of a relationship," writes Ed Welch.

> Being open about it, at least with someone who is a wise encourager, is part of the way out of shame. . . . When in doubt, go public. Speak to *someone*. . . . If you speak to the Holy Lord but won't speak to mere human beings, don't you think it's possible that your shame remains very much alive? It will offer many persuasive reasons to stay silent. But since the kingdom of God brings all things to the Light, you

> should speak to someone as a way to express your confidence in Jesus Christ.[7]

Brene Brown agrees: "Shame hates it when we reach out and tell our story. It hates having words wrapped around it—it can't survive being shared. Shame loves secrecy. The most dangerous thing to do after a shaming experience is to hide or bury our story. When we bury our story, the shame metastasizes."[8]

Bonhoeffer puts it even more forcefully:

> Sin demands to have a man by himself. It withdraws him from the community. The more isolated a person is, the more destructive will be the power of sin over him, and the more deeply he becomes involved in it, the more dangerous is his isolation. Sin wants to remain unknown. It shuns the light. . . . In confession the light of the Gospel breaks into the darkness and seclusion of the heart. The sin must be brought into the light. . . . It is a hard struggle until the sin is openly admitted. But God breaks gates of brass and bars of iron (Ps. 107:16).
>
> Since the confession of sin is made in the presence of a Christian brother, the last stronghold of self-justification is abandoned. The sinner surrenders; he gives up all his evil. He gives his heart to God. . . .[9]

In other words, it is not merely the help of others that enables us to escape from sin—their prayers, their wisdom, and their encouragement, along with our accountability to them. No; what *really* clinches it is the incredibly difficult mortification of self: In wrestling your sin into the light, you make a public and very painful admission that you have not been able to tackle it yourself—that your spirit is willing but your flesh is weak; and with this admission, you join the blessed ranks of those who "have crucified the flesh with its passions and desires" (Gal. 5:24). Confession to others literally breaks the power of sin. It mortifies the flesh, crushes pride, kills the self. It is hard, painful, humiliating work.

But it is work we will gladly do if we are truly committed to holiness. It may not feel that way, but in truth it is a small price to pay for the freedom from sin that you claim you want so desperately.

> When our "repentance" functions in isolation rather than in community, it almost always indicates that we remain more concerned about personal appearances than the resolution of sin . . . . The fact that our sin remains hidden from others proves we still favor presenting a nicely packaged life to others, while keeping sin quasi-managed and submerged. Yet genuine repentance desires to resolve *anything* and *everything* about our sin. No cover, no posturing, just pure repentance.[10]

When we are willing to downplay sin, as though it were not a serious enough problem to mandate transparency and confession, then we may be falling into the trap of those false preachers in Jeremiah, who "have healed the wound of my people lightly, saying, 'Peace, peace,' when there is no peace. Were they ashamed when they committed abomination? No, they were not at all ashamed; they did not know how to blush" (Jer. 6:14-15).

Sharing our sins with others reminds us to blush, and keeps us nailed to the cross of self-denial and sanctification. Without it, we cannot pretend that we are truly serious about the work that God has called us to.

OPEN FOR DISCUSSION

1. In addition to the verses quoted at the beginning of this chapter, cite some other Scripture passages that enjoin us to pursue holiness with vigor and sincerity. Discuss these briefly.

2. Discuss the Hawthorne quote under the subhead "Know Thyself" above. When we conceal our sins from others, does this

contribute to self-delusion about our own true nature? How does this happen?

3. In what ways can confessing to others help us understand ourselves better?

4. Do you agree with Powell and Tournier that introspection is a dead end, and does not really help with self-knowledge? If so, why do you think this is the case? If you *disagree*, can you share some ways in which you have found introspection useful or helpful?

5. Bonhoeffer insists that only by confessing to others can we make a true break with sin. Do you agree? Explain.

6. Take a few minutes now to consider a recurrent and problematic sin in your life. Are you willing to begin discussing this with someone else? Perhaps you could even make a commitment to be accountable to that person, admitting when you've failed and asking for continued prayer. (Be careful, however, not to choose someone who struggles with the same sin; in these cases, it can sometimes be a stumbling block for the other person to know that you have committed the sin they themselves are also drawn to.)

7. Can you think of a time when you confessed a sin to someone else? How hard was it? How did you finally manage it? What was her/his reaction? Did you find the confession helpful in the long run?

8. Ask yourself how serious you are about sanctification; if you hesitate about confessing sin to others, how might your determination to please God overcome this reluctance?

CHAPTER SEVEN

"All Suffer Together"

One Body

"As it would be unnatural, absurd, frustrating and injurious for the hand not to communicate effectively with the foot, or the eye with the ear, so there is a violation of every law of our union with each other when Christians do not communicate with one another."

That's Bible commentator Charles Hodge discussing 1 Corinthians 12,[1] where Paul spends more than 25 verses enjoining unity and interdependence in the church. The apostle's image is of one unified organism in which every part is crucial to the functioning of the whole; all of its members rely on the others, working together to fulfill the church's identity as Christ's body. Every "body part" has a role to play—provided by a wise and loving father for our mutual help, strength, and encouragement.

> For the body does not consist of one member but of many. . . . The eye cannot say to the hand, "I have no need of you," nor again the head to the feet, "I have no need of you." On the contrary, the parts of the body that seem to be weaker are indispensable. . . . But God has so composed the body, giving greater honor to the part that lacked it, that there may be no division in the body, but that the members

> may have the same care for one another. If one member suffers, all suffer together; if one member is honored, all rejoice together. Now you are the body of Christ and individually members of it. (1 Cor. 12:14-27)

It is the contention of this chapter that we cannot fully achieve Paul's vision of church life without transparency and openness. For if we fail to share our concerns with one another, it is as though one body-part were saying to another, "I have no need of you." We cut ourselves off from our fellow-members, foolishly ignoring the fact that, just as in human physiology, no single part of the body is designed to operate independently. In the words of Henry Cloud and John Townsend, sharing and seeking help reminds us that "we are incomplete, that we are needy, and that we are to seek outside of ourselves to take in what we need."

Citing such verses as Matthew 21:22, James 4:2, and 1 John 3:22, Cloud and Townsend go on to assert that "God places a high premium in the value of asking directly for help." The word *ask*, in its various forms, appears almost 800 times in Scripture—in such verses as "Ask, and it will be given to you" (Matt. 7:7), "You do not have, because you do not ask" (James 4:2), and "We know that he hears us in whatever we ask" (1 John 5:15); even Jesus himself asked his disciples for help in the Garden of Gethsemane.[2] If there were ever a human who manifestly did *not* need human help, it was this peerless man who fed 5,000, raised the dead, stilled the sea, and told his captors, "Do you think that I cannot appeal to my Father, and he will at once send me more than twelve legions of angels?" (Matt. 26:53). Yet facing crucifixion—and facing, in particular, the wrath of his father directed toward the sins of the world—Christ told three disciples, "My soul is very sorrowful, even to death; remain here, and watch with me" (Matt. 26:38).

Sisters and brothers, if Jesus Christ could open up like this in his moment of grief and vulnerability, we can do it too. Like our savior, we also must transparently admit our needs: We must openly declare these needs to others, and boldly ask for help. And we must ask in confidence that a gracious God—through the church, the precious body of his precious son—has already provided for us the resources, the individual strengths, the skills and insight and wisdom and experience, to minister to one another. For "we are to grow up in every way into him who is the head, into Christ, from whom the whole body, joined and held together by every joint with which it is equipped, when each part is working properly, makes the body grow so that it builds itself up in love" (Eph. 4:16).

NEEDY AND NEEDED

As we earlier discussed at length, such transparency helps us kill off that deadly and unbiblical penchant for self-sufficiency—while at the same time putting us in reach of the help and support we need in our struggle with sin (see Chapters Five and Six above).

More important for the current discussion, we also communicate to others that they are needed—that they have a key role to play in our lives and thus can contribute to the building up of Christ's body. In his fine book *Side by Side*, Ed Welch highlights both of these aspects of church life by organizing his material into two major divisions: Part I, "We Are Needy," and Part II, "We Are Needed."

Part II is nearly twice as long.

Call out to others, confessing your helplessness and asking for their love, prayers, and support; rather than saying, "I have no need of you," this affirms their value to the church and to Christ, who longs for unity in his body and insists we recognize that even the weakest member is "indispensable" (1 Cor. 12:22).

Let me give you an example.

Years ago, I was struggling with sleeplessness, depression, anxiety, and a sense of utter helplessness even in the face of simple tasks like cooking, driving, and grading papers for the high school classes I teach. As I wondered just how heavily to lean on my wife through all this, I asked my counselor and therapist what kind of husband she preferred:

one who was strong and would tough it out no matter what, or one who shared with her all his fears and feelings of inadequacy. Not in the habit of making blanket pronouncements, this counselor would often respond to such questions by making me think it through myself and come up with my own answer. In this case, however, he instantly responded that in virtually every marriage, the wife invariably preferred a man who needed her and wasn't afraid to admit it.

This "need to be needed" may be especially true for the woman, who was originally created because it was "not good that the man should be alone"; God wanted to "make a helper fit for him" (Gen. 2:18)—and in this way, helpfulness seems to be hard-wired into the feminine psyche. But of course, men need to be needed, too; what guy doesn't relish helping a friend fix something, or sharing with others the benefit of experience and knowledge in some area of specialty? As 1 Corinthians 12 suggests, we *all* have this need—and it can be met in the body of Christ, where fully leaning on one another might begin to give friendships the precious bond of unity that is generally found most fully in marriage.

DRAWING CLOSER

One of the best resources on godly interdependence is the work of Larry Crabb—particularly his helpful book *Becoming a True Spiritual Community.* Formerly named for Crabb's description of an ideal church—*The Safest Place on Earth*—this 1999 work begins with an anecdote in which the author and his wife walked past a home for retirees in Miami Beach. On the broad front porch, at least 100 aging women and men were resting in chairs—all facing forward; every single person sat staring straight ahead, with no sign of interaction, friendship, or conversation. Deeply saddened as he recalls this incident, Crabb begins urging a healthier, face-to-face community:

"A spiritual community, a *church*, is full of broken people who turn their chairs toward each other because they know they cannot make it alone. These broken people journey together with their wounds and worries and washouts visible. . . ." What's more, it is this very visibility that fosters the sense of community:

> It is our weaknesses, not our competence, that moves others; our sorrows, not our blessings, that break down the barriers of fear and shame that keep us apart; our admitted failures, nor our paraded successes, that bind us together in hope. . . . We often *hear* that brokenness is the pathway to a deeper relationship with God, but we rarely see it modeled. I sometimes think we want others to believe that we know God by demonstrating how unbroken we are.[3]

Yet what is it that God requires of us? A "broken spirit" and a "contrite heart" -- *these* are the things that bind us more closely to him (Ps. 51:17); and they will bind us to one another as well.

IN THE HANDS OF "EXPERTS"

Since many of us have trouble admitting our brokenness to others in the church, we often turn to professional counselors and therapists. In fact, Crabb asserts that contemporary Christianity has ceded its venue for spiritual and emotional help to the psychotherapy industry—and that this is probably not our best option. For the past several decades, the Christian community has assumed that chronic personal problems result from some underlying psychological cause and therefore need to be addressed by experts. Thus, believers wrestling with a profound internal crisis or problem will often turn first to a Christian psychiatrist—and they will sometimes find it tough to get an appointment, because counselors working from a biblical perspective are in very high demand these days. If on the other hand, a Christian senses a gift for counseling or listening, she or he will often work through a college program in psychology, therapy, or social services, together with the usual round of standardized tests, grad school, and clinical work in classrooms and offices.

Where is the church in this process?

Crabb goes on to cite research indicating that what we really need is "someone who *relates* well." Someone like this, in fact, is actually "more capable of promoting meaningful change than a trained professional who 'does therapy' to a patient as a set of clinical techniques. . . ." Rather than requiring some approved array of academic skills, the successful counselor needs mostly to convey three things: 1) that he or she cares; 2) that she or he is competent to help; and, 3) that there is no hidden agenda or ulterior motive. These three requirements, Crabb concludes, translate more simply as love, wisdom, and integrity; and if this is what's required for successful therapy, then a church or spiritual community is fully and uniquely gifted to provide just such an environment.[4]

While not disputing the need for professional help and perhaps even medication in the case of serious and life-threatening issues like anorexia and clinical depression, we would do well to ask ourselves the long-term cost of ignoring the community God has provided, where people know us, where they've often been through the same sorts of struggles, where there is no counseling fee—and no 50-minute time limit.

If we learn to call on others in the church for help with sin, we can begin to develop the "true spiritual community" of Crabb's title—where, as Paul writes, "the members may have the same care for one another"; for "if one member suffers, all suffer together" (1 Cor. 12:25-26). Isn't this the biblical ideal—the fellowship we long for but fail to cultivate as we refuse to share our weaknesses and ask for help? As Crabb puts it, "Self-protection is the silent killer of true community. Like untreated high blood pressure, it is rarely recognized but it drains the health and life out of relationships."[5] For a moment or two, try to imagine instead what that perfectly open and interdependent body might look like.

> Think of a time when you were in a group and someone spoke openly about a struggle in daily life. What happened

> next? In most instances, the group suddenly became more like a family. Other people opened up about their lives, and the prayers of the group sounded more and more like the Psalms. When something like this happens, the myth that we all have life figured out is exposed, and we begin to share one another's burdens, which is the way God intended it to be. We spend too much time concealing our neediness. We need to stop hiding.[6]

COROLLARY #1: THAT YOU BE NOT JUDGED

This chapter has been urging transparency as one way to make Christ's body look more like it does in 1 Corinthians 12. If we should actually manage to create such a spiritual community—one whose members depend on one another, bestowing both value and support on every brother and sister—we will likewise foster three corollary effects to help the church function even better as God's holy household.

The first of these is that by openly sharing, you can begin to cut back on your own judgmental attitudes. "Judge not, that you be not judged," commands Christ in a frequently quoted passage (Matt. 7:1). This verse has too often been used to sidestep any sort of proper Christian discernment; after all, the same Greek verb is used in other verses where we are *commanded* to judge (see, for instance, 1 Cor. 10:15 and 11:13). Nonetheless, what we call "being judgmental"—a scornful, belittling, contemptuous attitude—smacks of "holier than thou," of putting someone else down in order to elevate yourself. And many other Bible passages roundly condemn it—perhaps most pointedly James 4: "Do not speak evil against one another, brothers. The one who speaks against a brother or judges his brother, speaks evil against the law and judges the law. But if you judge the law, you are not a doer of the law but a judge. There is only one lawgiver and judge, he who is able to save and to destroy. But who are you to judge your neighbor?" (James 4:11-12; see also Rom. 2:1-3 and 14:1-11; Col. 2:16; James 2:4).

Condemning one another in this way grieves the Spirit of Christ and wrecks Paul's vision of church unity, where there should be "no division in the body" (1 Cor. 12:25). It thus keeps church members at a distance from one another—and perhaps even more tragically, it often leaves outsiders and visitors feeling unwelcome in our congregations.

Suffice it to say that if I were being wholly honest and transparent—if, for example, I had just shared my struggles with losing my temper and cursing over inconsequential matters—then how much harder would it be for me to condemn and judge others for their sin! To paraphrase Christ in the same judgment passage cited above: Why would I obsess over the speck in someone else's eye if I'm still battling a log that is lodged in my own? (Matt. 7:3).

Judgment divides, setting us against "those people over there"—the ones not like us, the ones we're "better than." Openness and transparency, on the other hand, put us all on an equal footing, reminding us that we all share the same struggles, the same needs, the same temptations, the same failures. To tell someone else frankly about my sins is a mortifying reminder that I am *not* better than anyone else. In this way, it helps foster the spirit of humility and brokenness that is essential to true church unity—a unity ineffably precious to Christ himself, who prayed that all his disciples should "become perfectly one" (John 17:23).

COROLLARY #2: "LET THE CHILDREN COME"

In Mark 10, Jesus became "indignant" at his disciples for trying to keep children away from him. "Let the children come to me," he said—"and he took them in his arms and blessed them, laying his hands on them" (Mark 10:13-16). At the same time, Christ described little ones by saying, "to such belongs the kingdom of God" (verse 14). In this statement, I always hear an implied rebuke to the disciples for thinking they themselves were any less problematic than children: Perhaps the disciples feared that the kids would disturb Jesus with their fuss and need and messiness, their tendency to ask a ton of questions and say the first thing on their mind. And Jesus is saying to this disciples, "This is the kingdom of God—this is what we're *all* like! It's just that some of us—like you guys right now!—are trying to pretend otherwise; what on earth makes you think you are any different from a little kid? For the kingdom of God belongs to people like this!"

We too may need to hear Christ rebuking our pretense—our assumption that we're "better than"—if this has made it harder for the church's children to get to Jesus. To put it more positively, another corollary to acting like Christ's true body is that it creates an environment in which children are more welcome—in which they can thus be more easily be blessed by their savior.

Here's Don Miller expounding on this in his inimitably frank and thoughtful manner:

> I've noticed parents who don't admit their faults have children who are troubled and emotionally restless as though they secretly want to be free from their families so they can be themselves. . . .
>
> If you think about it, parents who are open and honest with their kids create an environment in which children are allowed to be human. And, sadly, parents who hide their flaws unknowingly create an environment where kids feel the need to hide. . . .
>
> Some of the most troubled people I know were raised in fundamentalist environments with parents who felt the need to act more righteous than they were. I don't know if I've ever met a person from a legalistic family who didn't struggle. Environments in which we are encouraged to hide our faults are toxic.[7]

Of course, Miller is focused less on the church here, and more on families. But if families must create an environment of honesty and authenticity, rather than feigning perfection, surely churches must do so too.

I grew up in congregations where everything and everybody seemed just fine, where no one ever talked about the real problems we were having (except perhaps behind one another's backs!), and where children were swiftly whisked out halfway through the worship service—ostensibly to learn about the Bible in a more kid-friendly environment, but also perhaps to keep things quiet and controlled during the more grown-up sermon time. As a result, it took me years to let down my guard in church, to be "messy" before my brothers and sisters, and to let my kids be messy too. I can't be the only parent who ever felt consternation and embarrassment at my toddlers' often uncooperative attitude during worship or other church activities.

Now, no one will deny that some level of quiet reverence is necessary in church; but if we erect an artificial environment of mere external perfection, this will surely be communicated to our children. I often wonder if mothers and fathers don't spend an enormous amount of time actually training their children *not* to be transparent. Doesn't it seem to you that we do this in many areas of their public lives, but most especially in church? And so the message they sometimes get about church is: You cannot be yourself in this place. You must repress it, put on a front, leave your real self outside. And course, you're welcome to pick it up afterwards—which his how young people grow up learning that the person you present in church can and should be very different from the person you are outside of church. And in this case, don't we perhaps deserve the label "hypocrites," so often pasted on us by a contemptuous generation with no desire to be judged by folks who only pretend to be better than everyone else?

If, as Miller suggests, parents who act like they have no faults create children who are dying to get free and "be themselves," then churches without openness and transparency will likewise create their own generation of discontents—"expatriates" who soon learn to see behind the hypocrisy and strike out on their own for a more authentic life. As my pastor once said in a sermon, "You have to be real with your children, or the gospel is never going to develop traction in their lives."

May God forgive us adults in the kingdom if this is behind the mass church-exodus we've seen among youth in the past 20 years.

COROLLARY #3: THEY'LL KNOW WE ARE CHRISTIANS

That charge of hypocrisy so often hurled at the church really hurts—especially because our pretense and lack of transparency suggest that it just might be accurate. Perhaps this charge would become less justified—and more infrequent—if our churches were less like social or entertainment events and more like recovery centers, where we admit our problems and seek help. Jesus insisted that a watching world should be able to recognize our discipleship by the love we have for one another. What better way to show this than by the interdependence Paul enjoins in 1 Corinthians 12—demonstrating that here is a community of authentic love, one where you don't have to pretend to be someone you're not, where love is truly unconditional because our relationships are not founded on some artificial external standard, but on genuine acceptance of the beloved—no matter how messy or broken or sinful.

"Millions of people have yet to meet the King of Love. When they see us living in blame, shame, fear, denial, and anger, with no real answers, it confuses them. When they see us attempting to mask those dysfunctions, it tells them not to trust us—or the God we follow."[8]

By contrast, here is Crabb's vision of what he wants in a church—the sort of community that would make outsiders feel at ease rather than turning them off:

> I want to be part of a church that will greet me as I walk in the door and know I'm a mess, maybe a well-socialized mess, perhaps a devoutly religious mess, maybe a therapeutically rearranged mess, perhaps even an actively missional mess—but still a mess. I want to know that I'm

> seen and still wanted, that I can drop the pretense, shed the masks, and enjoy the soul-enlivening experience of looking bad in the presence of love. Then I'll be more grateful for blessings, more passionate about missions, and more eager to share the gospel with lost people.[9]

The book *TrueFaced*, by Thrall, McNicol, and Lynch, offers a similar picture of the church as it is healed by genuine love and becomes a beacon to the world:

> Closed, broken, frightened, bluffing men and women come squinting out of the dark corners into the light and start singing songs they didn't know were in them. They begin to feel alive—secure in his embrace, seeing life for the first time in full color. Actually allowing this love beyond their double-bolted defenses, they wonder out loud what took them so long. Each one becomes real, safe, creative, and refreshingly untamed. They drink this love in like those gulping down cold, fresh lemonade for the first time. And they almost involuntarily begin to offer to all around them a love as rich and freeing as what they are taking in. They discover a waiting, thirsty community everywhere they look. And the world around them dramatically changes, one drink at a time. . . .[10]

THE POWER AND THE GLORY

Let me conclude this chapter with the words of my friend Len Richards, a long-time church deacon who has often lamented the difficulty of trying to serve and help Christians who won't admit their needs:

"When people are transparent, it's so easy to reach out and help. When they're not, when there's a façade, we're clueless. . . . But when the walls come down, and people open their hearts and lives, God is glorified every minute of the day."

I guess that would be corollary #4: A church where members confess and listen and help and pray for and lean on one another—this glorifies God, because it is becoming a more perfect reflection of Christ's perfect love. Such a community allows God to manifest his goodness, wisdom, and faithfulness, as humble and ordinary fellow-believers become channels for his glorious provision—rather than isolated self-sustainers with no apparent need for human or divine assistance.

OPEN FOR DISCUSSION

1. Reread Paul's description of the church in 1 Corinthians 12. Discuss what this passage tells us about church life. In what ways does the modern church fail to fulfill this vision? It what ways does it succeed?

2. Think of a time when you had to ask for help. What were the circumstances? How did it feel? Were you glad you did it, and if so, why?

3. Do you think people "need to feel needed"? Explain.

4. Think of a time when someone asked *you* for help or prayer. What were the circumstances? How did you feel when you were asked?

5. What do *you* think about the author's question on wives: Do they want a husband who is "the strong and silent type," or one who shares his needs and weaknesses? Explain.

6. The idea that women are hard-wired to help others is not an especially popular one in our culture. What is your response to this? Does it seem to be a biblical idea? Why do you think there is so much resistance to it nowadays?

7. Are judgmental attitudes a problem in the contemporary church? Discuss and explain.

8. How might openness and confession help curtail this?

9. Are our churches the sort of place where children feel free to be themselves? Or are they learning to put up a front? If so, how can we work to improve this situation?

10. What is the balance between letting kids be themselves and maintaining proper reverence during worship?

11. Does interdependence in Christ's body glorify God? Explain.

CHAPTER EIGHT

"How Can One Keep Warm Alone?"

Real Intimacy

In the introduction to this book, we looked briefly at 1 John, where the beloved apostle insists that "if we walk in the light, as he is in the light, we have fellowship with one another. . . ." As we saw in that discussion, the very next verse helps clarify the concept of "walking in light": "If we say we have no sin, we deceive ourselves, and the truth is not in us. If we confess our sins, he is faithful and just to forgive us our sins and to cleanse us from all unrighteousness" (1:7-9).

From this conjunction of light, fellowship, and confession, we can conclude that "walking in the light" means a "perfect openness and transparent honesty": It means I have nothing to conceal and disguise, and am "willing to have all that I do and all that I am brought out and placed in the broad clear light of truth."[1] If we desire "fellowship with one another," we simply must be open about our faults, needs, weaknesses, and sins. The communion of saints can never be complete without this key element.

The reason is simple, and it forms the central thesis for our current chapter: If you aren't being honest about yourself—if you aren't letting others see the true, whole, wonderful, broken, hopeful, helpless you—then those other people cannot love the person you truly are. As a result, you will not experience the kind of genuine intimacy we all need and want. Deep and meaningful relationships are possible only in the context of deep and meaningful openness. To quote Brene Brown, this sort of vulnerability "is the birthplace of love, belonging, joy, courage, empathy, and creativity. . . . There is no intimacy without vulnerability."[2]

SPEAKING THE TRUTH

Most of us are familiar with the passage in Ephesians where Paul adjures us, "Be angry and do not sin; do not let the sun go down on your anger." In the first half of this verse, Paul says it's OK to be angry—while in the second, he urges us to *do* something with the anger by seeking reconciliation with whomever we're mad at. And doesn't this—sharing anger—require a certain vulnerability, as we are forced to admit a negative and perhaps even embarrassing reaction to another person? Indeed, that may help shed light on Paul's preceding statement: "Therefore, having put away falsehood, let each one of you speak the truth with his neighbor, for we are members one of another" (4:25-26). Because of the intimate bond we have in Christ—we are members of one body!—we must not be false with one another; we must rather "speak the truth." If, as the following verse suggests, this sometimes involves sharing angry feelings, then perhaps it should also involve a whole range of honest interaction: Any sort of "false" self must be put away in favor of the openness and "truth" that should characterize those in the family of Christ.

Paul is not the only Bible writer to urge that sort of closeness. In Ecclesiastes 4, the Preacher offers this moving meditation on companionship: "Two are better than one, because they have a good reward for their toil. For if they fall, one will lift up his fellow. But woe to him who is alone when he falls and has not another to lift him up! Again, if two lie together, they keep warm, but how can one keep warm alone?" (4:9-11). Students of the Bible generally recognize that Old

Testament passages on physical things—such as a land of milk and honey—often take on deeper spiritual meaning in the New Testament age. Paul, for example, can quote an ancient adage about muzzling oxen (Deut. 25:4) and apply it to honoring church leaders (1 Tim. 5:17-18; see also 1 Cor. 9:9-11). And so, in the same way, can we not see a more emotional, relational dimension to the Preacher's discussion in Ecclesiastes 4? Falling, lifting up, and keeping warm must surely describe dynamics not merely in our bodies but in our spiritual lives as well. Two are indeed better than one—for in an intimate, transparent relationship, we find the love, belonging, joy, courage, empathy, and creativity that Brown mentions. But how can one keep warm alone?

The recent book *TrueFaced* takes this a step further by asserting that our very neediness is precious, for it gives us the capacity to feel loved by others. Rather than pretending we do not fall, or get cold, or need to be raised up, perhaps we should welcome and *embrace* our weaknesses as touch-points for experiencing the Christ-like love of the church body: "We know or experience love when our needs are met. . . . Sadly, if we cannot identify our needs, we cannot know love. If we deny we have needs, we will not experience love. If we withhold our needs, we can't receive the love others have for us."

ELIMINATE THE NEGATIVE

Sadly, if I refuse to open up and allow others to meet my needs, I am not the only one who suffers. My attitude of invulnerable strength spreads lovelessness to those around me. As *TrueFaced* observes, a false front not only prevents me from *receiving* love, but also, "I also cannot give love from behind a mask, at least not love from the real me. The ones I long to love experience the cloying attempts of someone who doesn't exist."[3] In other words, any love I offer in these circumstances tends to feel artificial, since it isn't coming from a place of honesty and vulnerability.

And that is only one of the profoundly negative effects I can have on others when I try to seem like I have it all together. In their book *Safe People*, Henry Cloud and John Townsend describe what happens to a relationship in which one person opens up while the other pretends to have no needs: The more open person begins to feel inferior, weaker than she or he actually is, and overly dependent on this "perfect" friend; eventually, the "weaker" soul will grow tired, resentful, and angry over the façade of this supposedly stronger person. Needless to say, true intimacy is vitiated for *both* parties in such an unequal and dishonest relationship.

Furthermore, any relationship with a supposedly perfect person will be at best unsatisfying, and at worst hurtful, because such persons will generally work to dodge or ignore anything "imperfect" in the friendship.[4] Rather than seeking to resolve conflicts, the person who has it "all together" winds up blaming or judging the other for what went wrong, and thus misses out on an important phenomenon in close relationships: Such friendships are often better at healthy managing of conflict; for when both parties are honest about disagreements and problems, and willing to admit that *both* bear some blame—then healing and resolution can take place.

Indeed, in the same way that personal needs can serve as opportunities for intimacy, so likewise conflicts in relationships, however painful, should perhaps be seen as a chance to address deep-seated, unresolved issues—thereby leading to greater closeness and intimacy. Isn't that what spouses often experience after they've had a quarrel—after they've fought their way, through pain and tears, back to mutual love and understanding? Don't they often feel closer than ever at this point? And wouldn't it be amazing if we could do this with everyone in the church body—rather than stifling conflicts and thus remaining distant, estranged, perhaps even angry? Yet this sort of reconciliation is possible only with the most courageous honesty—that is, when we speak "truth" rather than "falsehood," and when, for example, we refuse to let the sun go down on our anger.

ACCENTUATE THE POSITIVE

In his influential 1957 work *The Meaning of Persons*, psychologist Paul Tournier writes:

> The man who keeps secret his most painful memories, his bitterest remorse, and his most private convictions, must needs show also, in his whole demeanor and in all his relationships with other people, a certain reserve which they all intuitively feel. This reserve is contagious, and sets up an obstacle to the development of personal relationships. On the other hand, the liberation experienced by the man who has confessed his sins is also contagious, even if he says nothing about the burden that has been lifted from his shoulders. All who come into contact with him find themselves becoming more personal.[5]

In other words, tight-lipped "perfection" is easily transferred to those around us, so that our unwillingness to speak honestly about our own needs likewise discourages others from opening up about theirs. At the same time, the man or woman who can confess—who has walked into the light, or spoken truth with his neighbor—begins to spread this light around, drawing others into a spirit of openness and liberation, so that they too feel comfortable simply being themselves in the presence of such a person.

Just imagine how it might feel if every church had several such people exuding a sort of "contagious" transparency, turning us all into those who truly have the kind of "fellowship with one another" that John describes in his first letter. If we did, says Larry Crabb, we could "enjoy the soul-enlivening experience of looking bad in the presence of love." Indeed, Crabb has written extensively on this subject, urging us to make church the kind of place to which we can bring our deepest struggles and problems. "I see a huge disconnect between what we do in church and what we're longing for and struggling with the most as we live our lives. . . . I long to be part of a church that somehow connects what we do when we meet together to who I am when I'm alone."[6]

Wouldn't you find it easier to worship with people you knew well—people who had been open with you—people who in turn knew you also with a deep and abiding intimacy?

In Luke 7, a Pharisee rebukes Jesus for allowing himself to be served by a woman who was a well-known "sinner"—to use the Pharisee's term. Here is a man who thinks he has it all together, as opposed to this mess of a woman washing Jesus' feet with her tears and hair after also expending on him a fabulously expensive vial of perfume. Jesus tries to reorient the Pharisee's attitude—telling the story of a man who learned to love his master after the master forgave a colossal debt. Like that grateful debtor, Jesus says the woman "loved much. But he who is forgiven little, loves little" (Luke 7:36-47). Translation: If you feel like you are perfect and don't need much forgiveness, then you will be greatly shortchanged in your experience of love. People who think they're better than everyone else—or who insist on seeming and feeling "perfect"—people like this Pharisee, for instance—such people have trouble internalizing grace, and so they will not feel loved at a deep level. For this reason, as Jesus pointed out, they also do not have a lot of love to give others.[7]

If, by contrast, we admit to imperfection—or if we have such a tear-inducing sense of our unworthiness that, like the woman in Luke 7, we can only worship Jesus with a wordless, selfless adoration—then in that case we will naturally have a much stronger love for God, a much stronger sense of his love for us, and concomitantly, a greater capacity for living in love with the body of Christ.

Intimacy, which swiftly dies in the dry heat of "perfection," flourishes in the soil of need, weakness, and vulnerability.

NAKED AND UNASHAMED

I have long averred that marriage is one way in which a gracious God offers us a glimpse of life before the Fall. When Adam admits, in Genesis 3, that he hid from God because he was naked, we understand that he and his wife have lost the precious, guileless innocence they had in Genesis 2—when "the man and his wife were both naked and were not ashamed" (verse 25). To some degree, when a man and woman marry even now, they are able to reclaim this, at least on a physical level—through a healthy sexuality that should be marked by shamelessness before one another in intimate communion. And if, as we did earlier, we can take physical terms like "keeping warm" and "being lifted up" to include the internal life as well, then surely matrimony is a place where spouses should be comfortable shedding not just clothing but also artifice—sharing the unabashed spiritual nakedness that characterizes real intimacy. In a good marriage, we enter that rare and glorious state where our true self, with all its passions, weaknesses, and vulnerabilities, is both well known and well loved.

I believe this kind of intimacy can, should, and will characterize life in the body of Christ. Isn't that what everyone wants in a church? To be known for what you truly are, yet also loved? To be spiritually and emotionally naked before one's sisters and brothers, yet unashamed? Shouldn't we be laboring to create this sort of haven in at least a few of our church relationships? Or should I say "heaven"? My wife would. For she and I are both convinced that in heaven, things will be like this *with everyone.*

Years ago, as we were learning what a treasure we had in our marriage, we struggled with the idea that it would be dissolved in heaven, where—as Jesus told the Sadducees—"they neither marry nor are given in marriage" (Matt. 22:30). As we began to reflect on this idea, we had to believe that whatever heaven was actually like, it would be better than marriage—that even those who had remained single on earth would not go on longing for it, feeling that they'd somehow missed out. Well, we wondered, what if the afterlife offered a sort of universal marriage to everyone—not physical, of course, but a state in which we were fully known and fully loved by all: a state of complete transparency before God, Jesus Christ, and one another?

After all, the Bible's greatest passage on love ends by observing that in this earthly life, "we know in part and we prophesy in part, but when the perfect comes, the partial will pass away. . . . For now we see in a mirror dimly, but then face to face. Now I know in part; then I shall know fully, even as I have been fully known" (1 Cor. 13:9-12).

Surely God will know us, and we will know God—and this knowledge will have in it not a trace of fear, as it so often does in this life. If that is the case, then might it not also be true of heavenly relationships with other souls? Fully known and fully loved. That is what we can look forward to in the next life. So why not begin working to bring some of that into this life, too? In our friendships; in our marriages; in our churches—wouldn't it be wonderful to understand, at least a little bit, how it feels to be both naked and unashamed!

OPEN FOR DISCUSSION

1. Brene Brown claims "there is no intimacy without vulnerability." Do you agree? If so, how does vulnerability facilitate or nurture intimacy?

2. What does it mean for every person to "speak the truth with his neighbor" (Eph. 4:25)?

3. Is it hard to tell others you are angry with them, as we are told to do in Ephesians 4:26? Why is this the case? Have you ever done it? What was it like?

4. Should our needs be seen as an opportunity to experience love from others? What about conflict in a relationship? Could that also be an opportunity? Explain.

5. Are vulnerability and openness contagious? If so, how and why? Have you ever known anyone who was contagious in this way? Can you describe her or him? How was this transparency communicated to others?

6. Consider Cloud and Townsend's statement, "'Perfect' people cannot internalize grace, so they will not feel loved at a deep level." Do you agree? Discuss.

7. What do you think of the author's assertion that heaven will be a place of universal transparency, where we are both fully known and fully loved? Do you agree? Is it possible to begin making our churches look like this?

CHAPTER NINE

"My Grace Is Sufficient"

The Virtue of Weakness

For Christians, weakness is a virtue—it's as simple as that.

But then again, maybe this idea isn't so simple; for like any virtue, weakness in our lives needs to be cultivated—and that sounds weird.

To help us with this counterintuitive idea, let's begin by examining Paul's approach to his own weakness in 2 Corinthians. After discussing his call to ministry and the amazing visions that were granted to him (12:1-4), Paul says a "thorn was given me in the flesh" (vs. 7); this was apparently some unknown personal issue that had been plaguing him—perhaps a demonic assault, an inward struggle, the constant rejection of opponents, or even a physical ailment such as the eye problem he mentions elsewhere (see Gal. 4:15, 6:11).[1] It may be best that we *don't* know the precise nature of Paul's problem—for we can then more easily apply his reflections to our own weaknesses and afflictions:

"Three times I pleaded with the Lord about this, that it should leave me. But he said to me, 'My grace is sufficient for you, for my power is made perfect in weakness' Therefore I will boast all the more gladly of my weaknesses, so that the power of Christ may rest upon me. For the sake of Christ, then, I am content with weaknesses, insults, hardships, persecutions, and calamities. For when I am weak, then I am strong" (12:8-10).

Who on earth would "boast" about their weaknesses? In a culture that has trouble with transparency, this sounds almost beyond belief. Yet what Paul is getting at in this striking passage is not hard to understand: When man is weak, that is the time for an almighty God to intercede and carry out his will in spite of our frailty and powerlessness. When we are forthright about weakness—when we honestly accept and publicly admit our inability—then a watching world can be sure that our perseverance and victory rest solely on divine power, rather than anything in ourselves. In this way, God gets the glory—and Paul is thrilled with these opportunities to show forth the goodness, power, and faithfulness of his savior. As the ESV Study Bible says, it was not Paul's glorious revelations but rather his "earthly weakness" that would be "the platform for perfecting and demonstrating the Lord's power."[2] "The abject weakness of the human instrument serves to magnify and throw into relief the perfection of the divine power in a way that any suggestions of human adequacy could never do."[3]

How different this is from the way we 21st-century believers approach our own frailties! As we've already seen in Part One of this book, Paul's Corinthian ministry had been dogged by accusations of weakness and inadequacy. By the time we reach 2 Corinthians 12, he has already dealt with this issue at length; see, for instance, 2 Cor. 10:10, where Paul quotes what that church was saying about him: "His letters are weighty and strong, but his bodily presence is weak, and his speech is of no account." Rather than fly off the handle at such personal remarks—as many of us might do—Paul's response is to *emphasizes* his weakness; unlike us, he doesn't *want* others to think too highly of him! As 2 Corinthians 12:7 makes clear, Paul felt that his afflictions were designed "to keep me from exalting myself" (NASB). It's a response we would do well to emulate when we struggle—as Paul did—with "weaknesses" and "insults."

And also when we struggle—as we do—to make ourselves look good at the expense of God's glory.

What's more, this "thorn-in-the-flesh" passage isn't the only one in which Paul shows a commitment to weakness for the glory of Christ. See, for instance, 2 Corinthians 11:30: "If I must boast, I will boast of the things that show my weakness." Or the famous "jars of clay" verse in 2 Corinthians 4, where the apostle again declares his willingness to accept frailty—as an opportunity for heavenly strength and faithfulness to shine: "We have this treasure in jars of clay, to show that the surpassing power belongs to God and not to us" (verse 7).

This text, with its fragile earthen vessels, always reminds me of the lyric from Leonard Cohen's 1992 song "Anthem": "There's a crack in everything. That's how the light gets in."

You see, this willingness to live with our inability does more than just highlight the goodness of God to a watching world. It also puts us in a better place to receive and experience this goodness. Indeed, self-abandonment is the only true route to living fully in the love of God. As Charles Hodge puts it in his remarks on 2 Corinthians 12, "When really weak in ourselves, and conscious of that weakness, we are in the state suited to the manifestation of the power of God. When emptied of ourselves we are filled with God."[4]

Other writers have likewise commented powerfully on this phenomenon. "My flaws were the ways through which I would receive grace," writes Don Miller. "Grace only sticks to our imperfections." Or consider these words from Henry Cloud and John Townsend: "Make friends with your needs. Welcome them. They are a gift from God, designed to draw you into relationship with him and with his safe people. Your needs are the cure to the sin of self-sufficiency." Thrall, McNicol, and Lynch put it more succinctly: Jesus is never closer to us than "when we come face to face with our failure."

> Weakness—or neediness—is a valuable asset in God's community. Jesus introduced a new era in which weakness is the new strength. Anything that reminds us that we are

> dependent on God and other people is a good thing. . . . When we see our sin, we are seeing the Spirit's conviction, which means we are witnessing spiritual power, but that power feels different from what we expect. It's not like worldly power. Spiritual power feels like a struggle, or weakness, or neediness, or desperation. It is simply, "I need Jesus," which is the most powerful thing we can say. . . . "Help" spoken to the Lord is power.[5]

THE FIRST STEP . . . IN A THOUSAND MILES

Why do we have such a hard time accepting, admitting, and even embracing our neediness? As born-again Christians, isn't that supposedly where we *started* this journey? Every believer knows that the first step to Christ is admitting your sins; there's no way you're going to grasp his sacrifice—and no way you're going to prize it with appropriate awe and gratitude—unless you first understand the depth of your own need for a redeemer. And so, having come to Christ in this way, how is it that we expect to move away from this sense of sin and weakness as our sanctification progresses? Hasn't your own experience been just the opposite? Don't you have a far *greater* sense of your own sin now than when you first believed? And is it possible that God wants it this way, so that we may go on depending wholly and entirely on him alone, just as we first depended on grace alone for our salvation?

That is the contention of Barbara Duguid's 2013 book *Extravagant Grace: God's Glory Displayed in Our Weakness*. If you have a hard time understanding why you still struggle with sin after so many years, I commend to you this wise and wonderful little volume. Working largely with ideas developed by John Newton, Duguid points out that God, in his infinite power, certainly *could* heal us of all our sins; in fact, he could do it fully at the very moment we're converted.

> Instead, he chose to save us and leave indwelling sin in our hearts and bodies. . . . Yet Newton also points out that since

> we know God does all things for his own glory and the good of his people, his decision to leave Christians with many struggles with sin must also somehow serve to glorify him and benefit his people. . . . God thinks that you will actually come to know and love him better as a desperate and weak sinner in continual need of grace than you would as a triumphant Christian warrior who wins each and every battle against sin. . . .
>
> John Newton shows us from Scripture that true sanctification is all about growing in humility, dependence, and gratitude. Joy blossoms in our hearts not as we try harder and harder to grow, but as we see more clearly the depths of our sin and understand more fully our utter helplessness. Only then will we take our eyes off ourselves and look to Christ for all that we need in life and in death. Only then will we truly cherish our savior and believe that we need him every minute of every day, and that without him we can do nothing (John 15:5).[6]

Using these ideas, Duguid helps resolve an issue that has bothered me for a long time: If God does, in a sense, want us to accept and "live with" this ongoing sin in our lives, then why are both the Old and New Testament simply chock-full of commands that set the bar so high—commands that are well-nigh impossible to keep, such as Christ's insistence that we love God with all our heart, soul, mind, and body (Luke 10:27)? If we must accept our powerlessness to fully obey such commands, is it not mere frustration and torture to make them in the first place? To put it more plainly, if God knows we're going to fail, why does he keep telling us to try so hard?

Duguid's answer is simple: God sets the bar so high precisely in order to confirm and deepen our sense of sin. Since the proud human heart is always hard at work denying that it is "desperately sick" (Jer. 17:9), any sort of milder or more "do-able" commandments would have us believing that we could meet the standard—or worse, that we actually *had* met it. "If we don't try hard and still fail, we might delude ourselves into thinking that we could obey God if we chose to make the effort. Yet when we try hard and fail, and try hard and fail again, we truly learn to ascribe our entire salvation to the work of Christ."[7]

Brothers and sisters, only in this way can we subdue our persistent, self-centered self-sufficiency; only in this way will we learn to cling desperately to Christ every moment of our lives. It's a desperate battle to let go of any and all hope in ourselves—to crush the pride that opposes Christ. And, having fought this battle all my life, I finally had to face this unhappy but very helpful fact: The miserable sense of my own sin, the constant hair-pulling over "I did it again, for the 98th time!"—the wallowing obsession with my own repeated failures; this is just an inverted type of pride, and a worse one than the more obviously smug and boastful types. I say "worse," because the person who goes about constantly mourning and moaning over his sin, to the point of single-minded fixation, might *sound* as though he's being humble; but in fact he is likely even more narcissistic than someone who is vain or proud—because all he does is think about himself. All the time.

If I'm constantly shocked and perhaps even angry that I can't stop sinning, it merely shows that I have not yet come to the end of hoping in myself; somewhere deep down, there still lurks the man-centered certainty that I *ought* to be able to do it, if I just try a little harder. The subconscious thought is, "I'm better than this"—but the truth is, I'm not. After nearly four decades in the Lord's kingdom, I should surely be able to acknowledge this more readily. I should have abandoned this insidious form of selfish pride and cast my lot with Christ, affirming both my own utter inability and his gloriously sufficient grace to cover all my sins. You may have to do the same thing.

For when we are weak, then we are strong.

OPEN FOR DISCUSSION

1. How is weakness a virtue? Is this idea countercultural? That is, does modern American culture see weakness as a virtue? If not, in what ways does our culture suggest otherwise?

2. What does it mean to "boast" about our weaknesses? Why should we do this?

3. As Ed Welch suggests in *Shame Interrupted*, try identifying some of your weaknesses, and then ask how you can boast about them.[11]

4. What as Barbara Duguid's answer to the puzzling issue of why we still sin after so many years in the kingdom? In other words, if God has all power and hates sin, why doesn't he just rescue us fully so that we no longer fall into sin?

5. If God wants us to "live with" our sins, then why does he make such extreme demands on us, such as loving him with all our heart, mind, soul, and body?

6. Do *you* struggle with frustration over your inability to stop sinning? Do you ever get angry about it? Is there a possibility that pride, rather than humility, could be at the bottom of your misery and frustration? If so, how can you get beyond this?

CHAPTER TEN

"My Burden Is Light"

Rest and Reassurance

Which is worse—going through some sort of trauma, or refusing to tell anyone about it afterwards? Research indicates it could actually be the latter. In the words of Brene Brown, "the act of not discussing a traumatic event or confiding it to another person could be more damaging than the actual event."

What's especially striking about this statement is that it's based on a study of victims recovering from rape and incest. Even in the case of such unspeakable trauma, researchers found that refusing to open up about our most damaging wounds can actually be more harmful than the wounds themselves.

"Conversely," Brown adds, "when people shared their stories and experiences, their physical health improved, their doctor's visits decreased, and they showed significant decreases in their stress hormones."[1]

As this material suggests, openness is good for you—physically, emotionally, psychologically, and spiritually. And this goes beyond mere openness about trauma. As this chapter will assert, letting people see the real you—while dropping the pretense of being cool, perfect, "together"—is restful and reassuring; it reduces stress while it also closes that crippling chasm between what we really are and what we would like others to think. Discontentment, exhaustion, and loneliness can be greatly relieved through personal sharing with others—for this cultivates, conversely, "a sense of excitement, involvement, security, warmth, and affirmation."[2]

"I THOUGHT IT WAS JUST ME"

By now, perhaps I've convinced you to take advantage of Brown's work, which offers a largely secular but useful and informed approach to many of the problems we've discussed. A favorite of mine is her 2007 book *I Thought It Was Just Me*—and doesn't that title alone so clearly highlight one reason why trauma, weakness, and distress are so debilitating? Even in a theoretically "safe" community like church—where entry is supposed to *begin* with an admission of sin and dependence on Christ—even here, you look around during fellowship time and feel certain you must be the only one who's struggling so badly.

Or perhaps instead of "even here," I ought to say "*especially* here."

Indeed, the "it's-just-me" syndrome actually seems worse in church than in many other social groups like Alcoholics Anonymous, the VFW, book-group discussions, or even your Tuesday night bowling league. Somehow—despite the unilateral testimony of Scripture that God's people are pretty messed up—we foolishly pretend that church really ought to be a cut above: We want to believe that here, if nowhere else in culture, all struggles and failures are susceptible to a quick fix that makes Christianity look like the answer to all of life's problems. It sometimes seems as though we want to *prove* that Christianity is so much better than the surrounding culture—as though the gospel truths of Scripture were insufficient, they somehow need our help to demonstrate God's power. Instead, by faking perfection, all we manage to "demonstrate" is that you can't be yourself in church; that timid, busted-up sinners don't belong; and that if you come in, you must quickly learn to suppress your struggles and put on your best Sunday face. Behavior becomes more important than belief; and *that's not the gospel.*

Sisters and brothers, if we want to feel truly at home church; if we want to get help and make progress in sanctification; if we want visitors to feel welcome when they come in—then we simply must drop the pretense and *be* who we really are: sinners saved by grace alone. Truly, as we saw in Chapter Six, it is the very *hiddenness* of shame, sin, and struggle that gives it continuing power over us. In their extensive work on shame, both Brown and Ed Welch insist on this idea. "Shame works only if we think we're alone in it," writes Brown. If on the other hand we come to find that others are struggling with similar issues, then the shame becomes "bankrupt."[3] By the simple but courageous act of sharing some deeply personal and perhaps even embarrassing problem, you can encourage fellow-believers to come out from behind their masks, to reconcile themselves to being life-long strugglers, to achieve the blissful rest of not having to *pretend* anymore.

STRESSFUL PRETENSE vs. RESTFUL MEEKNESS

In an oft-cited 1991 interview, the pop star Madonna told *Vanity Fair* magazine,

> All of my will has always been to conquer some horrible feeling of inadequacy. I'm always struggling with that fear. I push past one spell of it and discover myself as a special human being and then I get to another stage and think I'm mediocre and uninteresting. And I find a way to get myself out of that. Again and again. My drive in life is from this horrible fear of being mediocre. And that's always pushing me, pushing me. Because even though I've become Somebody, I still have to prove that Somebody. My struggle has never ended and it probably never will.[4]

While admiring this sort of drive and the goals it can achieve, one is nonetheless startled to learn that someone like Madonna, someone who had so clearly "arrived" atop the pop-culture pile, with millions of record sales, sold-out concerts, and a successful film career to boot—someone like this can still feel "inadequate"? Among other things, this interview confirms our sense that *everyone* struggles to "arrive"—and you should never classify yourself as some sort of oddball just because you also feel like you don't measure up.

It also confirms how exhausting is the race to keep convincing other people not only that you've arrived, but also that you are worthy enough to stay there—wherever "there" is! If we could all just get to the point where we *admit* we're inadequate—that we started out inadequate, that we will always be inadequate, that our sole adequacy is in Christ because *he's the only one who ever actually measured up*—if we could reach this point, we could lay down our burden of pressure, performance, pretense, and perfection, taking up instead a life of freedom. And authenticity. And belonging. And rest.

Perhaps this is part of what Jesus means when he tells us, "Come to me, all who labor and are heavy laden, and I will give you rest. Take my yoke upon you, and learn from me, for I am gentle and lowly in heart, and you will find rest for your souls. For my yoke is easy, and my burden is light" (Matt. 11:28-30). That is certainly how the great pastor and writer A. W. Tozer interprets it. In his famous 1948 work *The Pursuit of God*, he writes at length on the relief we can obtain from laying down the worldly burden of pretense in favor of the "meekness and rest" to be found in Christ alone. Speaking of how hard we work to keep others thinking well of us, he writes, "The heart's fierce effort to protect itself from every slight, to shield its touchy honor from the bad opinion of friend and enemy, will never let the mind have rest. Continue this fight through the years and the burden will become intolerable."

By contrast, the meek man, rather than working for the world's approval, has learned to accept God's estimate of his life:

> He knows well that the world will never see him as God sees him and he has stopped caring. He rests perfectly content to allow God to place his own values. . . . The old struggle to defend himself is over. He has found the peace which meekness brings.
>
> Then also he will also get deliverance from the burden of *pretense.* By this I mean not hypocrisy, but the common human desire to put the best foot forward and hide from the world our real inward poverty. . . . There is hardly a man or woman who dares to be just what he or she is without doctoring up the impression. The fear of being found out gnaws like rodents within their hearts. . . . I am sure that most people live in secret fear that some day they will be careless and by chance an enemy or friend will be allowed to peep into their poor empty souls. So they are never relaxed. . . .
>
> These burdens are real, and little by little they kill the victims of this evil and unnatural way of life. . . .
>
> Artificiality is just one curse that will drop away the moment we kneel at Jesus' feet and surrender ourselves to His meekness. Then we will not care what people think of us so long as God is pleased. Then *what we are* will be everything; what we appear will take its place far down the scale of interest for us. . . .

Citing "the easy yoke of self-forgetfulness," Tozer concludes, "The rest He offers is the rest of meekness, the blessed relief which comes when we accept ourselves for what we are and cease to pretend."[5]

ALL THAT AND REASSURANCE TOO

In an effort to model a modicum of transparency, I have already shared some of my struggles with pornography over many years. In

Chapter Six, for instance, I tried to indicate that by forcing myself to be accountable to my wife—that is, to be transparent with her whenever I succumb to this ugly sin—I have finally managed to get control over what was once a viciously persistent addiction.

Naturally, guilt is a huge part of any recurring sin-cycle like this: You sin, you feel guilty, you try to hide your guilt. And then this secret guilt, rather than discouraging further sin, merely becomes a prison from which it seems the only escape is more sin; at least that would take our minds off the guilt for a few minutes—so goes the diabolical argument. Thus, if we are trying to sidestep feelings of guilt by not sharing with others—"I just can't face telling someone about it!"—this concealment can actually backfire, leaving us more trapped than ever. I can't say exactly why, but it certainly has been my experience that deep-seated guilt somehow keeps us more firmly tied to the sin than ever. Paradoxically, the only thing that can set you free from this cycle is the grace of God: The knowledge that he has forgiven you and still loves you just the same. This alone fully and finally *severs* the bond of sin. *This alone* provides the strength to go on fighting temptation.

And believe it or not, one excellent way to experience this grace is by telling a trusted confidant.

My wife has had to forgive me for the sin of "lustful looking" more times than I can count. Yes, as time goes by these failures do tend to occur farther and farther apart, with somewhat less drastic sin in each case; indeed, at this point in middle age, most such confessions involve failure to "look away" during an R-rated movie or—similarly—allowing my gaze to linger too long on some immodestly clad lady, often in an otherwise innocuous magazine or Facebook post. Yet these are still serious sins—and every time it happens, I find myself thinking, with considerable anguish, "I just can't tell her one more time about yet another failure; surely she won't be willing to forgive me again!" Yet she does—and this serves as an unbelievably powerful confirmation that God does too. For isn't that just what we think of God—that he won't forgive us one more time, after so many similar sins in the past? And since this is so hard to believe and accept, don't we all need a compassionate friend who can, as it were, put real-world flesh and blood on God's astonishing grace and patience?

In the words of Henry Cloud and John Townsend, "When you have a friend with the ability to forgive you for hurting her or letting her down, something deeply spiritual occurs between you two. You actually experience a glimpse of the deepest nature of God himself."

Dietrich Bonhoeffer puts it even more clearly:

> Who can give us the certainty that, in the confession and the forgiveness of our sins, we are not dealing with ourselves but with the living God? God gives us this certainty through our brother. . . . Our brother has been given me that even here and now I may be made certain through him of the reality of God in His judgment and His grace. . . . The assurance of forgiveness becomes fully certain to me only when it is spoken by a brother in the name of God. Mutual brotherly confession is given to us by God in order that we may be sure of divine forgiveness.[6]

I'm not crazy about the word "only" in the penultimate sentence here; this way of phrasing it leans too heavily toward Roman Catholic confession, denying God the privilege of communicating such grace directly to his beloved children. Nonetheless, Bonhoeffer's point is one I have seen confirmed in my own life; honestly, I could almost weep when I recall how calmly and firmly my wife has assured me of her forgiveness for a sin that shows such disrespect toward her personally. Of course, I would never want to presume on her forgiveness as an excuse to sin—something that is even more unthinkable with God's forgiveness (see, for instance, Romans 6:1-2). Nonetheless, this embodiment of God's ongoing grace is the only way—yes, the only!—that I've been able to break the cycle of sin and guilt that has shackled me since I first encountered obscene pictures nearly 50 years ago.

To my fellow sinners, who all struggle with long-term temptations like this—of whatever sort they may be—I say that if you too want rest and reassurance, you must strip off the mask of pretense and be who you really are; tell someone—tell them again and again if you need to—and experience the amazing relief and true communion of knowing that no, it is *not* just you; and yes, God will *always* forgive those sins you hate so much.

Until you do this, it will be all but impossible to take up that light and easy burden of which Christ speaks so movingly.

OPEN FOR DISCUSSION

1. Research suggests that keeping quiet about trauma can be even more damaging than the trauma itself. Do you agree? If so, why do you suppose this is the case?

2. Have you ever had the "I-thought-it-was-just-me" syndrome, where you were sure you were the only one so messed up? Where does it occur it your life, and what is it like?

3. Have you ever experienced the above-mentioned syndrome in church? The author asserts that this syndrome is often *worse* in our churches. Do you agree? Why do you suppose this is the case?

4. Reread Madonna's description of constantly racing to overcome feelings of inadequacy. Do you struggle with this? How does it feel? Does it get in the way of transparency? Why is it that even famous people seem to struggle with these feelings?

5. Would it be restful to "drop the act" and just be yourself? Do you have friends in your life with whom you can do this?

6. Have there been times when you sinned against a friend, confessed it to him or her, and received forgiveness? What was that like? Have there been times when someone sought forgiveness from you? Were you able to model God's love by forgiving? How can we get better at both sides of this interaction?

Part Three

HOW WE CAN BE TRANSPARENT

CHAPTER ELEVEN

"He Will Quiet You by His Love"

Believing the Gospel

I'll wager that most folks reading this book have been Christians for quite some time—maybe years, maybe decades, maybe even going all the way back to childhood. So this chapter, including material on how and why we are saved through Christ, may seem like something that's already behind you—stuff you don't need to think much about anymore.

But we never get beyond the gospel. Even to the end of our lives we must keep working to recall our need for Christ—and his gracious, perfect, eternal provision for that need. Our failure to live in these truths is one reason so many of us struggle with assurance of salvation, with crippling shame and guilt; and it may well account for why we don't have the honesty, humility, and confidence to be open with others about our sins.

So let's begin with a brief review—keeping in mind that this may actually be new material for some readers:

The essential Christian message teaches that we are all sinners—that "none is righteous, no, not one"; for "all have sinned and fall short of the glory of God" (Rom. 3:10, 23). In other words, our sin unfits us to enjoy eternal life in God's presence; instead, it dooms to eternal death and damnation—"for the wages of sin is death." But as Paul tells us in this very same verse about wages and death, "the free gift of God is eternal life in Christ Jesus our Lord" (Rom. 6:23).

This is possible because on the cross, Christ took the punishment for our sins, not only dying for us but also suffering the curse of God's anger; "he himself bore our sins in his body on the tree," as Peter puts it (1 Peter 2:24); in the words of the Apostle's Creed, "he descended into hell" on our behalf. We can be healed of our sin and our lifelong fear of death by actively laying claim to Christ's provision—by turning our lives over to him and living in his righteousness, rather than our own. As Paul writes, "The life I now live in the flesh I live by faith in the Son of God, who loved me and gave himself up for me" (Gal. 2:20).

So while the gospel brings "good news," it also offers some very bad news: Namely, that we are far more sinful than we could ever imagine—so sinful that we can be saved only by someone else. We cannot erase or atone for our own sin. "No one comes to the father except through me," says Christ (John 14:6).

And that's the good news: Not only has this salvation been accomplished, but also, it's complete and irrevocable—a perfect salvation achieved by a perfect savior. "Christ also suffered once for sins, the righteous for the unrighteous, that he might bring us to God" (1 Peter 3:18).

Even if you already know all this, you may well need to keep reminding yourself of these important principles—especially if you struggle with transparency. Once we get these two key gospel truths imbedded in our hearts—namely, our catastrophic sin and his inestimable salvation—openness will be a lot easier. Believing in our utter lack of merit, together with the transcendent love of God through Christ, we won't worry so much about what other people think. In other words, as we saw in Chapter One, the pervasive "fear of man" can be driven out by proper reverence for what God says about us.

Let's flesh this out a bit more here.

POLLUTED GARMENTS

Just before the worldwide flood in Genesis 6-9, God looks down and sees that "the wickedness of man was great in the earth, and that every intention of the thoughts of his heart was only evil continually." Sadly, this pervasive sin was not cured by the flood; for many centuries later the writer of Ecclesiastes can also insist, "Surely there is not a righteous man on earth who does good and never sins" (7:20). Even in the New Testament era, humanity is described as "dead in sin"—"hostile" to God and literally unable to submit to his law (Eph. 2:5; Rom. 8:7-8).

Worse yet, this dire sin is not limited to unbelievers, but continues to rear its ugly head even after we have been saved and committed our lives to serving Christ.[1] This is perhaps shown most powerfully in Romans 7, where the Apostle Paul, for all his zeal for the kingdom, still describes himself as "wretched" and "sold under sin. . . . For I know that nothing good dwells in me, that is, in my flesh"—which he calls "this body of death" (Rom. 7:14-25). Of course, there are some scholars who believe Romans 7 describes Paul before his conversion; but the apostle, speaking in the present tense, uses 38 first-person pronouns in a mere 12 verses, confirming the contention of such authorities as Augustine, Luther, Calvin, John Owen, Charles Hodge, John Murray, James Boice, J. I. Packer, John Piper, and R. C. Sproul: Romans 7 does in fact discuss Paul's experience as a regenerated Christian.[2] In any case, the great apostle, writing several years later, can still describe himself as the world's "foremost" sinner (1 Tim. 1:15). Our depravity does not disappear simply because Christ has redeemed us; indeed, as most of us know from hard experience, our sense of sin—like Paul's—only seems to increase as we spend more and more time with Christ and his word.

This idea of pervasive sin is highlighted by powerful imagery elsewhere in Scripture. Isaiah, for example, famously insists that even "our righteous deeds are like a polluted garment"—which likely means clothing stained by menstruation (Isa. 64:6). In Zechariah, Israel's high priest—the nation's representative before a holy God—is likewise found to be "clothed with filthy garments," which likely means his attire was "soiled with excrement" (Zech. 3:3).[3] If the state of Paul, the high priest, and the nation of Israel can be described in terms of feces, death, and menstrual blood, why should we think we are any different?

But we do. While confessing our sinfulness and paying lip-service to our need for Christ, we constantly back-pedal: We compare ourselves to others, we minimize, we blame, we struggle to maintain a righteous front (especially in church!), and—perhaps most damning of all— if anyone is even the least bit critical of us, we react with alarm, rationalization, self-defense, even anger. Dietrich Bonhoeffer expounds on this subject with his usual hard-hitting phraseology: "The sin of resentment that flares up so quickly in the fellowship indicates again and again how much false desire for honor, how much unbelief, still smolders in the community." Bonhoeffer insists that by contrast, every true believer must work to consider himself the *worst* of all sinners—even though this "arouses all the resistance of the natural man. . . . There can be no genuine acknowledgment of sin that does not lead to this extremity. . . . If my sinfulness appears to me to be in any way smaller or less detestable in comparison with the sins of others, I am still not recognizing my sinfulness at all."[4]

TRANSPARENCY WITH ONESELF—FIRST OF ALL

If, like me, you suspect that lurking somewhere under all your confession and supposed humility, there is still some pride and self-righteousness—then you might consider David's prayer in Psalm 139: "Search me, O God, and know my heart! Try me and know my thoughts! And see if there be any grievous way in me, and lead me in the way everlasting!" (vss. 23-24). You cannot be transparent with others, or even with God, unless you are first transparent with yourself; yet ironically, it is God alone who can reveal to you the depths of your sin. And though it might not be pleasant, the Lord will surely answer a such a request—because he is holy, he knows what we are like, and he wants us to grow in humility, grace, and sanctification.

And if you also want this, then give God a channel to work in your heart by immersing yourself in Scripture. "The purpose in a man's heart is like deep water," says Proverbs, "but a man of understanding will draw it out" (Prov. 20:5). Working in conjunction with the Spirit, God's holy word can indeed "draw out" the unknown plans, motives, and sins buried deep in your heart. "For the word of God is living and active and sharper than any two-edged sword, and piercing as far as the division of soul and spirit, of both joints and marrow, and able to judge the thoughts and intentions of the heart. And there is no creature hidden from His sight, but all things are open and laid bare to the eyes of Him with whom we have to do" (Heb. 4:12-13).

The Greek word for "open" here is *gymna*, which literally means "naked"—stressing "complete exposure before God."[5] In other words, "every single detail and aspect of the human person is fully and inexorably open to the gaze of God." This in turn "discloses the futile superficiality of all the elaborate defenses which he seeks to erect against God"—for God's word "penetrates beneath the surface and beyond every specious façade to the radical heart of our being (cf. 1 Sam. 16:7)."[6] "Before Him all the superficial cover-up is stripped away. Before Him and His Word we appear just as we really are."[7]

At this point, I could easily show you how this works by listing a massive set of challenging verses to convict you of your sin; but for the sake of brevity, let's just look at the passage Jesus cited as a summary of the entire law: "You shall love the Lord your God with all your heart and with all your soul and with all your mind. This is the great and first commandment" (Matt. 22:37-38). Heart, soul, mind, and also body (if we include the phrasing from Luke 10:27). As your maker and redeemer—not to mention sovereign creator and lord of the universe—God has every right to demand this kind of allegiance. Yet you have never obeyed this commandment for even a few moments. You are, in fact, constantly fighting God's prerogative—every time you disobey a command, every time you covet, every time you give allegiance to something other than God, every time your mind wanders during prayer or worship, every time you make a decision or take credit without thinking of him first of all. Need I go on? Why do you think James, in chapter four of his letter, starts out by discussing things we want, and then goes on to use the terms "adulterous people" and "enmity with God"? A simple problem like the desire for something, or wishing to be "a friend of the world," constitutes an act of hostility toward your lord and savior (vss. 1-4).[8] And these are not isolated incidents; it's part of the very fabric of your life. It's not exaggeration to state that even Christians are ever struggling to put down a rebellious heart that daily wages war against the will, the goodness, and the sovereignty of God.

Psychologist Paul Tournier has a telling passage about this ongoing warfare. After a long course of psychotherapy, many of his patients admitted that they were in a state of open revolt against God. "And with all my heart I rejoice when these rebellions are brought out into the light of day, out of the deceptive silence behind which they have been muttering in secret. Do not let it be imagined that one must remain silent about one's feelings of rebellion in order to enter into dialog with God. Quite the opposite is the truth: it is precisely when one expresses them that a dialog of truth begins."[9]

Since your heavenly father already knows your daily struggle and your rebellious heart, you might as well admit it both to yourself and to him.

WHAT CAN TAKE AWAY MY SIN?

Like many in my circle of friends, I have a desperate and ongoing struggle with actually believing that my sins are paid for—constantly fearing that God is going to suddenly lose his patience and crush me, or that my sins have somehow finally outweighed the atoning sacrifice of Christ. That's why it's important to understand that only Christ could have achieved what I so desperately need—a complete and permanent obliteration of all the bad things I've done, am doing, and ever will do. His atonement can accomplish this monumental feat because my sin—like all human sin—is finite; it's big, but there is at least a fixed amount of it! Christ's righteousness, however, cannot be measured. He was *not* just a good man, a saintly man, a holy man. No; he was God himself—"God with us," "the true God," "the exact imprint of his nature" (Matt. 1:23; 1 John 5:20; Heb. 1:3; see also John 1:1; 1:14; 2 Cor. 4:4; Phil. 2:6). Because of this, his holiness is a divine holiness—perfect, immeasurable, *unending*. We cannot "out-sin" the righteousness of an infinitely perfect sacrifice.

One of my favorite sermon illustrations is a sort of mini-parable about a man struggling with sin and having to confess it over and over again. Coming back to God for the umpteenth time, he says, "Father, I know you just forgave me for this sin yesterday, but I have to confess it again." And God says, "What sin?"

Now this somewhat questionable anecdote does impugn the omniscience of God, who would certainly know what sin the poor man was referring to; yet in its limited way, it beautifully parallels a number of Scripture texts that insist on the thoroughness and permanence with which God, through Christ, has annihilated our sin—having "taken it out of the way, having nailed it to the cross" (Col. 2:14, NASB).

Perhaps the best known of these is from Psalm 103: "As far as the east is from the west, so far does he remove our transgressions from us" (verse 12). I once heard a Christian speaker point out that the compass directions here are especially significant, because one can move north or south only just so far before beginning to head in the opposite direction; but you can move east or west forever. Translation: There is no measuring the distance to which God has cast our sins away from us; it's infinite.

John 3:16 is another of the Bible's most famous verses—but even more precious to me is what follows: "God did not send the Son into the world to judge the world. . . . He who believes in him is not judged . . ." (vss. 17-18, NASB). Hallelujah! *He who believes is not judged!* Among many other words of assurance, my own favorites include two short, simple phrases, very easy to call up in a moral crisis when one needs a swift infusion of grace: Colossians 1 tells us we are "blameless and above reproach" (verse 22), while Romans 8 insists there is "no condemnation for those who are in Christ Jesus" (verse 1).

Hear that again:

Not judged.

Above reproach.

No condemnation.

This is God's truth, and you must cling to it—no matter how much trouble you have believing it.

Indeed, if we refuse, or deny, or shortchange the provision of God for our sin, then "we lay ourselves open to an endless variety of counterfeits peddling a promise of relief."[10] If we don't allow God to deal with our sin through the gospel of Christ, then we will inevitably find some other way to resolve it. Sadly, one of these false solutions is putting on a mask: trying to cloak our sin by convincing ourselves and everyone else that it isn't there, when God's word says it is. At the same time, God also says it isn't—for he has canceled the debt, wiped it out, cast it into a pit of oblivion, once and for all through Christ. There is no longer any reproach or condemnation—and thus, no need to escape from these threats by pretending we aren't sinners.

"THE BRIDEGROOM REJOICES"

I've been teaching adult Sunday school more than 25 years, covering such tough topics as gender, bioethics, and predestination—along with challenging Bible books like Judges, Esther, and Ecclesiastes. But by far the thorniest one I ever attempted, however, was Song of Solomon, with several issues that have stumped scholars for centuries. One such question runs as follows: Is this famous book to be read simply—and literally—as a romantic poem about two wildly passionate lovers? Or should we approach it more allegorically, as a symbolic depiction of divine love, with the husband and wife serving to represent

God and his people—and thus showing us what this relationship can, should, and does look like?

For centuries the church tended to prefer this latter more figurative interpretation, thus conveniently side-stepping some of the book's more erotic implications. In recent years, commentators have chosen to focus more on the literal approach—and I like that, too; for the Song then becomes an instructive, illuminating, and eminently hopeful portrait of passionate and devoted marriage—a portrait that seems to be increasingly rare in our culture.

Yet even when we look at it this way, the book can still teach us much about the way God loves and cares for his people; for the New Testament's key primer on marriage—Ephesians 5—repeatedly insists that good marriages are patterned on the relationship between Christ and his church: "Husbands, love your wives, as Christ loved the church and gave himself up for her. . . . This mystery is profound, and I am saying that it refers to Christ and the church" (see Eph. 5:22-33).

Thus, just as we come to understand the love of God the Father by reflecting on how earthly fathers love their children, so too we can get a firmer grasp on Christ's love for us by seeing how a good husband cares for his wife. And the blessed Song of Solomon certainly provides us with plenty of material for studying this.

Throughout the Song, the man praises very specific things about his beloved: her eyes, her breasts, her hair, her nose, her neck, her cheeks, her breath, her thighs—even her navel and her belly! (See, for instance, Song 4:1-5 and 7:1-9.) Clearly, he loves her for *who she actually is*—a unique person, not like anyone else. Most of us in my Sunday school class agreed that we want to be loved this way too. Just as we recognize what makes a good father, we all know what ideal married love is like: It's *person-specific*. A strong parent loves his or her child individually; and the man in Song of Solomon loves *this* woman the same way, separating her from all others and singling her out for who she is—and she rejoices in this specific commitment as he cherishes her. As commentator Iain M. Duguid puts it: "What is truly remarkable is that, although we each really are one among billions of ordinary people, he also treasures us constantly as individuals, delighting in the beauty that he has bestowed upon us as a glorious gift."[11]

Song of Solomon, after all, isn't the only Bible passage that points to marriage as the key to understanding God's love. We have already mentioned Ephesians 5, where Paul observes that a groom "nourishes and cherishes" his wife—"just as Christ does the church" (Eph. 5:29). And Isaiah declares, "As the bridegroom rejoices over the bride, so shall your God rejoice over you" (Isa. 62:5). Think of how thrilled a groom can be on his wedding day (and his wedding night!), when he has finally been united with this woman he prizes.

That is how God feels about us.

THE BENEFIT OF THE DOUBT

In his audio series called "Developing Christian Character," R. C. Sproul explains that one key aspect in practicing love toward others is giving people the benefit of the doubt.[12] If this is the case, then when 1 Corinthians says "love is kind," it's instructing us to give the best possible interpretation to others' actions, to trust their motives, and—rather than being skeptical, critical, and accusatory—to see them in a positive and favorable light as often as we can.

We are commanded to do this because it is analogous to how God loves us. In our imperfect knowledge of one another, we always hope for the best—while in his perfect omniscience, God views us as fully justified in Christ: Our future selves—sinless and glorified—are as much before his sight as our present selves (see, for instance, Rom. 8:29-30). Thus his holy word, in its descriptions of various flawed individuals, often sees them with this sort of kind and gracious love—in spite of their failures and transgressions.

The Old Testament figure Jephthah, for example, appears to have sacrificed his own daughter to keep a rash vow (Judg. 11:29-40);

meanwhile, his fellow Israelite Samson slept with prostitutes and twice fell for pagan women, allowing the second to strip him of his hair and his great strength (Judg. 14:1-2; 16:1-22). Yet these two figures, along with such other flawed Israelites as Gideon and Barak, are listed as heroes of the faith in Hebrews 11:32. Similarly, in his second letter, Peter describes Lot as a "righteous man" with a "righteous soul." This is indeed a surprising description, considering the way Lot is portrayed in Genesis, where he comes across as "greedy, cowardly and weak" (see 2 Peter 2:8 and Gen. 19:6-20).[13] Peter also holds up Abraham's wife, Sarah, as a model of feminine submission because she "obeyed Abraham, calling him lord" (1 Peter 3:6). Yet the only time Scripture records Sarah using this term is Genesis 18:12, where she cynically refers to her husband ("my lord") as "old"—after laughing because she didn't believe God's promise of a son. Not exactly a mountaintop moment of wifely submission for Christian wives to emulate.

Nonetheless, in all these cases, God's word is pleased to give these figures the benefit of the doubt—not ignoring or winking at their sins, but choosing instead to highlight the good that is working in them through his grace. That's because, just as a wife, for instance, is able to love her husband passionately and devotedly in spite of glaring sin in his life, so also God delights in his beloved people—as indicated by the Old Testament prophet Isaiah: "Can a woman forget her nursing child, that she should have no compassion on the son of her womb? Even these may forget, yet I will not forget you. Behold, I have engraved you on the palms of my hands. . ." (Isa. 49:15-16; for other verses on God's intimate and undying love, see Rom. 8:38-39 and 14:4; and Heb. 4:14-16).

As Isaiah suggests, the love of a mother or father is only a mini-portrait of God's relationship with us; his is that of a perfect father, a perfect mother—far more permanent and unshakable than the love of any human parent. For all we learn about Christ's love by studying marriage in Song of Solomon, his passion for us is likewise far greater than that of any flawed human groom for his bride. As Zephaniah puts it, "He will rejoice over you with gladness; he will quiet you by his love; he will exult over you with loud singing" (3:17).

DOUBLE IMPUTATION

In the last few pages, I have tried to stress the twin peaks of the gospel's good news—namely, that our sins are fully forgiven, and that God loves us like a holy bridegroom. These two truths are founded on what theologians call "double imputation." Yes, this kind of term sounds annoyingly intellectual; but it's actually quite straightforward and incredibly important. It simply means that our sin was placed upon Christ, while at the same time his righteousness was credited to us.

Most Christians know and accept the first truth so well that I'm not going to expound on it at length here. We know that Christ died in our place, bearing the punishment for our sins; and we can readily support this with such verses as Isaiah 53:5—"he was wounded for our transgressions; he was crushed for our iniquities." We understand that in this way, our "debt" to God has been canceled (see Col. 2:14), and thus we no longer live under the threat of hell and eternal death.

What we don't often consider is that this payment, this canceling of debt, merely brings us back to zero. We may not stand before God in the blackness of our sin—but that doesn't make us especially righteous, or any more worthy of his favor than a sinless rock or tree. In order to fully grasp God's love, we need to consider what is often referred to as the "active obedience of Christ." That is, he not only died for us—he also *lived* on our behalf. Because of this, we inherit and permanently possess his perfect righteousness; we stand before God not merely as "debt-free beggars," but as those laden down with the riches of Christ's glorious and holy obedience.[14] *This* is why God loves us with an infinite and undying love: As far as he's concerned, we possess all the righteousness of his own Son.

This imputation of Christ's obedience is made abundantly clear in a number of important passages. Take Romans 5:19, for example: "By the one man's obedience the many will be made righteous." Or Romans 4:6, which stresses "the blessing of the one to whom God counts righteousness apart from works." Other verses highlight both sides of the imputation: Speaking of the coming messiah, Isaiah writes, "by his knowledge shall the righteous one, my servant, make many to be accounted righteous, and he shall bear their iniquities" (Isa. 53:11). Perhaps clearest of all is 2 Corinthians 5:21: "For our sake he made him to be sin who knew no sin, so that in him we might become the righteousness of God." Since it is indeed the righteousness of God in Christ, it is complete, inviolable, spotless, absolute—and it lasts forevermore.[15] Many Christians spend considerable time thanking Christ because he died for their sins; personally, more of my own prayers express amazed gratitude for the perfect life Christ lived on my behalf, thus enabling me to come to God with the same rights and privileges possessed by his beloved and only begotten son.

To take it a step farther, this double imputation—our sin atoned for through Christ / his holy life ascribed to us—is actually what *enables* God to see us in the best possible light (even if this means doing it retroactively, as in the case of Old Testament saints like Lot, Samson, Sarah, and Jephthah). In his "divine forbearance" through Christ, he has "passed over former sins" (Rom. 3:25); and because we are now holy before him, he can say to us—like Solomon's love-smitten groom—"Behold, you are beautiful! . . . You are altogether beautiful, my love; there is no flaw in you" (Song 4:1, 7).

NOTHING LEFT TO PROVE

Surely such a gracious and loving commitment should encourage us to stop worrying what others think; we can rest in Christ and in the love of God rather than striving to seem good or look cool when we know deep down that we are not.

If we can grasp this incredible news—that we are hopeless sinners, even worse than we can imagine; that Jesus has fully paid for our sins, once and for all; that God loves us like a perfect husband and a perfect father—if we can really *live* in this and begin to experience it every day, then true transparency is within our reach. There is no need to pretend anymore; only to rest, trust, and worship Christ.

In *The Emotionally Healthy Church*, Peter Scazzero also expresses these ideas nicely: "God has given us the gospel to create a safe environment to look beneath the surface. I don't have to prove that I'm lovable or valuable. I don't have to be right all the time. I can be vulnerable and be myself, even if others don't accept me." And he then cites a favorite saying at his church; in this place, "You can be yourself because you have nothing left to prove."[16]

OPEN FOR DISCUSSION

1. In the first few pages of this chapter, the author cites several verses to indicate the profound sinfulness of mankind. Can you think of others?

2. Re-read Hebrews 4:12-13. Exactly how does Scripture penetrate to the deepest recesses of our being? Have you ever had an experience when some passage of the Bible helped you come to a better understanding of yourself? If so, describe it.

3. In your own life, do you see defensiveness and overreaction to snubs? Have you ever found yourself reacting this way only shortly after confessing to God how sinful you are? Could this indicate that maybe you don't *really* believe what the Bible says about your sin?

4. Re-read Romans 7:14-25. Do *you* think Paul is describing the experiences of a regenerated Christian in this passage? Why or why not? Have your own experiences with sin ever felt something like this? Explain.

5. Do you sometimes feel like you can "out-sin" the atoning sacrifice of Christ—or that you've already done so? How can we be sure that this is not possible?

6. What does it mean that God loves us like a bridegroom? In what ways is he the ideal husband and lover?

7. Under the subheads "What Can Take Away My Sin?" and "The Bridegroom Rejoices," the author cites verses suggesting how thoroughly God has wiped out our transgression, and also how much he loves us. Can you come up with any other verses to support these ideas? Pick one verse for each idea—atonement and love—and memorize it.

8. Have you ever asked for forgiveness from someone and not been granted it? In such cases, are you able to believe that God forgives you anyway?

9. What is meant by the terms "double imputation" and "active obedience of Christ"? The author asserts that we tend to downplay the latter, focusing more on the fact that Christ died for us and not enough on the fact that he also lived a righteous life on our behalf. Do you agree? Why is it important to stress that we are now in full possession of Jesus' righteousness? Consider memorizing one of the verses that supports this.

10. Do you think it helps with transparency if we have a full apprehension of the gospel—that is, of our deep sin, and our holy standing before God? Is it true that having grasped this, "we have nothing left to prove"? Explain.

CHAPTER TWELVE

"Whoever Loses His Life"

Dying to Self

In the final chapter of Galatians, Paul writes, "Far be it from me to boast except in the cross of our Lord Jesus Christ, by which the world has been crucified to me, and I to the world" (6:14). In other words, the world—with its passions and vicissitudes, its judgments and competition, its struggles for success, pleasure, fame, and fortune—is dead to the Christian; and the Christian has died to the world as well. Committed followers of Christ are to boast only in their savior, giving up everything that once meant so much to them. As Jesus famously put it in Matthew: "If anyone would come after me, let him deny himself and take up his cross and follow me. For whoever would save his life will lose it, but whoever loses his life for my sake will find it" (16:24-25).

Among the many worldly desires that must denied—lost, forsaken, and crucified—is our apparently bottomless desire for respect and admiration. If we could fully put this to death, transparency would follow as a matter of course.

That is the thesis of this current chapter.

In the Matthew passage above, the actual Greek verb for "deny" means "renounce" or "refuse," and thus "the call to discipleship demands that one completely abandon the natural desire to seek comfort, fame, or power." To put it another way, taking up the cross demands a "radical denial of self-interest and normal concern for one's own well-being."[1] Like Paul, I must remind myself that "I have been crucified with Christ. It is no longer I who live, but Christ who lives in me" (Gal. 2:20). This death will include the loss of all desire to be esteemed and well thought of. To the world, we are dead; and as Steve Brown has written, "Dead people don't have to 'do' anything. Dead people don't care what others think about them. . . . Dead people don't have anything to prove or to fake. They no longer have to be right. And dead people hardly ever have agendas or wear masks."[2]

Rather than putting up a front for the world, being lowly and despised should now be second nature to me—for as our master said, "If the world hates you, keep in mind that it hated me first" (John 15:18, NIV). Paul himself saw this being played out in his own life when he wrote, "I think that God has exhibited us apostles as last of all, like men sentenced to death, because we have become a spectacle to the world, to angels, and to men. We are fools for Christ's sake . . ." (1 Cor. 4:9-10). For this reason, the apostle and his coworkers lived as though "we had the sentence of death within ourselves" (2 Cor. 1:9, NASB).

You will find it easier to be transparent if you too pass a sentence of death on your public reputation—and if you determine to accept an inferior place in the world. True transparency means more than just opening up; rather, you must resolutely *refuse* to come across as better than you really are. Yes, I'm actually insisting you diligently work to ensure that others do not have an inflated or inaccurate view of what you are really like. You can, after all, bear false witness against yourself—if you try to pretend that you aren't a sinner. Exaggeration, deception, and misrepresentation all violate the truth—and thus break the eighth commandment.

This level of honesty and self-renunciation will be hard: shameful, humiliating, painful. It will often feel like death. Like crucifixion. It will require firm resolution and constant vigilance; but there are several things you can do to help nurture such a difficult lifestyle.

INJUSTICE AND CONFESSION

One sure way of dying to self—of nailing your ever-active flesh to the cross, and *keeping* it there—is to be more tolerant of insults and injustice. If someone does not treat you with the respect you feel you deserve—if you are snubbed or rejected or ill-used—try fighting that knee-jerk reaction of anger and self-defense; learn, like so many other religious leaders from Paul to Luther to Jim Elliott, that rejection, injustice, and hatred are the Christian's lot, his birthright—for it was part of our master's lot as well.

"The desire for one's own honor hinders faith. One who seeks his own honor is no longer seeking God and his neighbor. What does it matter if I suffer injustice? Would I not have deserved even worse punishment from God, if He had not dealt with me according to His mercy? Must it not be wholesome and conducive to humility for me to learn to bear such petty evils silently and patiently? . . . One who lives by justification by grace is willing and ready to accept even insults and injuries without protest, taking them from God's punishing and gracious hand." Rather than reacting with offense and indignation as we usually do, let us learn to see these snubs as an opportunity to deny the flesh, to step deliberately *away* from self-exaltation and pride. When such things happen, God is providing us with a perfect doorway to the death of self.

Another such opportunity for mortification is confessing sins to a sister or brother. "Confession in the presence of a brother is the profoundest kind of humiliation. It hurts, it cuts a man down, it is a dreadful blow to pride. To stand there before a brother as a sinner is an ignominy that is almost unbearable. In the confession of sins the old man dies a painful, shameful death before the eyes of a brother."[3]

My fellow strugglers, please learn to do this hard work of confessing. As we shall see later in Chapters Fourteen and Fifteen, there are many fine examples in the psalms—but one of these touches movingly on our current discussion. It's Psalm 32, where the writer is finding it hard to come forward with his sins; he kept silent about them for a while, during which time his bones "wasted away" and he was "groaning all day long"—for God's hand was heavy upon him, and his strength "dried up." After he eventually does acknowledge his sin and receive forgiveness from God, he later describes his initial reluctance as a sort of brute bull-headedness: "Be not like a horse or a mule, without understanding, which must be curbed with bit and bridle, or it will not stay near you" (Ps. 32:3-5, 9). My pastor once rephrased this as an injunction to "face the music," to own up to one's sins instead of acting like a dumb beast—especially since, as this psalm so clearly indicates, God will eventually bring you to a place of confession anyway, whether through groaning, wasted bones, or bit and bridle.

Of course, this confession of David is between himself and God—so it may not seem relevant to what we've been saying about transparency toward others. It's worth noting, however, that this penitential poem was intended to be read and used in public worship; so David actually is opening up to countless fellow-worshipers and other lovers of Scripture down through many centuries. Perhaps this is one of the things he learned to do when we was trying to hide his sin from God.

"HE MUST INCREASE, BUT I MUST DECREASE"

To some degree, these approaches—confession of sins, and self-restraint under injustice—are merely by-products of a sea-change that must take place if you are to crucify the fleshly need for affirmation and esteem. Though it's woefully hard to put into effect, this sea-change can be expressed quite simply: You have to stop caring so much about what others think of you.

In Chapter One, we looked briefly at 1 Corinthians 4, the key Scripture passage on what Tim Keller calls "the freedom of self-forgetfulness." In verses 3 and 4, Paul responds to criticism from the Corinthian church with an attitude we would do well to emulate: "With me it is a very small thing that I should be judged by you or by any human court. In fact, I do not even judge myself. I am not aware of anything against myself, but I am not thereby acquitted. It is the Lord who judges me."

In this bracing passage, Paul is not espousing complete indifference to what others think of him; he has some regard for their opinion, but in the end, this regard is "a very small thing." His emphasis, rather, is on the singular *un*importance of human judgment—on how fallible and relative it is, on its limitations and its unreliable nature as a guide to the truth about ourselves.[4]

Even in the secular world, many folks would love to attain an attitude like Paul's. As Keller observes, most contemporary counselors and therapists agree that we shouldn't be constantly aligning our lives to what others say or think; rather, these modern self-help gurus would generally have us scrap the false standard of others' judgment and replace it with our own internal goals: "Decide who you want to be," they tell us, "and then be it."

Naturally, one huge problem with this is that we can't live up to our own standards either.[5] Replacing others' judgments with our own is just another path to despair: Not only do we know too well how badly we fail to meet even our own lax standards—but furthermore, self-appraisal can be just as fallible and relative as the assessment of any other human being.

Of course, this dark and uncertain path is not the one Paul takes—for he insists, "I do not even judge myself." He will *not* fall into the trap of setting his own standard. Instead, Paul's only real concern is the final verdict of God—the only assessment that is sure, and the only one that ultimately matters. "All merely human judgments against him, be they of the Corinthians or of any others who may so judge him, are of little or no consequence whatsoever. The only judgment that counts is the final eschatological judgment administered by Christ himself. So much is this so that Paul includes personal 'judgments' of himself as equally inconsequential."[6]

"Notice the freedom Paul has. He does not have to make himself look better to other people. He is very satisfied with a resume that says, 'I am nothing, Jesus is everything.'" Ed Welch calls this the "great reversal, in which your reputation is of less importance and Christ's reputation is of utmost importance"; and if you can put this into effect, then you won't be controlled by what other people think.[7]

That is the key in ceasing to care so much for the opinions of others. First, we lean entirely on God's judgment and verdict—which, as we saw in the previous chapter, declares us free from sin and wholly loved as precious children. As Paul asks rhetorically in dismissing human judgment, "Who are you to judge the servant of another? To his own master he stands or falls; and stand he will, for the Lord is able to make him stand" (Rom. 14:4, NASB).

But that assurance of God's love is only part of the equation. Take another look at Welch's words on "the great reversal." It is not only God's verdict on us that must assume preeminence in our thinking. To focus solely on this would, in some degree, still leaves us stuck in the realm of narcissistic tunnel-vision; we're still obsessing over how we ourselves are being perceived and treated. No! What must rather take the top spot among our priorities is *God's glory*—the honor, reputation, and advancement of Christ and his kingdom. This is the true path to the death of self. As Paul found, "the surpassing worth of knowing Christ Jesus my Lord" makes everything else in life—including what others think—seem like mere "rubbish" (Phil. 3:8). The importance of others' esteem will not simply vanish by magic; that prized possession you value so much can be seen for what it is—worthless trash—only if you replace it with a deep and abiding knowledge of Christ in all his glory, grace, love, and majesty. In the words of John the Baptist, "He must increase, but I must decrease" (John 3:30).

As a final pointer along these lines, consider a few passages where encountering God's transcendent glory yields an instant outburst of transparency about sin. For example, Peter, witnessing the power of Christ to subdue the natural world, reacts by falling at Jesus' knees and declaring, "Depart from me, for I am a sinful man, O Lord" (Luke 5:3-

8). Job has a similar reaction after God speaks directly to him: "Behold, I am of small account; what shall I answer you? I lay my hand on my mouth. . . . I had heard of you by the hearing of the ear, but now my eye sees you; therefore I despise myself, and repent in dust and ashes" (Job 40:4, 42:5-6).

But of course the most famous of these reactions is found in Isaiah 6, where the prophet sees God in his throne room, with his robe filling the temple, and the house full of smoke, and the foundations quaking, and the seraphim declaring, "Holy, holy, holy is the Lord of hosts; the whole earth is full of his glory!" Isaiah reacts by crying out, "Woe is me! For I am lost; for I am a man of unclean lips, and I dwell in the midst of a people of unclean lips; for my eyes have seen the King, the Lord of hosts!" (verses 1-5).

In every case, the transparent declaration of sin and repentance seems entirely spontaneous, almost involuntary—as though a first-hand encounter with the holiness of God puts an instant end to any pretense we have about our own righteousness. Thus, if you do wish to cultivate greater humility and openness, one excellent step is to learn more about God! In the words of Andrew Murray, "Nothing but the presence of God can reveal and expel self. . . . The presence of Jesus will banish every desire to seek anything in ourselves, and will make us delight in every humiliation that prepares us for His fuller manifestation."[8]

As our knowledge of him increases, we must decrease—together with our pretensions, our pride, and all desire to conceal our sin or seem better than we are.

CHURCH AS FAMILY

"It doesn't really matter what I think," says Jack Miller. "Only what matters is God's honor and the welfare of others."[9] In this helpful life principle, Miller is pointing to a final key in dying to selfish worries about admiration and esteem. That key is, quite simply, concern for others. With this biblical focus on the glory of God and the needs of others, we move into the realm of the two great commandments in Matthew 22: "You shall love the Lord your God with all your heart and with all your soul and with all your mind. This is the great and first commandment. And a second is like it: You shall love your neighbor as yourself" (vss. 37-39).

As Welch observes, "There is something about love that crowds out our painful self-consciousness. You can't have one in your heart when the other is there. Consider the needs of others more than you consider your own, and guaranteed, the fear of other people will no longer suffocate you."

Indeed, Welch insists that we need to reach the point of *loving* others more than *needing* them—and that one way to do this is to think of your fellow believers as family.[10] We certainly *need* our families; yet in a truly healthy family, what we get from the others is not nearly as important as what we can do for them. Parents will go on loving their children even when the children are headstrong, insulting, rebellious—when, rather than doing something *for* their parents, they are actually making life more difficult and stressful. In these cases, we parents must set aside our own selfish desire to be respected and well treated by our children; like the heavenly father who pursues and saves a rebellious people, we go on loving them for their sake. Sisters and brothers, let us try to take this approach to those in our circle of fellowship. Let us die to our own desire to be liked and admired—to what others might be able to do for us; and let us rather commit to truly meeting the needs of those around us.

Just imagine for a moment how it might serve your Christian friends if you simply stopped pretending—if you gave them the priceless gift of honesty, intimacy, and true communion that comes when we share our sins and struggles. Isn't that also part of what characterizes healthy families? Even if the folks in church are fooled about who I am, my wife and kids know what I'm really like—and yet they love me anyway. This enables me to be myself and relax with them in a way that is much harder with people who don't know me well—and nearly impossible with those I've fooled into thinking what a great guy I am. If we could daily die to ourselves, and take up the cross of renouncing the fine public reputation our flesh covets, maybe we could achieve some of this familial intimacy in *all* our relationships.

And church might begin to feel more like home.

OPEN FOR DISCUSSION

1. What does Paul mean when he says he's been "crucified to the world, and the world to me" (Gal. 6:14)? What are some ways we can achieve this state?

2. What does it mean to "have the sentence of death within ourselves" (2 Cor. 1:9)?

3. How would achieving these things (in questions 1 & 2) aid us in transparency?

4. Describe a time when you suffered insult or injury from others—perhaps a snub, a rejection, a put-down, or outright injustice. What did it feel like? Have you ever had a time when you are able "swallow" something like this and get past it? How did that feel? Any idea how you managed it?

5. Does it help you "die to yourself" if you confess sins to a brother or sister? Explain.

6. In what ways are we controlled by the opinions of others? Describe Paul's attitude in this matter as expressed in 1 Corinthians 4:3-4.

7. How can proper love for God and others help us to "deny ourselves"? Can you think of a specific time when you had to die to yourself in order to help someone else?

8. The author asserts that family can be a safe place because these people know us best, yet still love us. Have you ever experienced

this sort of safety? How can we make our churches feel more like this?

CHAPTER THIRTEEN

"A Time To Refrain"

Accepting Limitations

Do you have trouble saying no to people?

Are you constantly acceding to some request, in spite of the fact that your schedule is already packed—plus, maybe you didn't even want to do it in the first place? And when you cave in this way, do you later find yourself getting resentful—wondering how you got talked into it? Worse yet, isn't this even more annoying when *you* are the one who talked yourself into it?

And in any case, what does all this have to do with transparency?

Well, go-getters who've said yes to those queries have many reasons for taking on extra tasks—among them, a laudable desire to serve. But I think that oftentimes we do it because it's hard to accept our limits; turning down a request or an opportunity means being vulnerable enough to admit that we can't do everything. If by contrast you want to feel like Superman—and you want others to see you that way—then you've got a problem with transparency: You have trouble accepting the limits of your own humanity.

THE BIBLE TELLS ME SO

At first, the notion of living within limits—of accepting our finite capacity—doesn't sound especially biblical. Aren't we, for example, supposedly able to "do all things" through Christ who gives us strength? Won't he lead us in "triumphal procession"? Aren't we supposed to move mountains, do "greater works" than Jesus, and become, in him, "more than conquerors"? (See Phil. 4:13, 2 Cor. 2:14, Matt. 17:20, John 14:12, Rom. 8:37.)

Truth to tell, I resisted this idea—and later in this chapter, we shall see that there are limits even on the idea of limitation. But Peter Scazzero finally persuaded me in his book *The Emotionally Healthy Church*—and he did so by amassing an impressive array of biblical proofs.

It starts right out with Adam and Eve, who were given virtually anything they wanted—with one limitation: They were not to eat from the tree of the knowledge of good and evil (Gen. 2:16-17); as Genesis 3:22 makes clear, they were not to seek to become like God, but rather to accept their limited humanness. "The fallout from their refusal to do so remains with us to this day."[1]

Indeed, it's easy to see the whole subsequent history of God's dealing with his people as a series of limits and curbs, often phrased this way: "You shall not." They were not to marry Gentiles, they were not to work on the Sabbath, they were not to eat a variety of forbidden foods; they were not to steal, lie, commit adultery, worship anything other than God, or covet—this final commandment admonishing us to accept what God has given without pining for more. Some of these limits have, of course, been lifted in the New Testament era—while others, like lust and murder, have been broadened and deepened.

There's no doubt about it: If you want to serve God, there are a lot of things you cannot do.

This includes wanting to be like God—which, as we noted above, seems to have been the idea behind the prohibition to eat from the tree in Genesis; for afterward, God laments that "the man has become like one of us in knowing good and evil" (3:22). One key to the severity of that first sin was Adam and Eve's decision to make their own rules, to put man in the place of God—a desire to know and determine for themselves those things that must necessarily remain the prerogative of God alone. As Moses puts it: "The secret things belong to the Lord our God, but the things that are revealed belong to us and to our children . . ." (Deut. 29:29). In the 131st psalm, David actually takes a positive approach to this limitation, finding comfort and rest in the fact that he doesn't have to be God—or Superman: "O Lord, my heart is not lifted up; my eyes are not raised too high; I do not occupy myself with things too great and too marvelous for me. But I have calmed and quieted my soul, like a weaned child with its mother; like a weaned child is my soul within me" (vss. 1-2). David had to learn this truth in a whole new way when Nathan told him that he could not build a house for God; to be sure, the king's desire was a good thing—but God said no: He set a clear limit. As David says elsewhere, "Our God is in the heavens; He does whatever he pleases" (Ps. 115:3, NASB).[2]

Even the famous "time" passage in Ecclesiastes 3 can be viewed as a series of limits: There are set times for birth and death, weeping and laughter, seeking and loss, "a time to love, and a time to hate; a time for war, and a time for peace"; even here, there is "a time to refrain" from certain activities (vss. 1-8). God has set each of these "seasons" at an appropriate place in human existence (cf. 3:11, NASB); and these beloved verses counsel us to accept this without wishing we could make more of life than God has ordained.

Moving to the New Testament era, we see John the Baptist peacefully accepting the fact that Jesus' ministry was outstripping his own. When some of his disciples came to report of Christ that "all are going to him," John replied contentedly, "A person cannot receive even one thing unless it is given him from heaven. . . . I am not the Christ . . ." (John 3:26-27). Similarly, Paul and his fellow-laborers had to accept the fact that "the Spirit of Jesus did not allow them" to go into the territory of Bithynia (Acts 16:7); the great apostle also suffered under a long prison term that would seem to have frustrated his desire to be out ministering to the nations at large. Moreover, he and nearly all the other apostles were forced into early martyrdom that would likewise—at least on the surface—seem to have curtailed further opportunities for the spread of the gospel.

Limitations like these are constantly manifesting themselves in the lives of God's people, and we must accept them just as Moses, David, and Paul did. For Jesus accepted them too.

LOOKING TO CHRIST

Of course, when one speaks of early death, it's hard not to think of Christ, who turned the world upside down (or shall we say, right-side up) despite a very short lifespan and a public ministry lasting only three years. Apparently, Jesus had limitations as well. Indeed, despite his astonishing miracles and world-changing ministry, it is not hard to see Christ's life as a lesson in limits:

Born to poor parents in a stable or cave, Jesus performed no miracles and apparently did no significant preaching for the first 30 year of his life. Even after he had begun working wonders, he constantly told his amazed eyewitnesses to keep quiet about it; in Mark 3, for instance, after healing many people, "he strictly ordered them not to make him known" (verse 12). The gospels, in fact, contain a dozen similar admonitions in which Christ placed limits on how quickly the news of his ministry could spread (see, for instance, Mark 1:44, 5:43, 7:36, 8:30, 9:9). Able to calm stormy seas and raise the dead, to address, feed, and captivate thousands at a moment's notice, Christ chose only 12 lowly followers to carry on his legacy; and he seems to have counted only three of these—Peter, James, and John—as close friends. This man through whom the worlds had been made (John 1:3, 10) restricted himself to a tiny backwater country dominated by a godless pagan empire. Jesus did not personally set off to meet the needs of every individual in Europe, Africa, and the Americas. He did not even heal or minister to every sick and needy person in his own small part of the world. He did not "run after crowds when they defected from him," and he did not—as he could have—call down legions of angels to save him from arrest and crucifixion (Matt. 26:53; see also John 18:36). Yet as Scazzero so sagely points out, all these limitations did not prevent Jesus from fully completing his mission. For at the end of his life, he tells God firmly, "I glorified you on earth, having accomplished the work that you gave me to do" (John 17:4).[3]

Even working within God-given limits, we too can still fulfill our calling from God.

SO WHAT'S IT ALL THIS MEAN?

Let's now draw a few implications out of all this biblical material.

First, as Scazzero observes, "the world's needs far exceed my supply"[4]—and thus, opportunity does not confer obligation. In other words, just because you *can* do something, that doesn't mean you should; we can certainly see this in the life of Christ. But it's a truism many of us have yet to learn, often with dire consequences. For Christians, it's an apt and humbling reminder of our humanity to have to choose a few important things rather than trying to "do it all."

Second, I would like to suggest that this sense of limitation applies not just to individuals but also to churches. If your own personal opportunities far exceed the time, energy, and abilities you possess, then this is equally true in the case of your church. Yet many churches just keep adding one ministry after another—until the weekly schedule is so crammed with activities and responsibilities that the members scarcely have time to tend to their families and their own devotional lives. Busyness is no indicator of spiritual health; in fact, it is sometimes quite the opposite.

Third, accepting limits allows us to be ourselves—to rest contented with who we are and where we are. It is true that God often calls people to some great ministry or to important missionary work in far-off lands; but perhaps more often, he asks us to go on serving and representing him in the often limited and ordinary places where he's put us. When, for example, some repentant Roman soldiers asked John the Baptist how to live, he did not tell them to leave their godless pagan army and go preach in Spain or Britain; rather, they were simply to do their job well by avoiding extortion and slander, and to be content with their wages (Luke 3:14). Later, speaking of whether Christians should seek to change their marital status or their position as slaves, Paul wrote, "Only let each person lead the life that the Lord has assigned to him, and to which God has called him" (1 Cor. 7:12-24). And finally, consider the ironic use of "ambition" in Paul's command to the Thessalonians: "Make it your ambition to lead a quiet life and attend to your own business and work with your hands . . ." (1 Thess. 4:11, NASB). Ambitious people don't usually mind their own business and work with their hands—unless their aspiration is to serve Christ right where they are.

ROOM FOR GOD

It may be that accepting limits is not merely good and healthy, but perhaps even vitally necessary to all effective Christ-centered work. As we noted earlier when discussing the virtue of weakness (see Chapter Nine), God has actually willed us to be weak and helpless so that we will learn to depend on him for all things—because he knows we cannot do it ourselves. If on the other hand we determine to be Superman—well, maybe the problem is that Superman doesn't need Jesus. As Scazzero puts it so concisely: "We can sometimes pass through our God-given limits and end up doing God's work without God."[5] To paraphrase Christ: What is the use of gaining the whole world through ceaseless superhuman activity if in the process we lose our soul's connection to God?

Even more important, if you are working without God, you will sooner or later run out of strength. Only by admitting that we cannot do it ourselves and getting out of the way—only in this manner are we able to access the divine power without which all work will eventually come to naught. To put it more simply: Only by accepting limits do we leave God room to work. As God himself told Paul, "My power is made perfect in weakness"—at which point, Paul resolved to be "content" with his limitations; "for when I am weak, then I am strong" (2 Cor. 12:9-10).

If limitation keeps us well versed in our own weakness, then perhaps we should start regarding it not as an obstacle but as a gift. For not only does it give us a proper dependence on God, but also, it keeps us from burning out. Citing the parable of various investments entrusted to three men (Matt. 25:14-30), Dwight L. Carlson asserts that we lay an impossible load on ourselves if we overestimate our God-given "talents": "Maybe God has entrusted you with two emotional talents. But if you and other individuals demand that you put out more than two talents' worth of performance, it will create tremendous emotional burdens for you. These burdens, which God longs to lift with his grace, can even prevent you from doing the two talents' worth you are able to do. Some people tend to expect more of themselves and others than God does. . . ."[6] Scazzero agrees: "We expect far too much from ourselves and each other and often live frustrated and angry lives. Much of burnout is a result of giving what we do not possess." And he then provides a helpful list of warning signs that we have taken on too much: anxiety, rushing, stomach tied in knots, not being fully present with others, irritability with simple tasks like waiting in line—and "skimming over time with God."[7]

DISNEY DELUSION, PART 2

Way back in Chapter Four, we looked briefly at what Barbara Duguid calls "the Disney Delusion"—that is, the notion that we can do and be anything we want. In countless commercials and children's films, we are told again and again that there is no end to what we can achieve if we believe in ourselves and "just do it." If some of us have a tendency to require too much of ourselves—to reach beyond our true abilities—then this tendency is exacerbated by a culture that constantly tells us to "be all that you can be." In magazines, on TV, and in films, we ingest a nonstop diet of messages insisting we can have our cake and eat it too—that we can, for example, enjoy a hearty and continual diet of Snickers bars, sugary Coke and never-ending pasta while also looking like Ryan Gosling, Scarlett Johansson, Beyonce Knowles, or Chris Hemsworth.

Yet movies often get the idea of limitation right. Even in the fabulously popular *Hunger Games* saga, beloved protagonist Katniss Everdeen finally chooses a life of simplicity and solitude over political power and prestige. In Woody Allen's acclaimed 2013 drama *Blue Jasmine*, Jasmine's sister comes perilously close to losing the love of her devoted blue-collar man because the title character has been pushing her toward the high life—a life, incidentally, that destroyed Jasmine by forcing her to put up an insupportable false front.

But perhaps Hollywood's best-known example of a man accepting less than he wanted is George Bailey in *It's a Wonderful Life*. It's an older film that remains a favorite because its message about what's really important is needed now as much as it was by those who first saw it in 1946. George desperately wants to get out of his provincial town and travel the world, rejecting the nickel-and-dime drudgery of his father's low-rent mortgage firm. In the long run, George stays, committing himself to a financially strapped existence in a run-down house—at the same time finding that all the smaller things he overlooked, like friendship and family, have made him rich in ways he never imagined.

THE LIMITS OF LIMITATION

I cited George Bailey intentionally, because while he accepted some limits on his life, he was, at the same time, often stretching himself beyond what he could bear. By the end of the film, he has expended so much time, energy, and money on others that he's reached the breaking point; yet that's part of what we admire about him. From this and from many of our own experiences, we know that God does sometimes ask us to go beyond our limits—that in fact, he *often* commands his people to do so. Consider Moses, charged with confronting Pharaoh and leading a massive nation through the desert despite his age and poor speaking ability; or Sarah and Abraham, called to be parents though nearly 100 years old. In the New Testament, Paul's co-worker Timothy, a man both young and apparently timid by nature, was nonetheless called to lead the sizable church at Ephesus, which had been plagued by conflict and false teaching.[8] We could multiply examples not only from Scripture, but also from our own lives; and it's not hard to see that in each case, it is indeed the very weakness which allows God to manifest his strength and power—taking us well beyond what we thought possible.

But the real question here is not whether we're sometimes asked to go beyond our limits; both experience and Scripture teach us that this is true. No; the puzzle is figuring out when "contentment," or saying "no," is a wise acceptance of our lot—and when it's just an excuse for laziness or unbelief. If we sometimes have to refuse a request, how can we know whether we turned it down just because we didn't feel like doing it? Was saying "no" an act of faith—or fear?

To some degree, this will be a matter between you and God and your own conscience; hard and fast rules aren't smart in such personal cases. But in general, when you are wondering whether to take on some additional task, or to do something that seems beyond you, it's probably a good idea to examine your attitude and your motives.

Are you approaching it with godly fear and trembling, all too aware of your own weaknesses, and fully committed to calling on God day by day, moment by moment? Will this task remind you of your own inability, and of God's faithful power as you depend on him to get you through it?

Or are you doing it because you just know how great you'll be at it, and how much people will admire you—how grateful they'll feel, and how you'll float off in self-satisfied ecstasy after you've added yet another task to your impressive schedule and pulled it off with your usual élan? Are you doing it because God has truly called you, or because you seek the approval of men? Will this task give you a greater understanding of your weakness and vulnerability—or is it just one more way for you to deny these things?

Sometimes you need to say yes because it will help you learn to depend on God. And sometimes you need to say no for the same reason.

THE ONE WHO "HAS DONE ALL THINGS WELL"

Personally speaking, one of my own constant stressors is the idea of "not measuring up." To be more specific, I never seem to complete my tasks and responsibilities with the sort of excellence that I feel is required. That, of course, is just another limitation that all of us must learn to accept—especially those of us who are perfectionists.

One of the great "Aha!" moments in my life occurred when I was counseling with my pastor on stress—on how worn out I feel because nothing I do ever seems to be good enough. My friend pointed me to a simple but little-known verse in Mark, where the crowd reacts to Jesus' astounding ministry by saying, "He has done all things well" (7:37). Pointedly, my counselor was implying that this is probably how I'd like people to feel about me; and he went on to insist that only one Person in the history of mankind deserves that statement. *Only of Jesus can it be said, "He does all things well."* If I want people to say such things about me, then my desire is not to serve God but to *be* God; and that's always been the problem with rebelling against limits—ever since the Garden of Eden.

"We can fail because of our own sin," writes Ed Welch, "but *most failure is simply a consequence of being a creature and not the Creator.* We are limited and finite. We make mistakes. We can't do everything perfectly. We can't even do things as well as our friends and neighbors. The fact that we don't compare well to other people is not a sin. It is a result of limitations we all experience. These are not a problem before God, but they certainly can preoccupy us if we are concerned about status and reputation."[9]

THE FALLOUT

If you want to seem mightier and more competent than you really are—if you want to seem as great as God—then that is a sure-fire sign that exceeding your limitations is not a matter of faith, but of pride, selfishness, and rebellion. Worse yet, far from serving those around you, it may have a negative effect on their faith as well. If they see you as some sort of invulnerable semi-deity, then rather than allowing God to display his grace and power through your admitted weakness, you have brazenly put yourself between them and God. This in turn urges them to focus on mere human ability, and—finally getting back to our topic in this book—it will make it harder for them to see and admit their own weaknesses. With your busy-ness and ability, you're just another roadblock on the difficult path to transparency—one more thing in life that makes others feel "less than."

If by contrast you publicly accept your limits and lean wholly on the strength of God, that enables others to do so too. When someone asks for help or a favor, or when you see an unmet need, you assume that saying "no" might be harmful to others. But in fact, hearing you say, "No, I can't do that" may actually enable them to see that you are *not* Superman, and that you don't want to be. It takes some vulnerability to admit that you can't do a certain thing; but it may be an act of faith—of belief that God can meet that need in some other way.[10]

You can't do everything; and you're not going to help others if you go on allowing them to think you can.

OPEN FOR DISCUSSION

1. Do you have trouble saying "no" to people? Why do you suppose this is the case?

2. Have you ever mustered up the courage to turn down a request? Can you describe that incident? What did it feel like? What was the other person's reaction? In the long run, were you glad you said no—or not?

3. The author describes several Bible passages that encourage us to accept limitations. Can you think of others?

4. Can you think of some Bible passages where men or women were asked to go beyond their strength?

5. Sometimes, saying no is a matter of laziness or unbelief; sometimes it shows that you have wisely accepted your limitations. How can we tell the difference?

6. Do churches need to accept limits too? Are some churches too busy, too ambitious, too committed to too many ministries? How can you tell when this has happened?

7. How can you tell when you yourself have become overcommitted?

8. The next chapter will discuss Bible passages where men or women are demonstrating transparency. Can you think of any passages like this?

CHAPTER FOURTEEN

"Confessing and Divulging"

Seeing Transparency in Scripture

If by any chance you remain unconvinced that transparency is vital in the Christian life, we are about to enter on what I consider the heart of this book: transparency in the word of God. Some of it might seem to belong more properly in Part Two; for one of the main reasons "why we should be transparent" is simply that, as we are about to see, *the Bible commands it.*

But much more often, the writers and major figures in Scripture are demonstrating godly transparency in ways we should emulate. In literally hundreds of passages, they show us what transparency can, should, and does look like. In fact, there is so much material on this subject that I've broken it into two chapters: one on the sorts of things we ought to be sharing, and a second examining a few particularly transparent Bible figures—in other words, case-studies of openness from the Old and New Testament. Naturally, there will be a bit of overlap between these two sections; but I hope it will make the copious material easier to digest—and more persuasive.

CONFESSING SIN AND FAILURE

As I've already suggested, the Bible both requires and models public confession of sin and failure. Perhaps the best-known of these passages has already been examined in this book—but it makes a fine jumping-off point for this current discussion: "If we say we have no sin, we deceive ourselves, and the truth is not in us. If we confess our sins, he is faithful and just to forgive us our sins and to cleanse us from all unrighteousness. If we say we have not sinned, we make him a liar, and his word is not in us." While not overtly clear, the public nature of this confession is suggested by the frequent use of "we," by the declaratory nature of *saying* something about our own sins, and by the preceding verse, with its emphasis on walking "in the light" and having "fellowship with one another" (1 John 1:7-10).

In any case, John is merely carrying forth a commitment to the public acknowledgment of sin that had been well established among God's people ever since the days of Moses. Leviticus, for example, cites a number of possible sins—such as rash oaths, uncleanness, or refusal to testify at a trial—and then insists that the man who commits these must step forward the moment he becomes aware of the sin: "When he comes to know it, and he realizes his guilt in any of these," he must bring a "sin offering. And the priest shall make atonement for his sin" (5:4-6). The public nature of such confession is even more apparent in Leviticus 16, where Aaron, acting as high priest, must make a sin offering of various animals taken "from the congregation"—a bull to "make atonement for himself and for his house," and then a goat "because of the uncleannesses of the people of Israel and because of their transgressions, all their sins." Later, a second goat is employed thus: "And Aaron shall lay both his hands on the head of the live goat, and confess over it all the iniquities of the people of Israel, and all their transgressions, all their sins. And he shall put them on the head of the goat and send it away into the wilderness by the hand of a man who is in readiness. The goat shall bear all their iniquities on itself to a remote area, and he shall let the goat go free in the wilderness" (vss. 5-22).

These ceremonies provide a platform for the *public* acknowledgement of sin—and for reassurance of atonement provided by the Lord himself.

But surely the Bible's best-known admonition to public confession is found in the New Testament letter of James:

> Is anyone among you suffering? Let him pray. Is anyone cheerful? Let him sing praise. Is anyone among you sick? Let him call for the elders of the church, and let them pray over him, anointing him with oil in the name of the Lord. And the prayer of faith will save the one who is sick, and the Lord will raise him up. And if he has committed sins, he will be forgiven. Therefore, confess your sins to one another and pray for one another, that you may be healed. The prayer of a righteous person has great power as it is working. (5:13-16)

In accord with the later emphasis of my current chapter, note how this lengthy passage urges us to share the whole realm of our emotional life—grief, joy, illness, and sin. Some may consider confession the hardest part of such sharing; but here James simply lists it right along with more common activities like praising God and asking for prayer. If you engage in those habits with biblical regularity, why not confession of sin as well? This should perhaps be second nature to us—just like those other communal acts of sharing.

Indeed, the imperative present-tense of "confess" suggests that "believers should be committed to confessing their sins to one another and praying for one another"—that James is encouraging such mutual confession "as a habitual practice." Commentator Joseph B. Mayor also points out how the phrase "one another" indicates that "no one may hear the confession of others unless he at the same time confesses his sin to them." Mayor adds:

> What a relief it would be to one of a sensitive self-conscious nature to lay his anxieties before another of whose wisdom and sympathy he felt assured! Might it not tend to increase

> the feeling of Christian fellowship, if those who were exposed to the same difficulties, anxious to conquer the same weaknesses and to practice the same virtues, could break through their Isolation and confirm themselves in their good resolutions by the knowledge that they were shared by others? Might it not help to diminish the miseries of life, and to change the course of thoughts which may be tending towards insanity or suicide if there were more of outspoken sympathy in the world, if people were sure that they might trust their secret feelings to others without fear of being despised or laughed at or shrunk from?

Mayor then quotes Thomas Arnold, who praises "this most divine system of a living Church, in which all were to aid each other, in which each man might open his heart to his neighbor and receive the help of his prayers, and in which each man's earnest prayer, offered in Christ's name, had so high a promise of blessing annexed to it. . . ."[1]

"Whoever conceals his transgressions will not prosper," says the writer of Proverbs, "but he who confesses and forsakes them will obtain mercy" (28:13). It's worth noting that the Hebrew verb used here for "confess"—*yadah*—nearly always has public overtones;[2] and thus we see the salutary public nature of confession modeled in other appearances of this Old Testament verb. For example, Solomon uses this term when beseeching God to forgive Israel if they admit their sin, turn to him, confess his name (*yadah*), and make supplication for "all their transgressions that they have committed." Here the newly crowned king of Israel envisions a time when all of God's people together will jointly acknowledge that they have "sinned and have acted perversely and wickedly" (1 Kings 8:33, 35, 47, 50). Much later, in what may be a fulfillment of Solomon's vision, the national leader Ezra "prayed and made confession [*yadah*]": He was "weeping and casting himself down," while "a very great assembly of men, women, and children, gathered to him out of Israel, for the people wept bitterly"; and at this point an otherwise-unknown figure named Shecaniah speaks for the people in citing specific transgression: "We have broken faith with our God and have married foreign women from the peoples of the land . . ." (Ezra 10:1-2).

If there was ever any doubt that the Bible endorses mutual public confession—or if you ever felt that confession of sins could be made only to a priest or pastor in perfect secrecy—it is to be hoped that these poignant passages resolve those doubts once and for all. But in case further proof seems warranted, let's look at a few more passages where this sort of thing is modeled.

Take, for example, the case of the prodigal son, who frankly told his father, "I have sinned against heaven and before you. I am no longer worthy to be called your son" (Luke 15:21). Even more specific in public confession is the Old Testament writer Asaph, who lays bare his sins in a psalm that was to be read by millions of fellow-believers for 30 subsequent centuries. Struggling to understand how God allows the wicked to prosper, he plainly tells us that he broke the tenth commandment: "For I was envious of the arrogant . . ."; and he goes on to describe his state of mind in the blunt terminology of true humbleness and transparency: "When my soul was embittered, when I was pricked in heart, I was brutish and ignorant; I was like a beast toward you" (Ps. 73:3, 21-22).

Similarly, Acts 19 offers a precious verse in which pagan magicians in Ephesus were converted under Paul—with the result that "many of those who were now believers came, confessing and divulging their practices" (verse 18). The verb for "divulge" in this passage implies "making a public announcement" and might best be rendered as "declared." And that particularly public disclosure has a special significance in this case, for pagan practice holds that "the potency of a spell is bound up with its secrecy; if it be divulged, it becomes ineffective. So these converted magicians renounced their imagined power by rendering their spells inoperative"—through open confession before other people.[3]

Thinking about the "power of secrecy" in Acts 19 always reminds me of what Brene Brown says on this matter: "Shame hates it when we reach out and tell our story. It hates having words wrapped around it—it can't survive being shared. Shame loves secrecy. . . ."[4] Brown urges the habit of making confession into a story, in which we narrate our shame and sin to others—somewhat as Asaph does in Psalm 73. But he isn't the only Bible figure to do so; the writer of Ecclesiastes also trots out a lengthy narrative of error and sin.

In Ecclesiastes 1 and 2, the Preacher describes his long and self-indulgent quest to find satisfaction in the pleasures of life—so that "whatever my eyes desired I did not keep from them." His excesses included "how to cheer my body with wine"; planting great vineyards, gardens, and parks; vast possessions of cattle, slaves, silver, and gold; "and many concubines" (1:16—2:10). This whole passage subtly portrays the Preacher as putting himself in the place of God: For one thing, the word "great" in 1:16 ("great wisdom") occurs elsewhere to describe what God himself has done—and it is also used "negatively of those who exalt themselves against God" (see 1 Sam. 12:24; Ps. 126:2-3; Jer. 48:26, 42; and Ezek. 35:13). Furthermore, the term for "parks" in 2:5 is from the Persian word that gives us "paradise"; together with the passage's references to trees (2:6) and its use of "male and female" (2:7), the whole narrative shows us a writer publicly impugning himself for assuming a God-like role in trying to re-create the perfect, Edenic world of Genesis 1-2.[5]

Yet none of it worked.

While I won't go so far as to suggest that all of Solomon's deeds here were sinful, the fact is that he did *not* succeed in finding the satisfaction he was seeking, and thus the story serves as a model for us in that it openly confesses failure. As he puts it, "Then I considered all that my hands had done and the toil I had expended in doing it, and behold, all was vanity and a striving after wind, and there was nothing to be gained under the sun" (2:11). The word "considered" is literally "faced"; it can mean "to look someone in the eye" or "face the facts." Thus, "the Preacher is not content to put a bold face on things; he must tell it the way it is"—and he describes his bitter disillusionment with a wide array of categorical terms: "all," "nothing," "vanity," and "striving after wind."[6]

In this way, the confession reveals what lurks beneath the glitzy appearance of cultural splendor: A "widespread sense of futility and weariness . . . underlies its confident, abrasive tone and its pretensions to divinity." So the Preacher's narrative contradicts the story we usually try to tell with our public persona; in so doing, it reveals the superficial nature of the worldly mindset, and the way its quests are doomed to failure.[7] In these revelations, the Preacher also serves as a model for those who hesitate to tell their own story of excess, failure, and transgression.

Moses was another Bible writer who apparently wanted all posterity to know about his sins. It has been the testimony of the historic Christian church—and of the New Testament itself—that Moses is the original human author of the first five Old Testament books (see, for instance, Mark 7:10).[8] And thus it is before all God's people that the great leader of Israel forthrightly describes his sin in Numbers 20; here, he strikes the rock instead of merely speaking to it as God had commanded—and God sharply reproves him "because you did not believe in me, to uphold me as holy in the eyes of the people of Israel" (vss. 8-12). Moses makes no excuses in bluntly exposing his sin to all posterity.

And as a final example of transparency before the children of God, we can look to the Apostle Peter. This may surprise readers who cannot recall many such confessions—with the possible exception of his public declaration, "Depart from me, for I am a sinful man, O Lord" (Luke 5:8). However, let us recall the almost unilateral tradition that Mark's gospel was written down at the dictation of Peter.[9] In this case, the apostle's openness about his sin becomes clearer—for it is Mark who so tellingly describes Peter's foibles, failures, and foolishness.

First comes the memorable moment when Peter, hearing Christ describe his forthcoming rejection and death, "took him aside and rebuked him"—as though this brash disciple somehow had a keener knowledge than his master of what was true and best; fittingly, Peter himself gets a more appropriate rebuke in this passage, with Jesus telling him, "Get behind me, Satan! For you are not setting your mind on the things of God, but on the things of man" (Mark 8:31-33).

This brief incident, however, is nothing compared to Peter's betrayal of Christ in the hours before the crucifixion. Indeed, even during the events leading up to Jesus' detainment in Jerusalem, Peter's failures are readily apparent. As one commentator puts it, he exhibits "rash self-confidence and scorn of others," insisting that his fellow disciples might fall away, but he will not (Mark 14:29). Then, when the soldiers come to arrest Jesus, Peter proves the silliness of his boast by panicking and fleeing right along with everybody else (14:50). Later, he does follow Christ—but only while carefully maintaining his distance and freely associating with his master's enemies (14:54).[10]

And then of course, when questioned about his association with Jesus, he thrice denies even knowing the man. In the first case, he fearfully refuses to understand the question when confronted by a mere servant girl; and he then moves out to the gateway—almost certainly to escape further questioning (14:66-68). The second denial is even worse, both because of the larger audience ("bystanders") and the verb tense (literally, "was denying"—which indicates an ongoing action) (14:69-70). And the third time, "he began to invoke a curse on himself and to swear, 'I do not know this man of whom you speak'" (14:71). One scholar has suggested that "on himself"—an interpolation based on the Greek verb—should mostly likely be "on Christ";[11] and even if this isn't the case, Mark's narrative of this event is in many ways the most detailed and damning account among all four gospels. Clearly, Peter pulled no punches when describing it to Mark; he must surely have wanted future generations to see and understand his radical failure at this key moment.

CONFESSING WEAKNESS

Sin may be the toughest thing to confess—but admitting weakness isn't easy either. In the Bible, however, it often seems a matter of course to confess a lack of strength. Indeed, the Old Testament is replete with statements where the writer feels "stunned, faint all the day long," where suffering has "caused my strength to fail" (Lam. 1:13-14). In Psalm 109, for example, David confesses profound helplessness and inadequacy: "I am poor and needy, and my heart is stricken within me. I am gone like a shadow at evening; I am shaken off like a locust. My knees are weak through fasting; my body has become gaunt. . . . Help, O Lord my God! Save me according to your steadfast love!" (vss. 22-26).

Similarly, many Bible figures frankly confess that they don't feel strong enough—or important enough—to accomplish what God is asking them do to.

When God commands Moses to confront Pharaoh about the oppression of Israel, Moses declares that he is lacking in the area of public speech—and, by writing this down in Scripture, he declares his weakness to future generations as well: "I am not eloquent, either in the past or since you have spoken to your servant, but I am slow of speech and of tongue" (Ex. 4:10). On at least three later occasions, Moses continues to confirm his weakness—by relying on Aaron to speak for him (Ex. 4:14-16, 30); by having Aaron and Hur hold up his "weary" arms during a battle (17:11-12); and by accepting advice from his father-in-law, who insisted that Moses needed help judging Israel ("The thing is too heavy for you. You are not able to do it alone," Ex. 18:18).

Other Bible leaders expressed similar doubts about their own sufficiency when asked to lead God's people. Barak refused to go to battle without the help of Deborah (Judg. 4:8), and Gideon responded to God's call by asking, "Please, Lord, how can I save Israel? Behold, my clan is the weakest in Manasseh, and I am the least in my father's house" (Judg. 6:15). David likewise prayed, "Who am I, O Lord God, and what is my house, that you have brought me thus far?" (2 Sam. 7:18). Even the great Solomon felt unable to begin his reign without first asking for wisdom: "And now, O Lord my God, you have made your servant king in place of David my father, although I am but a little child. I do not know how to go out or come in. . . . Give your servant therefore an understanding mind to govern your people, that I may discern between good and evil, for who is able to govern this your great people?" (1 Kings 3:7-9).

A similar but even more thorough admission of inability can be found at the end of Proverbs, where the little-known Agur surprisingly declares, "Surely I am too stupid to be a man. I have not the understanding of a man" (30:2). I once had a friend who insisted that Christians should never say this sort of thing, since we have the Spirit of Christ to make us wise. But if Agur wrote Scripture, he had the Spirit too; and I think anyone who's ever come to the end of his rope—anyone who's dropped the ball, who's had to confront misguided assumptions, or acknowledge a wrong decision when they were initially sure it was right—in short, anyone who's tried and failed; we can all can find great comfort in knowing that even Bible-writers felt wholly inadequate to the tasks they were facing. Yes, "too stupid to be a man."

CONFESSING GRIEF AND DISTRESS

Painful emotions such as sadness, anger, fear, and distress also find frequent expression in Scripture. In fact, an entire book—Lamentations—is named for its public expression of grief over the destruction and exile of Judah in the sixth century B.C. "Look and see if there is any sorrow like my sorrow," says the writer (1:12)—and he goes on to articulate his feelings in the most graphic terms: "my heart is wrung within me . . ." (1:20); "my groans are many, and my heart is faint" (1:22); "my eyes are spent with weeping; my stomach churns; my bile is poured out to the ground . . ." (2:11); "my eyes flow with rivers of tears . . ." (3:48); "my soul is bereft of peace; I have forgotten what happiness is" (3:17). He urges his fellow-sufferers to grieve along with him: "Arise, cry out in the night. . . . Pour out your heart like water before the presence of the Lord!" (2:19); and in keeping with these adjurations, he often speaks in the plural voice: "we are weary; we are given no rest" (5:5); "our heart has become sick, . . . our eyes have grown dim . . ." (5:17). There is thus a public, corporate nature to this grief, as indicated by this similar reference to the exile in Psalm 137: "By the waters of Babylon, there we sat down and wept . . ." (vs. 1).

Since the psalms were to be used in public worship, they regularly show us writers who were perfectly willing to let countless others see how they felt; what's more, these expressions of grief were then shared as God's people sang them together in worship—and as they continue to be sung, recited, studied, and discussed even in the contemporary church.

Psalm 77, for example, has been called a "community lament," with each person acknowledging participation in the shared grief of God's people. As in Lamentations, this grief is thus corporate, public, and profound: "I cry aloud to God. . . . I moan; when I meditate, my spirit faints. . . . I am so troubled that I cannot speak" (vss. 1-4). The tense of "cry" here indicates "the perpetual nature of the speaker's praying. It is not a passing sorrow or even a sudden tragedy that has caused this distress; the speaker's life has become defined by doubt and anguish." And as verse 4 indicates, "The disturbance is so great that the sufferer cannot even speak of it, but broods instead."[12] Furthermore, insisting that "in the night my hand is stretched out without wearying," the writer describes those sleepless nights of ongoing grief and terror that so many of us struggle with (see also Psalm 6:6); in this way, he shows us that there is no shame in confessing fear, anxiety, and panic along with grief and distress.

Psalm 102 also uses potent language in its expression of suffering and misery. There is a note of desperate urgency as the writer asks God to "answer me speedily in the day when I call!"; and he goes on to describe bones that "burn like a furnace," "loud groaning," loss of appetite, insomnia, and a desert-like sense of desolation; "I eat ashes like bread," he writes, "and mingle tears with my drink" (vss. 2-9). "All are vivid images of what it feels like to be consumed by sorrow and tempted by despair."[13]

And indeed, despair may be one way to describe what is surely the Bible's deepest and darkest expression of soul-anguish: the well-known 88th psalm. The heading informs us that it was written "to the Choirmaster" by one of the "Sons of Korah," some of whom were "in charge of the service of song in the house of the Lord" (1 Chron. 6:31). So keep the public nature of this document in mind as you read its narrative of suffering and woe:

> My soul is full of troubles,
> and my life draws near to Sheol. . . .
> I am a man who has no strength,
> like one set loose among the dead,
> like the slain that lie in the grave. . . .
> You have put me in the depths of the pit,
> in the regions dark and deep. . . .
> I am shut in so that I cannot escape;
> my eye grows dim through sorrow. . . .
> O Lord, why do you cast my soul away?
> Why do you hide your face from me?
> Afflicted and close to death from my youth up,
> I suffer your terrors; I am helpless.
> Your wrath has swept over me; your dreadful assaults
> destroy me. . . . my companions have become darkness.
> (vss. 3-6, 8-9, 14-16, 18)

As the *ESV Study Bible* points out, most laments in the Book of Psalms "let in a ray of sunshine, usually closing on a confident note; Psalm 88 is distinct from all the rest in that there is no explicit statement of confidence."[14] It sounds at times like a discussion of clinical depression; and indeed, its concluding verse—with the telling final word, "darkness"—can also be translated as one author did in the title for her recent Christian book on mental illness: *Darkness Is My Only Companion* (Kathryn Greene-McCreight, 2015).

FRUSTRATION, BEWILDERMENT, AND COMPLAINTS

In a 2015 article on the *Reformation 21* website, cancer patient J. Todd Billings had some hard-hitting reflections on Scripture's frequent expressions of pain and grief:

> In a Christianity always seeking to be upbeat, centered on helping us to discover and fulfill our dreams, I had missed the centrality of lament: raw complaints and protests before the Lord. As a cancer patient whose life expectancy had likely been chopped off by decades, I felt grief and anger. But am I supposed to "bring those emotions to church," and risk being a complainer? The prayer of Psalm 102:23-24 was clear enough: "In the course of my life he broke my strength; he cut short my days. . . ." Apparently, God can handle our complaints. The Psalmist not only brings anger and grief before the Lord. He *blames* God.

At the same time, Billings goes on the reflect that such bold laments and complaints cannot occur in a vacuum:

> The psalmist complains, but not as a self-indulgent "complainer." On the one hand, the Psalmist does not seek to bottle up his emotions before God; on the other hand, his lament is also more than simply "venting" before God. The Psalmists bring all of their emotions—their whole selves—before the Almighty, not simply in order to "feel better," or to get an intellectual answer to the problem of evil. The Psalmist offers complaints—and thanksgiving for deliverance—because they trust in God's covenant promise.[15]

So as we move from grief and distress to outright complaining—to wrestling with God, expressing deep frustration, and challenging him with blunt questions—it is vital that we balance two important ideas: First, the gut-wrenching transparency of these men in divulging their dire struggles and doubts; and second, the way virtually all of them stop short of actual sin against God or other believers. Psalm 73, for instance, frankly unveils the writer's inner turmoil as he looks enviously upon the easy life of sinners. He wonders pointedly why "they have no pangs," why "they are not in trouble as others are," and why they seem to get away with pride, violence, malice, and oppression. His puzzlement is only exacerbated by the fact that he himself has maintained holiness ("I have kept my heart clean"), but has nonetheless been "stricken and rebuked every morning" (vss. 3-13). Asaph even goes so far as to suggest that this righteousness of his was "all in vain"—before admitting to God that his angry complaints would have harmed fellow Israelites: "If I had said, 'I will speak thus,' I would have betrayed the generation of your children. . . . I was brutish and ignorant; I was like a beast toward you" (vss. 73:15, 21-22).

In the following paragraphs, we shall see grief, frustration, and even anger expressed in strident, fiery words; but we will also note that like Asaph, the anguished speakers never curse God or accuse him of sin. That is, they never assign wrong deeds or evil motives to our heavenly father. If we see these passages as an excuse to accuse God, we have moved from transparency to sin—and foolishness. For in doing so, we would damage the relationship that is our only hope—while also causing others to stumble by publicly maligning God's reputation.

HABAKKUK AND JEREMIAH

The prophet Habakkuk, for example, sounds a lot like Asaph in Psalm 73, demanding to know why God seems to ignore sin and evil: "O Lord, how long shall I cry for help, and you will not hear? Or cry to you 'Violence!' and you will not save? . . . For the wicked surround the righteous; so justice goes forth perverted. . . . Why do you idly look at traitors and are silent when the wicked swallows up the man more righteous than he?" (1:2-4, 13). With "anguished questioning" that is both prolonged and importunate, Habakkuk is not content to blithely accept an outrageous state of affairs; rather, like Job, he argues and expostulates with God in no uncertain terms. Yet after doing so quite bluntly, the prophet then declares: "I will take my stand at my watchpost and station myself on the tower, and look out to see what he will say to me, and what I will answer concerning my complaint" (2:1). In this way, Habakkuk indicates that his questions are asked in expectation of an answer—posited on faith in God's goodness, and in the kind of relationship where true feelings are communicated honestly, in hopes that the painful issue can be resolved. Thus, when the anticipated response comes, Habakkuk "reaches a clearer understanding of God's character and a firmer faith in him."[16] And the prophet then records this process for the benefit of future believers, so that we too can learn to bring questions, doubts, and frustrations to our heavenly father.

Jeremiah's complaints and protests, however, are more personal, more strident—and more problematic. They come to a head in chapter 20, most of which seems understandable and legitimate, with the weeping prophet lamenting that "the word of the Lord has become for me a reproach and derision all day long" (verse 8). Later, he carefully avoids the sin of denouncing either his parents or God—choosing instead to curse the day of his birth and the messenger who brought his father the news; this lengthy, five-verse diatribe concludes with Jeremiah asking, "Why did I come out from the womb to see toil and sorrow . . . ?" (vss. 14-18). Wishing one had never been born isn't necessarily a sin; Job expresses similar feelings in 3:11-13, and so does the Preacher in Ecclesiastes 4:2-3.

No, what's problematic here is the prophet's opening statement: "O Lord, you have deceived me, and I was deceived; you are stronger than I, and you have prevailed" (verse 7). To accuse God of deception is bad enough—the verbs used here for "deceive" and "prevail" are found elsewhere in passages about sexual seduction, such as Deuteronomy 22:25 and 2 Samuel 13:11-14. Exodus 22:16 uses it in the context of having to marry a woman after illicit sex—with the implication that Jeremiah feels like he had been lured into bed and then tossed aside.[17]

While my current chapter exhorts you to go ahead and be transparent with God and others about your feelings, no one would defend this sort of language; it ascribes wrongdoing to God and could be a stumbling block to others. Nonetheless, however ill-advised and perhaps even sinful this statement is, God does not reprove or punish Jeremiah for it; instead, he has allowed these words to stand as part of Holy Scripture. And in any case, the broader context is important: The entire lament depicts a man "loudly complaining about his lot in life, yet showing that he is still submissive, loyal and obedient to God's will."[18] For even in the midst of these laments, the prophet declares, "The Lord is with me as a dread warrior. . . . Sing to the Lord; praise the Lord! For he has delivered the life of the needy from the hand of evildoers" (vss. 11-13); and in this way, the passage provides "a strong picture of Jeremiah's assurance that Yahweh was with him in all such crises, even if he lost heart momentarily at times." Perhaps, as commentator J. A. Thompson puts it, "Only one who walked intimately with God would dare to speak as Jeremiah did."[19] And perhaps only God himself could make the decision to permit such speech in his holy book.

THE EXAMPLE OF JOB

Job is another Bible figure whose laments sometimes seem to exceed the bounds of spiritual propriety—with one major difference: At the end of the book, God tells him it was okay. Please try to remember that as we look at what Job actually says.

Having seen unparalleled misery in the loss of his property and his children (1:13-19), in the lack of support from his sarcastic wife (2:9), and in "loathsome sores" all over his body (2:7), Job also curses the day of his birth and, like Jeremiah, wishes he had never been born: "Let the day perish on which I was born, and the night that said, 'A man is conceived.' Let that day be darkness! . . . Let gloom and deep darkness claim it. Let clouds dwell upon it; let the blackness of the day terrify it. . . . Why did I not die at birth, come out from the womb and expire? . . . Or why was I not as a hidden stillborn child, as infants who never see the light? . . . For my sighing comes instead of my bread, and my groanings are poured out like water" (3:3-5, 11, 16, 24).

Linguistically, Job conveys the depth of his anguish here in the first sentence, which contains three different tenses and also inverts chronology (birth before conception). Similarly, the very end of this long speech in chapter 3 is "so unintelligible in the Hebrew original that translators have had to take various liberties to secure reasonable English. The words *sighings* and *groanings* are not strong enough. The latter describes the roaring of lions . . ."—and the whole phrase might better be rendered "my bellowings cascade like the sea. . . . The impression is given that groans come from his whole body."[20] Later, Job expands on this by asserting, "My face is red with weeping, and on my eyelids is deep darkness. . . . And now my soul is poured out within me; . . . the night racks my bones, and the pain that gnaws me takes no rest" (16:16; 30:16-17)

Such powerful language is a blatant rejection of the "bourgeois etiquette" sometimes found in the western Christian church—and likewise of some misguided stoicism that strives to be "pure mind with no feeling. The Bible knows nothing of such dehumanizing philosophy." Job, by contrast, "rightly grieves for his bereavement; he is authentically depressed by his illness. He is human. The untrammelled serenity which some prescribe as the goal of 'victorious living' is a negation of whole areas of our experience as God has made us."[21]

Given the trouble we all have with transparency, it's not too surprising that Job's friends express alarm over what he has said; but Job insists he will go on complaining, using terminology that repeatedly emphasizes bold, open, declarative speech: "I will not restrain my mouth; I will speak in the anguish of my spirit; I will complain in the bitterness of my soul" (7:11). And he will do so not only before these friends, but also directly to God himself: "I will give free utterance to my complaint. . . . I will say to God, Do not condemn me; let me know why you contend against me" (10:1-2). He will question God in language that sounds harsh and sarcastic: "Am I the sea, or a sea monster, that you set a guard over me? . . . What is man, that you make so much of him, and that you set your heart on him, visit him every morning and test him every moment? How long will you not look away from me, nor leave me alone till I swallow my spit? . . . Though he slay me, I will hope in him; yet I will argue my ways to his face" (7:12, 17-19; 13:15).

Later, he employs the language of warfare to vent his feelings—with God as the assailant. Calling God "my adversary," Job uses military imagery to describe the divine assault: "He has torn me in his wrath and hated me; he has gnashed his teeth at me. . . he seized me by the neck and dashed me to pieces; . . . He slashes open my kidneys and does not spare; he pours out my gall on the ground. . . he runs upon me like a warrior. . . . I cry to you for help and you do not answer me. . . . You have turned cruel to me; with the might of your hand you persecute me" (16:9, 12-14; 30:20-21).[22]

At least one commentator has suggested that the famous statement "Though he slay me, I will trust in him"—stuck in the midst of all this protest—is not so much an affirmation of faith as an admission of fear that God will strike Job down for speaking so strongly.

But this never happens.

"Job's words certainly expressed deep anguish and frustration; but God does not count these words sinful."[23] True, God does rebuke him strongly in chapters 38-41, unleashing a litany of works and wonders so awe-inspiring that Job decides he will stop complaining: "I lay my hand on my mouth. . . . I will proceed no further" (40:4-5). After more revelations of God's might and power, Job does eventually "repent in dust and ashes" for questioning God and uttering "what I did not understand" (42:3-6).

But I don't think this should discourage us from responding to calamity in a similar fashion. For one thing, Job was always careful to avoid actually cursing God; and as several writers have noted, even though he asks God to take his life (6:8-9), he never contemplates active suicide.[24] Furthermore, the very strength and persistence of Job's complaint is what finally elicits the only thing that is able to finally assuage his pain: a face-to-face encounter with God himself.

But most important of all is God's final verdict on his relationship with Job. In the final chapter, he twice tells Job's friends, "You have not spoken of me what is right, as my servant Job has" (42:7-8).

Throughout the book, Job's friends keep reprimanding him for the way he speaks; but now God reprimands *them*, expressing approval for the way Job persevered in seeking answers—as opposed to these men who thought they already understood it all. "While they say all the right things *about* God, they never say anything *to* Him. Job wrestles with God and tells Him every doubt and fear. His relationship with God is vital while theirs consists of dead aphorisms."[25] This is why James, in the New Testament, can praise Job for his "steadfastness" (5:11). Such unflagging importunity as Job demonstrated—especially when expressed in such strong language—is itself a declaration of faith, a commitment to the relationship, a quest to understand and know God better.

"God's final endorsement of Job's speeches . . . silences the cant of those who remind us of the inscrutability of God, and smugly say, 'It is not for us to question the ways of the Almighty!' For that is precisely what Job does, and God says that he was fully justified in doing so. The Lord welcomes this exercise of moral judgment from man's side, even when it is directed in judgment on God Himself!"[26]

In a slightly different context—that of Psalm 77—the *ESV Study Bible* insists, "It does not offend God when his troubled people raise these questions with an interest in the explanation. Indeed, just putting the questions invites the answer. . . ." "Even Christ on the cross, making the words of one of the psalmists his own, could cry out, 'Why have you forsaken me?' But when the man or woman of faith cries out like this, it is from a fundamental conviction that God is all-righteous as well as all-powerful."[27]

Such laments and complaints are acceptable to God when they proceed from a committed relationship with him—from what we have learned about God in the past, what we believe about him now, and what we seek with him in the future.

PRAISING AND REJOICING

"Is anyone cheerful?" asks James in the passage quoted earlier. His own response: "Let him sing praise" (5:13). Because songs of praise would naturally be a public activity, this command provides an excellent opening to finish this chapter on a positive note. For we must be transparent not only about our sins, weaknesses, and griefs, but also about our joys, our happiness, our excitement—especially as these reflect the goodness and kindness of a gracious God. It may surprise you to learn that our word "enthusiasm" contains the well-known Greek base *theos*, meaning "God." In the early days of the English language, people understood the profound truth that all such excitement flows from the thrilling goodness of our abundantly generous father in heaven.

We are in fact commanded to rejoice in him—to do so loudly and enthusiastically, in the company of many other people:

"Sing to God, sing praises to his name; . . . exult before him!" (Ps. 68:4). "Sing aloud, O daughter of Zion; shout, O Israel! Rejoice and exult with all your heart . . ." (Zeph. 3:14). "Oh sing to the Lord a new song; sing to the Lord, all the earth! . . . Declare his glory among the nations, his marvelous works among all the peoples! . . . Ascribe to the Lord, O families of the peoples, ascribe to the Lord glory and strength!" (Ps. 96:1, 3, 7). In the apostolic era, Paul enjoins us to become a similarly worshipful body of saints—one that is always "addressing one another in psalms and hymns and spiritual songs, singing and making melody to the Lord with all your heart . . ." (Eph. 5:19; see also Col. 3:16).

Accordingly, many of God's saints model this public praise and worship in both the Old and New Testament. The psalms, of course, are rife with such praises, and since we shall examine several in the next chapter, perhaps two or three will suffice here. See, for instance, how transparent the sons of Korah are in professing their well-nigh desperate love for God—in words intended to be read, studied, and sung together by God's people: "My soul thirsts for God, for the living God"; "my soul longs, yes, faints for the courts of the Lord; my heart and flesh sing for joy to the living God" (Ps. 42:2; 84:2). Later in Psalm 42, the writer recalls "how I would go with the throng and lead them in procession to the house of God with glad shouts and songs of praise, a multitude keeping festival" (verse 4).

That's public, all right.

Even the narrative portions of Scripture reflect the people's penchant for public praise. After the exodus from Egypt, for instance, Moses sings to God in a lengthy psalm of 18 verses—at which point "Miriam, the prophetess, the sister of Aaron, took a tambourine in her hand, and all the women went out after her with tambourines and dancing. And Miriam sang to them . . ." (Ex. 15:1-21). After a similarly victorious intervention by the Lord in Judges, Deborah also professed her gratitude aloud: "Hear, O kings; give ear, O princes; to the Lord I will sing; I will make melody to the Lord, the God of Israel" (Judg. 5:3).

Likewise, the New Testament era finds people publicly rejoicing—like the lame beggar in Acts 3, who responds this way after being healed: "And leaping up he stood and began to walk, and entered the temple with them, walking and leaping and praising God"; one result of this transparent joy is that others "were filled with wonder and amazement at what had happened to him" (vss. 8-10). Likewise, upon Jesus' triumphal entry into Jerusalem, "the whole multitude of his disciples began to rejoice and praise God with a loud voice for all the mighty works that they had seen, saying, 'Blessed is the King who comes in the name of the Lord! Peace in heaven and glory in the highest!'" (Luke 19:37-38). Indeed, this sort of excited communal rejoicing is but a foretaste of what heaven will be like—as depicted, for instance, in Revelation, where John hears "the voice of a great multitude, like the roar of many waters and like the sound of mighty peals of thunder, crying out, 'Hallelujah! For the Lord our God the Almighty reigns. Let us rejoice and exult and give him the glory . . ." (19:6-7).

If this chapter seems overlong, don't blame me; for we see now that the Bible is chock-full of transparency, and that it encompasses the whole range of human thoughts and emotions—from sin to weakness to grief to anger to frustration to joy. It cannot consist of one or two isolated statements about a single feeling or action. It is a way of life, a characteristic openness before others. As such, it is most amply demonstrated by three of the greatest leaders in the history of God's people—David, Paul, and Jesus. In the next chapter, we shall see what these mighty men can show us about transparency.

OPEN FOR DISCUSSION

1. The author lists a number of situations in which we can be transparent: sin, failure, weakness, grief, distress, frustration, bewilderment, and joy or excitement. Pick one of these and come up with one additional example of someone sharing it in the Bible—that is, a passage not covered in this chapter.

2. Tell one story about sin or failure in your life.

3. Describe one time when you felt weak or inadequate and had to call on God for help. Were you able to share this weakness with others? What kinds of answers did God provide?

4. Are there other emotions or feelings about which we can be transparent, besides the ones listed above? Can you think of biblical commands or examples regarding these additional areas for sharing?

5. Do you think Jeremiah or Job went too far in expressing frustration and despair? Explain why or why not.

6. Have *you* ever "vented" your frustrations to God in such blunt and strenuous language? If so, what was it like? What are the limits on such vigorous expressions?

7. In the next chapter, we will examine the lives of David, Paul, and Jesus for moments of transparency. In preparation for that, see if you can think of one or two examples for each of these three men.

CHAPTER FIFTEEN

"Our Heart Is Wide Open"

Looking at Biblical Case Studies

King David: a man after God's own heart (1 Sam. 13:14; Acts 13:22).

Paul the Apostle: an evangelist who "turned the world upside down" (Acts 17:6).

Jesus Christ: "the image of the invisible God," the "exact imprint of his nature" (Col. 1:15; Heb. 1:3).

If you wish to model yourself after three of the greatest men who ever lived, then you must be transparent—for as we shall see, they lived lives of exemplary openness before God and others.

DAVID THE PENITENT

Going all the way back to the sixth century, the Christian church has generally identified a group of seven "penitential psalms"—that is, chapters from the book of Psalms expressing repentance over sin: These are psalms 6, 32, 38, 51, 102, 130, and 143.[1]

King David wrote all but two of these.

Keep in mind that he composed his psalms for use by temple choirs, and that the entire collection "served as the song book of the worshipping people of God."[2] So it's clear that David had no trouble telling others about his sins.

In Psalm 32, for example, he uses three different terms to describe his disobedience; they are translated in the ESV as "transgression," "sin," and "iniquity" (vss. 1-2). The first reflects "rebellion against God," the second designates "offense, or turning away from the true path," and the third suggests "distortion, criminality, or the absence of respect for the divine will." Together in such close proximity, these words "specify the full dimensions of human evil." Moreover, in spite of this thorough self-indictment, David goes on to admit that he had a lot of trouble bringing himself to confess; instead, he "kept silent" while his bones "wasted away," and he was "groaning all day long"—until, at last, he frankly opened up to God: "I acknowledged my sin to you, and I did not cover my iniquity" (vss. 3-5). "The 'groaning' is a consequence of living with guilt and a stifled conscience"—while the wasted bones show "the growing weakness of the spiritual life which follows the unhealthy practice of bottling up one's evil within the soul, steadfastly retaining silence, rather than finding the emancipation of forgiveness through speech."[3]

If that's not an argument for transparency, I don't know what is.

Psalm 38 takes a slightly different approach, reflecting not so much the nature of sin and the difficulty of confessing, but rather the vast quantity and depth of David's transgression—"For my iniquities are gone over my head; as a heavy burden they weigh too much for me" (verse 4, NASB). Here too the writer frankly owns up to his transgression: "I confess my iniquity; I am sorry for my sin" (verse 18)—while also opening up about what appears to be literal illness that may be an effect of the sin. Perhaps due to the "rebuke" and "discipline" cited in verse 1, David writes of wounds that "stink and fester because of my foolishness. . . . For my sides are filled with burning, and there is no soundness in my flesh" (vss. 5-7). Yet this confession of guilt and suffering does not obviate what is worthy in him—nor has it wrecked his relationship with God; for the psalm concludes with David insisting, "I follow after good"—and using the covenant name *Yahweh* to refer to "my God" (vss. 20-21).

Surely the most famous of the penitential psalms is 51, whose heading declares that it deals with the sins of adultery and murder in the affair of Bathsheba and her husband. Here again, as in Psalm 32, David uses the three different terms for disobedience—"sin," "iniquity," and "transgression"—adding a fourth one ("evil "— vss. 1-4). Yet what's most remarkable about this oft-cited confession is the way its writer makes absolutely no excuses. The great Bible commentator Matthew Henry thinks the phrase "take not your Holy Spirit from me" (verse 11) recalls David's predecessor, Saul, whom the Spirit did in fact abandon (1 Sam. 16:14).[4] This abandonment may have been due partly to the fact that Saul had so much trouble publicly admitting sin—as we see when he confessed, but in the same breath asked Samuel to "honor me now before the elders of my people" (1 Sam. 15:30).

David, by contrast, prostrates himself in this public document whose heading proclaims that it is written "to the choirmaster." Indeed, David's terms for sin all have "my" attached to them—five times in the first three verses—and for this reason, he insists God is both "justified" and "blameless" in judging him (verse 4); there is no finger-pointing, as though the responsibility could possibly lie with anyone else. Furthermore, David indicates that the transgression was not some isolated or uncharacteristic incident, but part of his intrinsic nature—for "I was brought forth in iniquity, and in sin did my mother conceive me" (verse 5). On top of all this, David affirms the public nature of this confession when he tells God that, having been forgiven, he will "teach transgressors your ways, and sinners will return to you" (verse 13). In other words, his confession is partly for the benefit of others; his battle with temptation, sin, guilt, and forgiveness has enabled him to help fellow-strugglers in similar predicaments.[5]

THE KING OF WEAKNESS AND DISTRESS

The previous chapter examined passages of weakness and grief, of which there were many; but in these areas, David's emotions rush forth in a frank and copious flood that is aptly summarized in Psalm 142: "I pour out my complaint before him; I declare my trouble before him" (verse 2, NASB).

"I am a worm, and not a man," writes the great king in Psalm 22. "I am poured out like water, and all my bones are out of joint; my heart is like wax; it is melted within my breast; my strength is dried up like a potsherd . . ." (vss. 6, 14-15). From Psalm 55: "My heart is in anguish within me; the terrors of death have fallen upon me. Fear and trembling come up me, and horror overwhelms me" (vss. 4-5). And Psalm 143: "The enemy . . . has crushed my life to the ground; he has made me sit in darkness like those long dead. Therefore my spirit faints within me; my heart within me is appalled. . . . My soul thirsts for you like a parched land. . . . My spirit fails!" (vss. 3-7).

Psalm 38 is particularly helpful, for here David indicates that we are *always* transparent before God, regardless of whether we actively open ourselves to Him: "O Lord, all my longing is before you; my sighing is not hidden from you." Yet David does open up—both to God and to those hearing or reading these meditations; for he says, "My heart throbs; my strength fails me, and the light of my eyes—it also has gone from me" (vss. 9-10). And later in this psalm of repentance, he describes himself as "ready to fall"—thereby confessing "the sinner's chronic instability, the only consistency he displays."[6]

Along with these admissions of weakness and frailty, David frequently expresses deep grief and desolation as well—often in the strongest and most poignant of terms. "I am lonely and afflicted," he writes in Psalm 25. "The troubles of my heart are enlarged; bring me out of my distresses. Consider my affliction and my trouble, and forgive all my sins" (vss. 16-18). In Psalm 31: "My eye is wasted from grief; my soul and my body also. My life is spent with sorrow, and my years with sighing; my strength fails because of my iniquity, and my bones waste away" (vss. 9-10).

Once again, a penitential psalm is perhaps most potent in this regard—specifically, Psalm 6, of which Derek Kidner writes, "Depression and exhaustion as complete as this are beyond self-help or good advice";[7] for here David declares, "I am weary with my moaning; every night I flood my bed with tears; I drench my couch with my weeping. My eye wastes away because of grief . . ." (vss. 6-7). It's likewise helpful to recall David's public lament over the death of Saul and Jonathan, expressed so powerfully in 2 Samuel. Here David not only articulates his woe ("I am distressed for you, my brother Jonathan," 1:26), but also insists that others share his grief—for "he said it should be taught to the people of Judah," and in the lament itself, he urges the daughters of Israel to "weep over Saul" along with him (1:17-27).

DAVID'S DREAMS, DESIRES, AND DELIGHTS

It almost goes without saying that the writer of nearly half the psalms would be extremely open and candid about his love for God; and thus, we find numerous such passages from the pen of King David—passages that show the true meaning of the word enthusiasm:

"I love you, O Lord, my strength. . . . I will praise you, O Lord, among the nations, and sing to your name" (Ps. 18:1, 49). "My soul will rejoice in the Lord, exulting in his salvation" (Ps. 35:9). "You have turned for me my mourning into dancing . . . that my glory may sing your praise and not be silent. O Lord my God, I will give thanks to you forever!" (Ps. 30:11-12).

David's love is so strong, in fact, that his "powerful, longing desire for the near presence of God" makes him feel, at times, like a wanderer in the Judean desert.[8]

> O God, you are my God; earnestly I seek you;
> my soul thirsts for you;

my flesh faints for you,
as in a dry and weary land where there is no water. . . .
Because your steadfast love is better than life,
my lips will praise you. . . .
My soul will be satisfied as with fat and rich food,
and my mouth will praise you with joyful lips,
when I remember you upon my bed,
and meditate on you in the watches of the night;
for you have been my help,
and in the shadow of your wings I will sing for joy.
My soul clings to you. . . . (Ps. 63:1, 3, 5-8)

"The several references to 'my soul' (vss. 1, 5, 8) point to the intensely personal devotion to God that infuses the whole song." Indeed, the "soul" and "flesh" of verse 1 tell us that David's entire being is "deeply restless and unsatisfied without God," while he later expresses boundless satisfaction in the divine presence, as with a sumptuous meal. At the end, "clings" is same verb used to describe marital love in Genesis 2:24, where it's usually rendered "cleave" or "hold fast"—suggesting on David's part "the eagerness of a friend, almost a lover, to be in touch with the one he holds dear."[9]

This sort of untrammeled passion is also reflected in one of David's most vigorous and overt demonstrations of godly enthusiasm: his public dance of joy when the ark of the covenant finally returned to Jerusalem after an absence of more than 20 years. As the ark moved along, "David danced before the Lord with all his might . . . leaping and dancing before the Lord. . . ." Some commentators feel that the king, wearing the linen ephod instead of his usual royal garb, may actually have inadvertently exposed himself during the ecstatic display—but in any case, it was certainly a vigorous dance, as the word for "leaping" here is better rendered "whirling."[10] However, David's wife, Michal, was disgusted by this impassioned display, for upon seeing it, "she despised him in her heart"—and later, she reproached him sarcastically: "How the king of Israel honored himself today, uncovering himself today before the eyes of his servants' female servants, as one of the vulgar fellows shamelessly uncovers himself!" (2 Sam. 6:14-20).

In this way, Michal reveals the sort of superficial concern for public decorum that so often makes us clamp down on our passions and feelings—even those that are positive and loving! As Dale Ralph Davis suggests, we—like the king—supposedly have an image to preserve, and heaven forbid we should "expose" ourselves by fanatically flying off the handle in this embarrassing way—even if we sometimes do it for rock concerts and football games![11] Yet David, a genuine "Renaissance man" who is among the Bible's greatest leaders, responds to Michal by affirming his willingness to risk shame and scorn for the sake of divine love: "It was before the Lord," he explains, ". . . and I will make merry before the Lord. I will make myself yet more contemptible than this, and I will be abased in your eyes" (2 Sam. 6:21-22).

It's a revealing look into the soul of a man after God's own heart—one who was always willing to disclose his sins, his weaknesses, his griefs, and his joys, no matter how it made him look before others.

PAUL THE OPEN-HEARTED

Paul's ministry to the first-century churches is another case of guileless transparency and self-revelation.

Much of this openness can be found in the poignant Corinthian letters, where Paul so often bares his soul about weakness and struggle in his ministry. We have, for example, already discussed 2 Corinthians 12, in which the apostle several times cites an unidentified weakness that he learned to accept and even embrace (see Chapter Nine). Thus, he tells the Corinthians elsewhere, "I was with you in weakness and in fear and much trembling, and my speech and my message were not in plausible words of wisdom, but in demonstration of the Spirit and of power, that your faith might not rest in the wisdom of men but in the power of God" (1 Cor. 2:3-5). As David Garland observes, this "fear and trembling" refers to a public demeanor exactly the opposite of that era's ideal for the strength and boldness that a cultured orator should possess.[12] In the same way, this prince among evangelists also came across as the opposite of what *we* usually seek—when we want others to be impressed by how cool and capable we are. "In his ministry and in his interpersonal relationships, Paul didn't put on airs. He didn't pretend to be something he wasn't."[13] That's because undue emphasis on one's own ability impedes the gospel, with its necessary focus on the helplessness of man, and our resulting need for the all-sufficient provision of God in Christ.

For this reason, Paul often stresses his own weakness and desperation—as in, for instance, his second letter to the Corinthian church. Describing afflictions that beset him and his fellow-laborers during their missionary work, he writes, "But we have this treasure in jars of clay, to show that the surpassing power belongs to God and not to us. We are afflicted in every way, but not crushed; perplexed, but not driven to despair; persecuted, but not forsaken; struck down, but not destroyed; always carrying in the body the death of Jesus, so that the life of Jesus may also be manifested in our bodies" (4:7-10). This expands on an earlier passage in which he writes, "we were so utterly burdened beyond our strength that we despaired of life itself. Indeed, we felt that we had received the sentence of death. But that was to make us rely not on ourselves but on God who raises the dead" (1:8-9). Paul thus shares some of his deepest personal feelings, knowing that he can most effectively encourage churches to depend on God if he stresses that he himself always has to do so.

PAUL THE PENITENT

Along with weakness, Paul makes no bones about his own sins, either. Most Bible readers are familiar with 1 Timothy 1:15, in which the apostle identifies himself, in the *present tense*, as the "foremost" of sinners; and this confession is all the more remarkable, as it follows directly on a blood-curdling list of sins that God condemns—including perjury, lying, sexual immorality, murder, and the capturing and selling of men into slavery (1 Tim. 1:9-14).[14] Paul apparently considers his own sinfulness as even worse than all this!

But that's still only part of the story.

Earlier in his life, around 54 A.D., Paul had referred to himself as "the least of the apostles" (1 Cor. 15:9). This sounds humble—but at that point, at least he still had a place in the top 12! Several years later, in writing Ephesians, he calls himself "the very least of all the saints" (Eph. 3:8); and shortly afterward, much closer to the end of his life, he writes, "Christ Jesus came into the world to save sinners, of whom I am the foremost" (1 Tim. 1:15). Not only is Paul boldly affirming his own unrighteousness before God—but also, we can see that his sense of sin, and his transparency about it, have *grown*, to the point where he does not call himself an apostle or even a saint, but simply the world's worst sinner.[15] As James Boice once said in a talk on these passages—*that's* sanctification!

But of course, the chief passage in which Paul reveals his sin is Romans 7, discussed earlier, in Chapter 11. Though a few scholars insist Paul is portraying his pre-conversion experience here, I've already cited the long church tradition that sees this passage as an accurate description of ongoing sin in the life of a committed Christian. As such, it is packed with the strongest imaginable language about Paul's struggle, and well worth quoting at length:

> . . . I am of the flesh, sold under sin. For I do not understand my own actions. For I do not do what I want, but I do the very thing I hate. Now if I do what I do not want, I agree with the law, that it is good. So now it is no longer I who do it, but sin that dwells within me. For I know that nothing good dwells in me, that is, in my flesh. For I have the desire to do what is right, but not the ability to carry it out. For I do not do the good I want, but the evil I do not want is what I keep on doing. Now if I do what I do not want, it is no longer I who do it, but sin that dwells within me. . . .

> For I delight in the law of God, in my inner being, but I see in my members another law waging war against the law of my mind and making me captive to the law of sin that dwells in my members. (vss. 14-23)

J. I. Packer observes that the fact of being "sold under sin" is "stated categorically and without qualification."[16] We might also note that Paul's description here covers both sides of the famous distinction between sins of commission ("I do the very thing I hate") and omission ("I do not do the good I want").

Furthermore, earlier in the chapter, Paul actually names one of the specific sins he's been battling: "I would not have known what it is to covet if the law had not said, 'You shall not covet.' But sin, seizing an opportunity through the commandment, produced in me all kinds of covetousness" (vss. 7-8). Some may feel that Paul is merely pulling a theoretical sin out of the air in order to formulate an example—but let's not forget that before his conversion, Paul *had* been a very zealous and ambitious Pharisee (Phil. 3:4-6); at that time, he may well have coveted higher position and status in Jewish leadership—actively *wanting* something that he then had to give up, eventually counting it as "loss for the sake of Christ" (Phil. 3:7-8).

In any case, Paul's long description here is of special use in dealing with transparency—not only because of its frankness, but also because he affirms a crucial idea in handling our own sins. He has carefully balanced two key concepts by expressing both in the strongest terms, and if I also wish to be transparent, I must likewise fully accept both truths about myself: first, that this terrible sinner *is* indeed who I really am; and second, in the long run, this is *not* who I really am.

On the one hand, Paul repeatedly uses the emphatic pronoun *I*: "I do the very thing I hate"; "evil . . . is what I keep on doing." One scholar explains this to mean "I by myself and apart from any new or other power"[17]—and thus, like David in Psalm 51, Paul takes full responsibility for his sins. *He* alone and no one else has done evil—or failed to do good, as the case may be.

On the other hand, he consistently avers that it is not the real Paul doing it—not his deepest and most characteristic self: "I do the very thing I hate"; "it is no longer I who do it" (the latter is stated twice). He can say this because, as he puts it, "I have the desire to do what is right," and "I delight in the law of God, in my inner being." While Paul frankly admits to sin, yet at the same time, these sins are somehow dissociated from his truest self—from what he really wants, likes, and loves, from the "inner being" that was once hostile to God but now yearns to obey through a transformation made possible by the spirit of Christ (see Rom. 8:7-10).

Would we not also find it easier to be transparent if we were able to make this distinction: to frankly assert the *I* of sin, while also seeing the deeper, truer *I* that has an identity in Christ—that wants so desperately to be free of sin, to serve God in spirit and in truth?

In examining a different Pauline passage—1 Corinthians 4:3-4—Tim Keller writes that Paul "knows about his sins but he does not connect them to himself and his identity. . . . He refuses to play that game. He does not see a sin and let it destroy his sense of identity." Though we are sinners, our true and eternal identity is in Christ, and we will find a healthy admission of sin far easier if we understand that this wrongdoing does not define who we really are. If on the other hand we consider sin the truest representation of self, we will have a much harder time admitting it and letting go of it—because it is too closely associated with our identity; rather than insisting "this is not who I am," we will want to keep the iniquity covered and concealed lest anyone discover "the real me." And in avoiding transparency, we will think we are protecting our *selves*—when all we are doing is protecting our sins.[18] By contrast, true Pauline transparency says: "Yes—this is who I really am; but in truth, this is not who I really am."

DANGERS, FEARS, ANXIETIES, AND TEARS

Like David, Paul also felt free to admit his worries, fears, and distresses. Eight times in his letters, Paul specifically cites fear in connection with his church work—describing, for example, "fighting without and fear within" (2 Cor. 7:5; see also 1 Cor. 2:3; 2 Cor. 11:3, 12:20-21; Gal. 2:2 [NASB], 4:11; 1 Thess. 3:5).

Likewise, Paul speaks frankly in 2 Corinthians about "afflictions, hardships, calamities, beatings, imprisonments, riots, labors, sleepless nights, hunger"—of "having nothing," of being "sorrowful" and being "treated as impostors" (6:4-10); he expands on these sufferings later in the letter, speaking of "countless beatings," and of being "often near death":

> Five times I received at the hands of the Jews the forty lashes less one. Three times I was beaten with rods. Once I was stoned. Three times I was shipwrecked; a night and a day I was adrift at sea; on frequent journeys, in danger from rivers, danger from robbers, danger from my own people, danger from Gentiles, danger in the city, danger in the wilderness, danger at sea, danger from false brothers; in toil and hardship, through many a sleepless night, in hunger and thirst, often without food, in cold and exposure. And, apart from other things, there is the daily pressure on me of my anxiety for all the churches. (11:23-28)

The final verse is especially illuminating for the way Paul puts it last—as though this special concern for his converts was the most distressing burden of all. What's more, the word "anxiety" here is a form of the same one used in Philippians, where the apostle commands us, "do not be anxious about anything . . ." (Phil. 4:6). Clearly, there is a very thin line between godly concern and ungodly fretfulness—and Paul has no hesitation in telling others how close he often got to that line.

Similarly, the life of Paul in Acts and his letters is marked by frequent public weeping—as in Philippians, where he describes unbelievers by saying that "many, of whom I have often told you and now tell you even with tears, walk as enemies of the cross of Christ" (3:18). In Romans 9, Paul offers similar sentiments about fellow-Jews who had not accepted Christ: "I have great sorrow and unceasing anguish in my heart. For I could wish that I myself were accursed and cut off from Christ for the sake of my brothers . . ." (vss. 2-3).

Even more revealing are the episodes in Acts where Paul is departing from the churches he founded, knowing that he and his beloved children in the faith will probably never see each other again. Speaking in Ephesus, Paul twice points out that his heart-felt public ministry to them was accompanied by weeping ("I did not cease night or day to admonish everyone with tears," 20:31; see also 20:19); when it finally comes time to leave, there is "much weeping on the part of all" and "they embraced Paul and kissed him" (20:37). The following chapter shows us a similarly woeful departure from Caesarea, with Paul's converts begging him not to leave for Jerusalem—to which he responds poignantly, "What are you doing, weeping and breaking my heart?" (21:13).

LOVE AND PRAISE

This level of unabashed and tender-hearted passion reaches its apex with the Corinthians, to whom Paul made the statement that provides the title of this current chapter: "We have spoken freely to you, Corinthians, our heart is wide open" (2 Cor. 6:11). We do not have space here to recount Paul's long struggle with this church that alternately loved and spurned his ministry, but he repeatedly makes himself vulnerable to them as he begs for a rightful place in their lives, saying, "you are restricted in your own affections. . . . widen your hearts also. . . . Make room in your hearts for us" (2 Cor. 6:12-13; 7:2).

Commentator Philip Edgcumbe Hughes describes these exchanges in lavish terms, referring to the warmth and enlargement of Paul's heart, the "genuineness and whole-heartedness of his affections." Uninhibited and unconfined, the apostle expresses himself freely and without restraint—with no reservations or "inward barriers"; Ralph P. Martin adds that 2 Corinthians 6:11 might perhaps be better translated "I have let my tongue run away with me."[19]

The same warmth and enthusiasm is apparent in Paul's relationship with his God and Savior—marked by a tendency to burst into David-like doxology right in the midst of a passage where he's discussing something entirely different.

In Ephesians 3, for instance, while praying for the strength and growth of believers, he suddenly breaks out with a heartfelt hymn of praise: "Now to him who is able to do far more abundantly than all that we ask or think, according to the power at work within us, to him be glory in the church and in Christ Jesus throughout all generations, forever and ever. Amen" (vss. 20-21). He does the same in 1 Timothy, moving right to enthusiastic words of praise while talking about the divine mercy he received: "To the King of ages, immortal, invisible, the only God, be honor and glory forever and ever. Amen" (1:17).

Perhaps the strongest such example occurs in Romans 11, where, after talking at length about how the Jews have been temporarily cut off as the Gentiles come into the kingdom, Paul suddenly exults, "Oh, the depth of the riches and wisdom and knowledge of God! How unsearchable are his judgments and how inscrutable his ways! 'For who has known the mind of the Lord, or who has been his counselor?' 'Or who has given a gift to him that he might be repaid?' For from him and through him and to him are all things. To him be glory forever. Amen" (vss. 33-36).

David's many ecstatic praises are generally uttered in the context of public worship—a song written specifically for use by God's people; but with Paul, almost any occasion can lead to a spontaneous outburst in which he vigorously blesses and glorifies God—as though he simply can't help himself.

Paul was ever open-hearted—whether in petition, fear, doxology, distress, love, or confession. Praise God that we have this glorious record of one so willing to show his true self, both to the churches of his time and to all the believers who would read his transparent words down through many ensuing centuries.

ACQUAINTED WITH GRIEF—AND WITH JOY

Like Paul and David, Jesus too was "a man of sorrows, and acquainted with grief"—as Isaiah described the Messiah many centuries before his birth (53:3). But I would like to start this portion of my chapter by affirming our Savior's joy as well, since that aspect of his life doesn't usually get much emphasis.

We see some of this in his interaction with those who believed his message—especially the surprised pleasure he felt when Gentiles displayed more faith than the sons of Israel. He "marveled," for instance, at the Roman centurion who instinctively understood Jesus' great power and authority (Luke 7:9). This verb, also used of Christ in Mark 6:6, can alternately be translated "amazed," "surprised," or "astonished."[20] Similarly, Luke 10 tells us that upon the return of the 72 disciples he'd sent out, Jesus "rejoiced in the Holy Spirit" and praised God, saying, "I thank you, Father, Lord of heaven and earth . . ." (verse 21).

The upper-room discourse in John 14-17 contains similarly public declarations of love between Jesus and his heavenly father (see especially 17:4-5 and 22-26). Twice in this passage Christ refers to his own joy, and to his desire that the disciples would share it—"that my joy may be in you, and that your joy may be full" (15:11; see also 17:13).

At this point, it may be well to recall Jesus' assertion that "I and the Father are one" (John 10:30)—a truth he reaffirms twice in the upper room ("we are one," John 17:11; see also 17:21). Thus, the word of God is also the word of Christ, superintended by a loving savior for our benefit. So when Scripture declares that Jesus felt a certain way, this is

Christ himself telling us, for he himself is the eternal Word of God (see John 1:1-2; 14). When you communicate about yourself so directly and forthrightly—that's transparency.

Jesus wants us to know that he has joy, that he marvels and rejoices—and that he is sometimes indignant. That's the term for his reaction when the disciples tried to keep little kids away from him ("when Jesus saw it, he was indignant"—Mark 10:14); interestingly, this is the same word used to describe the response of contemporary religious leaders when Jesus performed miracles on the Sabbath (Luke 13:14) and when his followers were crying out during the triumphal entry (Matt. 21:15). At times, Jesus' indignation crosses over to outright anger, as when he made a "whip of cords" and drove the money-changers out of the temple. This cleansing of God's house appears to have occurred twice (John 2:13-17; see also Matt. 21:12-13, Mark 11:15-17, Luke 19:45-46[21]). Though the word "anger" is never used in these passages, Jesus' feelings are not hard to infer, especially as John applies Psalm 69:9 to the way he was feeling at that time: "Zeal for your house will consume me" (2:17). In any case, the term does appear clearly in Mark 3, where Jesus reacts with indignation to religious leaders who did not want him to heal on the Sabbath: "And he looked around at them with anger, grieved at their hardness of heart . . ." (Mark 3:5).

And so we come at last to grief in the life of Christ. Surely the best-known example of this is Jesus' reaction to the death of his friend Lazarus. At first, this touchingly transparent terminology describes his reaction to the weeping friends and family: "he was deeply moved in his spirit and greatly troubled." Then follows the so-called "shortest verse in the Bible," which our forefathers in the faith saw fit to set off as a separate unit: "Jesus wept" (John 11:33-35). It is thus a pointed, public declaration of a very public action—as indicated by the witnesses who remarked, "See how he loved him!" (John 11:36). And there are other moments of public weeping in Jesus' life—including the tears he shed over Jerusalem; for "when he drew near and saw the city, he wept over it. . . ." (Luke 19:41). The distress he thus articulates—distress over the doom that awaited the city and its children—gets poignant emphasis in

Matthew, where Christ says, "O Jerusalem, Jerusalem, the city that kills the prophets and stones those who are sent to it! How often would I have gathered your children together as a hen gathers her brood under her wings, and you were not willing!" (23:37).

But of course the most powerful description of our Savior's grief and distress occurs at the cross, when he takes up the words of Psalm 22. These laments are uttered for all to hear, as Jesus "cried out with a loud voice, . . . 'My God, my God, why have you forsaken me?'" And later, in yielding up his spirit, "Jesus cried out again with a loud voice . . ." (Matt. 27:46, 50). Earlier, in contemplating these future agonies, Jesus tells his disciples, "Now is my soul troubled" (John 12:27). That's a transparent declaration of distress—one that becomes even more marked in the Garden of Gethsemane, as Jesus considers the terrifying prospect of bearing all our sins and thus enduring the mighty wrath of a mighty God:

> And they went to a place called Gethsemane. And he said to his disciples, "Sit here while I pray." And he took with him Peter and James and John, and began to be greatly distressed and troubled. And he said to them, "My soul is very sorrowful, even to death. Remain here and watch." And going a little farther, he fell on the ground and prayed that, if it were possible, the hour might pass from him. And he said, "Abba, Father, all things are possible for you. Remove this cup from me. Yet not what I will, but what you will." (Mark 14:32-36; see also Matt. 26:36-39 and Luke 22:39-44)

In bringing along his three friends, Jesus is revealing that "he seeks the fellowship and encouragement of his disciples as he faces the most difficult experience of his life. He wants them to recognize his turmoil and suffering. . . ." Moreover, since standing was "the usual posture for prayer in ancient times," falling to the ground is "indicative of extreme spiritual anguish." And the double verbs in verse 33 add emphasis to this, with the first of them expressing "deep emotional distress" (it is translated "alarmed" in Mark 16:5-6). "This extreme sorrow unto death can mean a sorrow that is almost killing him; a sorrow so great that he wants to die. . . ."[22]

Christ's suffering at this moment is even more apparent in Luke's version, where an angel arrives to strengthen him; "and being in an agony he prayed more earnestly; and his sweat became like great drops of blood falling down to the ground" (22:43-44). This may indicate a condition called "hematidrosis," in which extreme anguish causes burst capillaries, mingling sweat and blood together.[23] In any case, we see here what one commentator calls "agony of soul"—possibly even "fear." To Peter, James, and John—and to all subsequent disciples who read these words—"Jesus shows how deep and real is His anguish at this time: He is not portrayed as a Stoic who cannot suffer. . . ." He is, by contrast, a man in anguish and distress, a man who felt great need for the help and companionship of friends in an unimaginable an ordeal.[24] It may be these moments—along with those on the cross—that the writer of Hebrews had in mind when he wrote, "In the days of his flesh, Jesus offered up prayers and supplications, with loud cries and tears, to him who was able to save him from death. . ." (5:7).

INFINITE TRANSPARENCY?

Surprise, surprise.

All along, I've been saying this chapter would cover three case studies in transparency—but I now have one important addition; and if you know the doctrine of the trinity, it should not be hard to guess the identity of this fourth and final example.

According to the Westminster Shorter Catechism—an esteemed 17th-century summary of what the Bible teaches—"God is a Spirit, infinite, eternal, and unchangeable, in his being, wisdom, power, holiness, justice, goodness, and truth." The well-known pastor and author James M. Boice once said that he would like to see "God's desire to reveal himself" included in this list of attributes that are "infinite."[25]

While I'm not sure I would go that far, it's easy to see how Boice arrived at this conclusion.

What if we were to compile a comprehensive list of Bible passages in which God reveals himself to mankind? How many verses would we finally come up with? I can give you a precise answer to that question: 31,102—every single verse in the Old and New Testament.[26] In a very real sense, all of these embody God's revelation of himself. That's why Jesus Christ is called "the Word" (John 1:1-2, 14). Indeed, since Christ is in fact the ultimate revelation of God's nature, perhaps God really *is* infinite in his desire to reveal himself to us: Christ himself is an infinite being. After all, Christ is truly "God with us" (Matt. 1:23). As Jesus tells his disciples, "I and the father are one" (John 10:30)—and Scripture affirms that he is indeed "the image of the invisible God," the "exact imprint of his nature" (Col. 1:15; Heb. 1:3). It's startling to think about this in light of what we learned above through Jesus' transparency—his grief, his love, his joy, and his anguish.

Does God feel anguish, and does he rejoice over his people? I'd like to conclude this chapter by looking at a couple of answers to such questions—just a few, since we clearly don't have time or space to examine everything God reveals about himself in Scripture. (His anger and wrath alone, for example, occupy hundreds of entries in any exhaustive concordance.)

In considering God's openness about his own feelings, let's start with Genesis 6, in which he contemplates destroying the world with a flood—for "the Lord was sorry that he had made man," and the sight of man's wickedness "grieved him to his heart" (vss. 5-6). Even more striking are passages in Isaiah and Jeremiah, where God's lament is so personal that you actually have to look back through earlier verses to make sure it's God talking and not his human prophet (it is, in both cases): "My heart moans for Moab like a flute, and my heart moans like a flute for the men of Kir-hareseth" (Jer. 48:36 [see also 48:1, 33]; also Isa. 16:11-13). And this over the destruction of a pagan nation that repeatedly harassed God's people for centuries!

"VULNERABLE AND PASSIONATE"

When it comes to his own chosen nation, God's feelings are even stronger. Take this passage from Hosea, for example: "How can I give you up, O Ephraim? How can I hand you over, O Israel? . . . My heart recoils within me; my compassion grows warm and tender" (11:8). The Hebrew verb for "recoils" here is the one used of Saul when "God gave him another heart" (1 Sam. 10:9). Translated elsewhere with such terms as "changed," "overthrown," "turned back," and "reined about," it often describes the overthrow of wicked cities in the Old Testament (see Gen. 19:25 and 29; Deut. 29:23). Keeping in mind that the preposition "within" here is literally "against," the passage indicates what commentators call a "wracking ambivalence" in God's heart—a "self-struggle"—one in which "compassion wins out."[27]

Considering how freely God reveals this struggle in the passage, it has been called "a soliloquy" to which "readers and hearers are invited to listen. . . ." "It connotes something *gut-wrenching*. God is saying that his insides are in turmoil on behalf of his people." In this way, Yahweh reveals "his intense compassion" and "the depth of his desire to bring his people back to himself." As expressed in 2 Timothy 2:13 ("if we are faithless, he remains faithful"), God's steadfast love "is not a stoic faithfulness. It is vulnerable and passionate. It is a faithfulness so intense that God describes it as tearing at his insides."[28]

It is also the faithfulness of a mother toward her child, as indicated in this famous passage where God addresses his beloved city of Zion: "Can a woman forget her nursing child, that she should have no compassion on the son of her womb? Even these may forget, yet I will not forget you. Behold, I have engraved you on the palms of my hands; your walls are continually before me" (Isa. 49:15-16). In fact, his affection in these verses is even greater than that of a loving mother, for some mothers do grow cold in their devotion—but God does not; and the extent, the far-reaching permanence of his steadfast love, is beautifully reflected in the obvious reference to Christ's redeeming wounds on the cross.

As Edward J. Young observes, "This is one of the strongest, if not the strongest expression of God's love in the Old Testament, and it is often compared with Jeremiah 31:20": "Is Ephraim my dear son? Is he my darling child? For as often as I speak against him, I do remember him still. Therefore my heart yearns for him. . . ."[29]

Other passages clearly articulate the delight God takes in his creation—including his firm proclamation in Genesis that all creation is "good" and "very good"; like us, God also enjoys this beautiful world—for he says so seven times in one chapter! (See Genesis 1:4, 10, 12, 18, 21, 25, and 31.) In the same way, God exults over his people, too—as in the book of Isaiah: "I will rejoice in Jerusalem and be glad in my people . . ." (65:19; see also 62:5 and Deut. 30:9). But surely the most touching revelation of God's deeply personal love for his people is in Zephaniah: "The Lord your God is in your midst, a mighty one who will save; he will rejoice over you with gladness; he will quiet you by his love; he will exult over you with loud singing" (3:17).

The word used for "exult" here is the very same one that often describes God's people rejoicing or delighting in him (Ps. 68:3 and Isa. 61:10; see also Ps. 35:9, 40:16, 70:4, 119:14, 162); yet here God displays this same excited rapture for his precious daughters and sons. As he "bursts forth in joyful divine celebration," Yahweh also reacts "as an abandoned parent or a jilted lover to whom the beloved has returned."[30] Bible scholar Alec Motyer points out that the Hebrew word *hesed* is most often used of God's covenant love, whereas this passage employs the term *ahaba.* Citing other uses of this word, Motyer suggests that it recalls "the passionate love of Jacob for Rachel (Gen. 29:20) and of Michal for David (1 Sam. 18:28), the fond love of Jacob for Joseph (Gen. 37:3), Uzziah's devotion to gardening (2 Chron. 26:10), Jonathan's deep friendship with David (1 Sam. 18:3), the devotee's delight in the Lord's law (Ps. 119:97)." Motyer also feels that the adjective "quiet" in this passage actually refers to God himself, and thus this love "makes him contemplate his beloved with wordless adoration"; it's a love that "cannot be contained," and so the passage "bursts into elated singing."[31]

These, of course, are only a few of the key passages in which God is surprisingly transparent about his inward feelings. But I guess that should not be terribly surprising after all. As I already asserted, every single verse in God's word serves to tell us what he is like—and so does the whole realm of creation (see Rom. 1:20). Indeed, he has done so many things to show himself to us that "were every one of them to be written, I suppose that the world itself could not contain the books that would be written" (John 21:25).

OPEN FOR DISCUSSION

1. What does it mean to be "a man after God's own heart," like David? Does transparency play a part in this?

2. In Psalm 51, David makes no excuses for his sins. Have you been able to reach this point in your life? Do you try to make excuses for yourself when you sin? Would you be willing to share any of your experiences along these lines?

3. Is it hard to be transparent about love for God? If so, how do we overcome this? If not, what are some ways in which you have shown such en*thus*iasm?

4. In our culture, is it OK to be excited at sporting events and rock concerts but not in church? How has this happened? How can we bring more David-like enthusiasm back into our worship?

5. The author asserts that while taking full responsibility for sin, we must, as Christians, also understand that it does not define us—it is not key to our deepest nature and our true identity in Christ. Why is it important to make this distinction? What happens to our thinking if we believe sin is part of our ultimate identity?

6. What do we learn about God through the transparency of Christ? Be as specific as you can.

7. Is God "infinite" in his desire to reveal himself to man? Even if you don't agree, what might make someone think along these lines?

8. The author covered just a handful of passages in which God is revealing things about himself. Find a few others and discuss what they reveal as well.

CHAPTER SIXTEEN

"Becoming Visible"

Making It Work

While the two previous chapters constitute the heart of this book, some readers are probably still waiting for the meat-and-potatoes—the practical, hands-on material about what transparency actually looks like: How do I make it happen in everyday life? *To whom* am I supposed to be transparent? How much do I tell them? And when? And in what context?

This chapter has some answers to those questions; but let me first express a good deal of wariness about systematic Christian programs—about some sort of format or formula with a bunch rules and guidelines that Scripture itself has not laid down as a clear requirement for all. Oftentimes, too much structure actually gets in the way, becoming an end in itself and limiting the Spirit's work, rather than freeing us to grow in grace according to the individual needs of each person—or each group, as the case may be.

In other words, don't go looking for "Joe Smith's 40-Day Program for Transparency"—together with the requisite handouts, workbooks, videos, leader's guides, and other revenue-generating impedimenta. For some of this material, you'll just have to think and pray about how to apply it in your own daily life.

That said, let's examine several practical considerations for making transparency work. And even if you've been anxious to hear such detail, you might not like the first one very much.

CONFESSING SPECIFIC SINS

A major question in this area involves opening up about our sin: Will it suffice to identify ourselves as sinners—as frequent sinners, as awful sinners, as the worst of sinners—without ever specifically naming any actual sins we've committed? My answer is no. Or rather, yes: At some point and in some contexts, you simply *must* discuss particular sins—those you struggle with, and those you've actually committed.

In the following pages I shall insist that this does *not* mean total sharing about all your sins with everybody; that would be dangerous, stupid, and absurdly narcissistic. But on the other hand, you can't just go around saying what a sinner you are without ever sharing any of the things you actually did.

On the most basic level, you certainly must confess particular sins when they have been directed against another person. Jesus insists that if you are performing an act of worship and suddenly recall some unresolved conflict with a fellow believer, you must "first be reconciled to your brother" (Matt. 5:23-24)—just as he also told the disciples to keep on forgiving those who came to them repenting of their sins (Luke 17:4). Such reconciliation is never going to occur unless the sinner humbles himself by identifying the particular sin and asking for forgiveness. This pretty much goes without saying—and the same principle requires us to confess publicly and specifically if the sin affected not just one individual but perhaps a larger group, or even the entire congregation. Someone who lost his temper and swore during Bible study, for example, is going to have to apologize to that group—and she or he must do so by naming the sin itself. The same thing would apply, for example, to an elder who belittled or insulted the pastor during a congregational meeting. Needless to say, biblical healing is not going to occur unless the sin itself is identified and confessed to all who were affected by it.

More to the point, our real question here refers not to this sort of interpersonal forgiveness—where the naming of actual sins is basically a no-brainer—but rather with the need to be specific when sharing more general struggles, failures, and personal idols with other Christians. And again I say yes—at some point, you are going to need to be specific. While it's true that the writers of Scripture don't always divulge particulars, yet the two preceding chapters show us that several of them do just that. Asaph names envy, and Paul cites coveting (Ps. 73:3; Rom. 7:8). Shecaniah publicly confesses pagan intermarriage (Ezra 10:2), and Moses writes about his disobedience in striking the rock at Meribah (Num. 20:8-12; see also 27:14). In Ecclesiastes, the Preacher specifies the grandiose and sometimes sinful projects—for instance, "many concubines"—that failed to substitute for godly contentment (2:1-11; see especially 2:8). And Peter, in dictating the gospel material to Mark, laid out his own boasting, cowardice, and betrayal in shocking detail (14:31, 50, 53-72).

The need for specific confession also seems to lie behind some of Paul's commands in Ephesians 5: "Take no part in the unfruitful works of darkness, but instead expose them. . . . But when anything is exposed by the light, it becomes visible, for anything that becomes visible is light. Therefore it says, 'Awake, O sleeper, and arise from the dead, and Christ will shine on you'" (vss. 11-14). Like John in his first letter (1:6-10), "Paul stresses that the way to walk in the light is to expose the darkness to light. There is no way for you to walk righteously while concealing the darkness from the shining light of Christ." These remarks are from Denny Burk and Heath Lambert, who are specifically addressing same-sex temptation and sin. Nonetheless, their words also apply to a wide variety of similar struggles—and to the necessity of identifying specific sins:

> If you are like most people, you know that this is true but find it hard to actually do it. You believe you can't share the secret struggle that you face. You are tired of burdening

> your friends with your secret thoughts. You lie to yourself that the current inner struggle isn't a very big deal and will eventually go away.
>
> All these excuses are deceptions that keep you from doing what God commands in Ephesians. They will eventually lead to your downfall. To combat this, one of the most important things you can do is to find a fellow Christian . . . with whom you can be close and completely honest. . . . When you find this person, you need to resolve to follow his or her counsel and to tell him or her *everything.* You need to say when you're tempted, how regularly you're tempted, what your past struggles have been, who tempts you, and any other relevant details.[1]

Using some of the same language about light and darkness, Dietrich Bonhoeffer goes a step further in confirming the particulars of confession: "Confession should deal with *concrete* sins. People usually are satisfied when they make a general confession. But one experiences the utter perdition and corruption of human nature, in so far as this ever enters into experience at all, when one sees his own specific sins. . . . Otherwise it might happen that one could still be a hypocrite even in confessing to a brother. . . ."[2]

Indeed, in some way that is hard to articulate, specific confession of specific sins to a specific person actually helps mortify that particular predilection. As I suggested earlier, the process of fessing up is *so* hard—so agonizing, so severe, so drastic—that it actually helps sever us from the sin, reminding us in the most painful terms just how very *bad* it is, how shameful, how scandalous to others; and in this way, we are all the more confirmed in our desire and determination not to do it again.

The more specific it is, the harder it will be—and the more complete will be the severing that can finally begin to free you from your sin.

KILLING HYPOCRISY

Despite all these persuasive arguments, I still got some push-back on this idea when I was teaching about transparency; people didn't like the idea of having to confess so specifically. And just as I was struggling to come up with the clincher—with something that would convince them once and for all to name specific sins—I happened to be reading Nathaniel Hawthorne's *The Scarlet Letter*, in which one character is terribly burdened with guilt but cannot bring himself to confess.

Sadly, this struggling man is a pastor, and his sin was adultery with a member of his flock. So he is painfully aware of his hypocrisy before the congregation. And in his sermons, he tries to tell them the truth by declaring what a terrible sinner he is. Yet because he won't reveal what he actually did—because he won't identify the specific sin—the result is to make him feel even more hypocritical than ever; for the vague, generalized confession merely causes his listeners to be all the more impressed by his apparent humility:

> He had told his hearers that he was altogether vile, a viler companion of the vilest, the worst of sinners, an abomination, a thing of unimaginable iniquity. . . . Could there be plainer speech than this? Would not the people start up in their seats by a simultaneous impulse, and tear him down out of the pulpit which he defiled? Not so, indeed! They heard it all, and did but reverence him the more. . . . 'The godly youth!' they said among themselves. 'The saint on earth!' . . . The minister well knew—subtile, but remorseful hypocrite that he was!—the light in which his vague confession would be viewed. . . . He had spoken the very truth, and transformed it into the veriest falsehood.

This half-baked confession is worse than useless; it doesn't really expose his sin to the light. Readers can well imagine what might happen if he did: how those hearers would actually react if their beloved pastor specified the adulterous relationship that scandalized the entire community—especially since his lover, in pregnancy and single motherhood, has borne virtually all the opprobrium for their sin. Instead, by confessing only general instead of particular transgression, he merely makes himself look better. Since he wouldn't name the specific sin, his confession has the opposite of its intended effect. Worse yet, he causes those poor souls in his flock great consternation as they reflect that if their godly pastor can feel so bad about his sin, how much worse must be their own! And in this way, rather than uniting himself with them in what Bonhoeffer calls "the fellowship of the undevout," he merely increases the gulf they feel between themselves and their apparently pious pastor. Thus can Hawthorne conclude, "'Be true! Be true! Be true! Show freely to the world, if not your worst, yet some trait whereby the worst may be inferred.'"[3]

SOONER OR LATER

We've covered a lot of Scripture in this book, but we haven't really examined any Bible narratives that involve a blatant *lack* of transparency—the kind of thing Hawthorne decries in the passages above. If you try recalling some instances, you may notice a phenomenon that provides one final incentive for specific confession: When God's people stubbornly persist in concealing a sin, the Sovereign Lord often arranges events that force it into the public light—sometimes in ways that are quite unpleasant. As Moses says in Numbers, " . . . be sure your sin will find you out" (32:23). In the words of Steve Brown, "There is a direct correlation between a Christian's proclivity to wear a mask and God's proclivity to rip it off"—and in support of that statement, he cites Luke 12:2-3: "Nothing is covered up that will not be revealed, or hidden that will not be known. Therefore whatever you have said in the dark shall be heard in the light, and what you have whispered in private rooms shall be proclaimed on the housetops."[4]

This pattern of exposing sin is established with the very first transgression, where Adam and Eve literally try to mask their exposure with hand-made loincloths—after which, "the man and his wife hid themselves from the presence of the Lord God among the trees of the garden." But their creator pursues them, calling out and pressing them with questions—four, to be exact—until they finally have to admit what they did (Gen. 3:7-13). It's the same pattern of pursuit and conviction that we find after David commits adultery with Bathsheba and then has her husband killed before he can find out. Shortly afterward, David is confronted by the prophet Nathan; he describes for David a rich man with "very many flocks and herds" who steals the only little precious ewe belonging to a poor man. David then inveighs angrily against such selfish greed, saying that the rich man deserves to die—at which point, Nathan lays it on the line with his famous clincher: "You are the man!" (2 Sam. 11:1-12:7).

Much earlier, in Genesis, Judah has concealed his scandalous sexual relationship with an apparent prostitute who, unbeknownst to him, was actually his daughter-in-law in disguise. When he learns of the woman's illicit pregnancy—for her previous husbands, Judah's sons, were both dead—he threatens to have her burned alive. She then pulls out the signet ring and other items Judah had given her, forcing him into the painful public admission, "She is more righteous than I . . ." (Gen. 38:12-26).

This unsettling little vignette is actually tucked into the middle of a much longer story that also exposes sin—namely, the crime of Judah and his siblings against their detested younger brother Joseph; eventually, they sell him into slavery and then conceal this sin by making their heartbroken father think his beloved son had been devoured by a wild animal. But God brings this sin to light as well—for when the whole family seeks help in Egypt, Jacob eventually learns that Joseph is still alive. Indeed, the brothers themselves seem to recognize their divine comeuppance: When they first encounter Joseph in Egypt, they don't know who he is, and he doesn't tell them; instead, he feigns anger, accusing them of being spies and insisting they leave a brother with him. "Then they said to one another, 'In truth we are guilty concerning our brother, in that we saw the distress of his soul, when he begged us and we did not listen. That is why this distress has come upon us.' And

Reuben answered them, 'Did I not tell you not to sin against the boy? But you did not listen. So now there comes a reckoning for his blood'" (Gen. 42:21-22).

Perhaps the Bible's most drastic example of hidden sin brought to light is the New Testament narrative of Ananais and Sapphira, who sold some land and then boastfully pretended they'd given all the money to the Lord when in fact, they kept some back for themselves. Mind you, it was the hypocritical deception, not the keeping of some money, that offended the Lord; for Peter indicts Ananais by saying, "You have not lied to men but to God"—at which point, the deceiver instantly falls down dead. Shortly thereafter, Peter gives Sapphira a chance to confess as well—but she tries to perpetuate the hypocrisy and is also killed on the spot (Acts 5:1-10).

Of course the Lord had reasons for establishing policies of honesty at such an early stage in his nascent church, and I'm not suggesting that concealment of sins is always going to be fatal. But God does have a habit of disciplining his children (see Heb. 12:6); and even if he chooses not to unveil your sin—well, perhaps that in itself would be an even worse punishment.

Wouldn't it be better to just do it yourself and get it over with?

CAVEAT #1: OVERSHARING

Psalm 51 is probably the most famous confession in Scripture; but of course, David doesn't actually name his sin in this psalm (the heading does, but these were probably written much later, by someone else[5]). David in fact does not cite his actual sins in any of the five penitential psalms he wrote—nor is sin specified in the other two penitentials. Paul, in confessing himself "the least of the apostles," "the least of all the saints," and the "foremost" of sinners, likewise does not name any specific ongoing sin—only those committed before his conversion (1 Cor. 15:9; Eph. 3:8; 1 Tim. 1:15).

All of this suggests that large public contexts—sermons, whole-church functions, or widely disseminated writings—are probably not the best venue for detailed public confession. Larry Crabb cautions against turning the worship service into "a big Sunday morning therapy group where shamed sinners reveal all their secrets while grace-imitating voyeurs look on with empathy." Wayne Mack expresses similar reservations about widespread public confession of specific sins: Vulnerability, he writes, is "not oversharing, it's not purging, it's not indiscriminate disclosure, and it's not celebrity-style social media information dumps."[6] You have to be careful choosing the time, place, and people when you are confessing specific sins. Setting aside large-scale gatherings for the moment, even a small group can be the wrong context for some types of transparency.

I had a wake-up call along these lines during the years when I was teaching my adult Sunday school classes on transparency. Because the material was hitting home, the subject came up at a Sunday afternoon meal I'd been invited to; as I discussed how helpful my wife had been in holding me accountable for certain sins, our hostess urged me to put my money where my mouth was and identify the particular sin I was talking about. Now it just so happened that this involved my long-term struggle with pornography, which I don't have any special trouble discussing; but I looked around the table at my hostess's grandchildren, ranging in age from seven to 10 to 18—and I knew there was no way I could broach that sin in this context; I had no choice but to turn her down.

"We cannot tell others everything," writes J. Grant Howard. "Some things they don't need to know. Some things they can't take. Some things they won't take. Our words may depress them, confuse them, frustrate them, upset them, alienate them."[7] Of course it can be hard to know when it's okay and when it isn't, but Howard's quote starts us in the right direction by insisting that we ask whether the recipients can handle what we're about to say, or whether it will overwhelm them. That would certainly apply to discussing pornography with a seven-year-old girl; and I don't think her grandparents would have been too thrilled, either.

As I see it, the only time it's necessary to confess before a large group (the church, for example) is when the sin itself is a public one: when it has become widely known, or damaged the group in some way—or when, for instance, the person has been publicly disciplined by the church and now wants to indicate repentance. Examples of this might be someone who'd disseminated false teaching; two members who got into an angry shouting match during fellowship hour; someone who'd been spreading gossip and caused wide division in the body; or a woman who had left her husband, been excommunicated, and then decided to repent and return to her family.

For nonpublic sins, Mack insists that we'd best share hard details only with people who, as it were, "have earned the right to hear them"—and we shall say much more about this shortly when we ask what kind of people are safe for sharing. Crabb takes privacy a step further by strongly preferring one-on-one sharing when it comes to your deepest, darkest secrets.[8] I wouldn't necessarily go that far—I do think there are times when you can share some of your most shameful sins with a small group of trusted friends. But in general, we might float a guideline something like this: The more shameful and personal your sin is, the smaller the audience ought to be for your confession. Martin Luther, even after rejecting the compulsory and sacramental confession taught by the Roman Catholic church, still preferred private one-on-one confession, saying, "if any one is wrestling with his sins and wants to be rid of them and desires a sure word on the matter, let him go and confess to another in secret, and accept what he says to him as if God himself had spoken it through the mouth of this person."[9]

Perhaps one additional story will serve to clarify this issue. A young friend of mine went to a conference where one of the leaders shared with the entire group a number of personal, sexual sins. She had never met him before—nor had several others in attendance—and this made her profoundly uncomfortable. She said that after he'd shared these things, they were all she could think about every time she later ran into him; she literally knew nothing else about the man except "that's the guy who has thus-and-so problems with sexual sin." This brief but telling anecdote reminds us that there has to be a *context* for sharing. Especially in the case of detailed personal matters, confession properly occurs against the backdrop of a trusting, long-term friendship with many other facets besides just divulging sins!

So: Not everyone needs to know about your struggles with, for instance, alcohol, adulterous lust, or stealing things from work; nonetheless, public confession might be okay for less embarrassing but perhaps even more pernicious sins—things like pride, insensitivity, man-fearing, laziness, anger, cowardice, and selfishness. And in any case, you need to be transparent with yourself and your listeners about the limits of transparency—as I had to when little ears were listening around the dinner table. It was actually a bummer to tell my hostess "no"—partly because I wanted to impress everyone with my willingness to fess up. But this sort of boastfulness can never be a goal of transparency—and that leads to my second important disclaimer.

CAVEAT #2: FALSE CURRENCY

Transparency has many worthwhile goals and effects. When we share our own struggles, this enables others to see that they are not the only ones who feel weak, sinful, distressed, or afraid. Better yet, it can help with assurance of forgiveness, as listeners speak the gospel to guilt-ridden confessors. Moreover, it can enable us to die to self: Not only does it nurture humility and underscore just how bad sin is, but it also points us away from our own misery—and toward the gracious love of an atoning savior.

We must be wary, however, if less noble intentions begin to filter in and foul up the process. Transparency for its own sake is usually just self-centeredness in disguise. There is always the possibility, for example, that by opening up, what you actually want is reassurance that your sins aren't really that bad. While there may occasionally be some false guilt that needs to be extinguished by a wise friend, the general goal of transparency is quite the opposite: Rather than reassuring us about our failures and transgressions, it should always be driving home our unrighteousness and rekindling our need for Christ.

For some, it seems, transparency may be having quite the opposite effect—becoming a sort of false currency that supposedly proves the genuineness of our walk. A 2014 article at the *Gospel Coalition* website asks, "Has 'Authenticity' Trumped Holiness?" Pointing to the recent explosion of books like *Messy Spirituality*, blogs posts titled "Dirty, Rotten, Messy Christians," and webpages such as "A Hot Mess" or "My Wreckage," writer Brett McCracken wonders if we have "turned 'being screwed up' into a badge of honor, its own sort of works righteousness. . . . It's almost as if our sins have become a currency of solidarity—something we pat each other on the back about as fellow authentic, broken people." In the process, McCracken insists, "We've become too comfortable with our sin, to the point that it's how we identify ourselves and relate to others."[10]

This is unbiblical. As we saw in the last chapter, Paul insists that his sinful impulses do *not* represent his true self—the "inner being" that takes "delight in the law of God" and desperately wants to put sin behind him (Rom. 7:15-24). Too much focus on transparency for its own sake can make us feel that we aren't being "real" unless we're wallowing in our failure and disobedience; but surely we are also being "real" when we pursue holiness, faithfulness, and love for God. After all, the most real Man who ever lived was entirely without sin.

Citing fellow writer Stephen Mattson, McCracken also suggests that Christians who overemphasize their sins before unbelievers are sending the wrong message to a broken world that wants and needs healing. "While we think self-deprecation causes us to be more relatable and empathetic to non-Christians, it's ultimately communicating a sense of disappointment, disillusionment, and discontentment," writes Mattson. "It thrives on negativity and kills our sense of hope."[11]

Transparency is not righteousness, and it is not an end in itself; if it becomes one, then it might seem like an excuse to avoid the hard work of sanctification: It might actually induce us to continue wallowing in sin—if this provides more opportunity for that all-important "authenticity."

Furthermore, there is always a danger that too much public confession will become a form of man-centered narcissism. Another friend told me the story of some Christian summer-camp counselors who met before the kids arrived in order to share and grow together as a team. When one young man confessed his struggles with fear and anxiety, he received so much attention and affirmation from the others that it was all he could talk about for the rest of the week; he would constantly button-hole fellow counselors and keep on talking about the same problems—with very little attention to the power of Christ in healing these difficulties.

The goal of transparency is love and growth, not attention, validation, or impressing others with your honesty and genuineness. If you have any fear that your own transparency is in danger of becoming a "badge of authenticity," or something to seek for its own sake, try remembering this: Even if you manage to "go public" with your sins and struggles, you still won't have told the half of it.[12] If you're honest with yourself, you know it would take hours, if not *days*, to describe all your sins to someone else. And you also know you've got sins in your life that you're not even aware of; indeed, these unconscious sins, so deeply ingrained in the way we think, live, and interact with others, are often far more harmful and insidious than the ones we know about.

Transparency is nothing to be proud of. Only God knows the whole truth—and it's probably far worse than we think.

SPREADING THE WORD—OR NOT

As Larry Crabb observes, the need to share is directly connected with the need to find the right people to share with. "We must admit to our community, to a spiritual friend or a spiritual director, who we are at our worst. We must tell our stories to someone without consciously leaving out a chapter. The response of community comes next. If the response is anything less than unconditional love, our brokenness becomes fragmentation. We present part of who we are to our unsafe community and hide the rest."[13]

In other words, if we are to come out of hiding and open up about our deepest needs and problems, we must find what Henry Cloud and John Townsend call "safe people." This section of our current chapter provides some guidelines for figuring out just who those people might be.

There's an old story about a rabbi, a Catholic priest, and a Baptist who went fishing together and felt the need to open up a bit when none of their charges were around to hear. The rabbi confessed that he sometimes enjoyed a few slices of bacon for breakfast, and a nice pork chop for dinner. The Baptist, who came from a teetotaling church, owned up to an occasional stop at the local tavern for a few beers. Turning to the Catholic, the first two asked if he had any questionable habits to divulge; they were horrified when he responded, "I can hardly ever resist a chance to gossip about others."

That's meant to be funny—but in real life, gossip is no joke. One of the swiftest and surest ways to wreck a church, gossip is constantly condemned in Scripture, often classed with such sins as malice, strife, and even murder (Rom. 1:29, 2 Cor. 12:20, Eph. 4:31, Col. 3:8; see also Prov. 20:19, 1 Tim. 5:13, 2 Tim. 3:3, and Titus 2:3). Clearly, no one with such a propensity can be trusted with your deepest secrets and sins. Likewise, if someone has shared personal information with you, please be terribly scrupulous about respecting his or her privacy (but see also my discussion under "Wisdom from Adams" in Chapter Seventeen). If you want to see division and heartbreak spread like wildfire through a group of believers, try sharing something that was told to you in strictest confidence.

Or not.

WATCH OUT FOR THAT STUMBLING BLOCK!

Besides avoiding gossip, you may also need to make sure that your confession is not tempting the other person into the very same sin.

Years ago, when I was young and not too smart, I struggled with a persistent and habitual sin. In an effort to get it under control, I asked a fellow-believer if he would help hold me accountable. Actually, since he also struggled with the same sin, we agreed to hold each another accountable, and we would sometimes make a desperate phone call when tempted. Problem was, we also agreed to confess to one another whenever we succumbed—which proved to be a terrible stumbling block, as confession of the sin would often cause the other person to succumb right afterward. Needless to say, this was a downward spiral that not only failed to curtail the problem but sometimes made it even worse.

There may be many cases in which people who struggle with the same sins can share these battles and encourage one another—battles with, for example, fear of evangelism or laziness at work; after all, that sort of sharing is partly behind the success of organizations like Alcoholics Anonymous. But we must also be careful not to place any stumbling blocks in a brother's way. If, for instance, you struggle with same-sex attraction, you must not seek accountability with another person of the same sex who shares your problem; this would clearly be a recipe for disaster.

TRULY SAFE PEOPLE

Besides the obvious pitfalls of gossip and stumbling-blocks, I think what we want and need most in a receptive listener is unconditional love—that is, someone who will go on loving us no matter what we tell her or him about ourselves. A passage near the end of Galatians is helpful in this regard: "Brothers, if anyone is caught in any transgression, you who are spiritual should restore him in a spirit of gentleness. Keep watch on yourself, lest you too be tempted. Bear one another's burdens, and so fulfill the law of Christ. For if anyone thinks he is something, when he is nothing, he deceives himself" (6:1-3).

Of course, this is confirmation that—as we saw above—the "restorer" might be tempted by the same sin himself; but it also points to the mindset required in our confidants: gentleness and humility, bred from recognition that the listener himself is "nothing"—is in fact just as susceptible to downfall as the one he is restoring. That may well be some of the thinking behind Jesus' famous injunction, "Judge not, that you be not judged" (Matt. 7:1). One book takes this a step further by lamenting that so many church-goers must seek out a professional counselor before they can find a sufficiently non-judgmental atmosphere in which to discuss their griefs, their wounds, and their transgressions. If this is the kind of person we seek, then it is also the kind of person we must be toward fellow-believers.[14]

For those who are married, one such confidant should probably be your spouse. Hopefully, you have the kind of marital relationship that is characterized by openness and safety grounded in a lack of judgment. If not, you may have some work to do—work that is somewhat beyond the bounds of this book. But I will say for now that with one another, husbands and wives must strive to be like Adam and Eve in the garden—"both naked" and "not ashamed" (Gen. 2:25). And I'm not just talking about sex! Indeed, you may find that even physical intimacy will be far richer and more rewarding when founded on emotional trust and openness. The qualifications for good confidants, as laid out in the following paragraphs, will be a good starting point in trying to transform any married friendship into a safe place for sharing.

In his 2015 book *Side by Side*, Ed Welch lays out some characteristic of "good helpers": They are first of all *present* with us—"which is a good thing when fears arise"; they really listen; they "avoid being impersonal teachers"; and they "never minimize, are never trite." Moreover, they should be people who enjoy us, who like spending time with us, who love us, ask questions, draw out our needs, remember what we've shared, and follow up on it. Welch then points out that these are all qualities perfectly modeled by Jesus Christ; ultimately, *he* is the type of confidant we must seek.[15]

Henry Cloud and John Townsend also see Christ as the model for a good listener and friend; they insist that such people must have an ability to connect with us—they must "dwell with us in the flesh," as Christ did. Like our Savior, they will show us grace or "unmerited favor," meaning they are on our side, providing unconditional love and acceptance—with no condemnation (Rom. 8:1; Eph. 4:32). Cloud and Townsend go on to offer this helpful set of characteristics found in healthy friendships:

* mutual struggles, though they needn't be the same ones

* loving confrontation

* both parties need other support systems as well [to avoid "toxic dependency"]

* mutual interest and chemistry; a genuine liking

* an absence of "one-up and one-down" dynamics [by which they mean an ongoing power struggle that puts one person in a controlling position and treats the other as something less]

* both parties in a relationship with God[16]

To take this a step further, Larry Crabb suggests that three key qualities are necessary in such "safe" friends: They must be "broken yet strong; vulnerable with hope; respectfully curious."

The first and most important of these—brokenness—means that we must find people who are ready to admit their *own* sins, who have perhaps already shown a willingness to share struggles with us. We know that we can trust people like this not to judge or rub it in our faces. As we then admit weakness, sin, or failure, such broken people "find no joy in the power of superior knowledge or superior morality." They have nothing at stake in listening to us and feel no need to dictate some program that will fix all our problems; they "*want* us to change, to grow, to mature, but we don't have to change for their sakes."

Indeed, as regards wanting the best for us, Crabb's strongest advice is to find someone who will keep seeing Christ in us no matter what we've revealed about ourselves. A true friend "will *celebrate* Christ in me, he will not judge me, and I will feel safe. He will *envision* the reality of my new identity as it is and will become."[17] Such "friends in need" can look at us and see—in spite of our ongoing sins and struggles—that Christ is being formed in us. They believe the best about us—and that this best will eventually emerge and triumph, revealing who we really are, the person God designed us to be: made in his own image and "being transformed into the same image from one degree of glory to another" (2 Cor. 3:18; see also Rom. 8:29).

Welch agrees. "As a general rule," he writes, "we will not be able to have growing relationships in which we help other people unless we see the good in them, and they know we see the good in them." In support of these assertions, Welch cites Paul's greeting to the Corinthian church. Though this congregation was badly plagued with division and a wide array of scandalous sins, Paul opens his first letter by saying, "I give thanks to my God always for you because of the grace of God that was given you in Christ Jesus . . ." (1:4). *This* is the only foundation from which he can launch a campaign to challenge and repair their dire condition.[18]

In this way, we must both find and *be* the sort of fellow-believers who go on "encouraging one another," who know how to "stir up one another to love and good works" (Heb. 10:24-25)—who see one another as God sees us: saints who have been not only justified but also sanctified and glorified through the redeeming blood of his Son (Rom. 8:29-30).

Crabb concludes: "A spiritual community consists of people who have the integrity to come clean. That happens only when we have the confidence that ugliness and conflict will not end a relationship, a confidence that grows out of an even stronger confidence that what is deepest within is not brokenness but beauty, the literal beauty of Christ."[19]

START AT THE TOP

Besides cultivating the right sorts of trusting, nonjudgmental relationships, there are a few other practical things we can do to create transparency in the local body of Christ. One of these is particularly focused on our spiritual leaders—leaders of the kind we looked at in the two previous chapters:

Moses. David. Peter. Paul. Jeremiah. Jesus.

That's a short list of some of the greatest leaders in the Bible—and they all demonstrated admirable openness. If we want our churches to demonstrate a similar transparency, then we need similar leaders who can show us the way.

"The strongest among us must communicate their weaknesses; else they will continue to perpetuate the erroneous conclusion that 'they've got it all together.' . . . Even the 'strong' need to be transparent about some less-than-perfect aspects of their lives." Indeed, transparency is a necessity in leaders—"not only to maintain their own emotional and spiritual health but also to foster an environment where the 'weaker brother' will feel safe. The creation of such an environment must start in the pulpit and permeate the ranks of everyone in the church."[20]

Paul Tournier makes a convincing case for the way truly open-hearted leaders might spread transparency among those around them: The reserve of a secretive and private person is contagious; in keeping quiet about his inmost thoughts and struggles, such a person creates "an obstacle to the development of personal relationships. On the other hand, the liberation experienced by the man who has confessed his sins is also contagious. . . . All who come into contact with him find themselves becoming more personal."[21] Surely this applies to leaders most of all!

In Chapter Four of her book *I Thought It Was Just Me*, Brene Brown identifies a syndrome she calls "Do Ask—Don't Tell." She is talking specifically about credentialed fields such as medicine, clergy, education, and therapy, where workers "have been trained to extract information from reluctant consumers while sharing as little as possible about their lives. The unspoken rule states the greater the credentials and status, the more you're allowed to know about others and the less you have to reveal about yourself. Think about it. Your doctor may know your sexual history, your weight and how many bowel movements you have per week. Yet it's questionable for you to ask if she's married or has children."[22]

Brown's point, of course, is the apparent paradox of authority figures asking you to be entirely transparent while revealing absolutely nothing about themselves. If this dichotomy is present with those who hold authority in church—with the pastor, the elders, the deacons, or other leaders—then it is not merely paradoxical but downright absurd.

In church, transparency starts at the top.

Right after becoming a Christian in the eighties, I attended a Navigators conference where one break-out workshop was led by an older student. He was someone I admired as a long-time leader in the local campus ministry. In fact, being new to the faith and still quite ashamed over my long history of sin, I was somewhat intimated by leaders like this. Fortunately for me, this young man, before a decent-sized group of fellow-believers, frankly and specifically shared his daily struggles with self-discipline, especially regarding his personal devotions. As a recent convert who was sure I must be the worst sinner in attendance, that upperclassman's public admission of weakness had the force of a revelation—one that made me feel like I really did belong at that conference, that I wouldn't have to go on feeling ashamed, pretending, and then being even more ashamed by the pretense.

If one key to true Christian spirituality is dying to self and admitting weakness, then church leaders should actually be *better* at this, not worse as it so often seems. They must regularly seek it, and model it: Pastors must model it in sermons. Teachers must model it in Sunday school classes—whether with young kids, teens, or other adults. Elders and deacons must model it when meeting officially with one another, and especially when counseling or praying with members in crisis. They must also model it when standing in the narthex talking about work, the sermon, their kids, or even next weekend's fishing expedition.

On the one hand, leaders cannot expect transparency in the flock if they themselves don't approach every interaction as an opportunity to demonstrate it. And on the other hand, if parishioners see even these supposed "leaders"—long-time Christians and admired saints—continuing to struggle with sin, temptation, weakness, and failure, then just think how this would enable them to open up as well: to drop the mask and start feeling like they actually *belong* in church. My word to church leaders is this: To a large degree, you and you alone can help set your people free in this way.

SMALL GROUPS—AND SMALL TALK

Given that subhead and the approach of contemporary evangelicalism, you are probably expecting this chapter to conclude by urging your church to start up small groups that get together regularly for the purposes of sharing sins, weaknesses, and fears, etc. But while I don't think that approach is strictly wrong, I can't recommend it very warmly.

In the first place, I don't see that sort of thing modeled anywhere in Scripture. Believers get together to study, sing, pray, and worship—to share meals, help the poor, and testify to God's goodness (see Acts 2:42-47, 4:32-37; Eph. 5:19-20; Col. 3:16). Even when James does include confession in a list of Christian activities (5:13-18), he does not seem to be describing a public gathering, since the suffering person has to "call for" the elders, suggesting a household visit of some kind. There is certainly no New Testament record of a group whose sole purpose is to divulge secret sins and struggles. Probably the reason for this is that, as an official church activity, it would far too easily degenerate into a public navel-gazing. Man-centered and often dizzying in its complexity, this would not tend to direct people's attention to Christ and his work.

Indeed, if you try to picture such a ministry, you can quickly see two other problems. One is that the group might soon get in over its head, unearthing deep psychological issues that may well require professional help—or at least some very experienced leadership. That's why Cloud and Townsend "generally discourage informal groups of hurting people who get together with no trained or experienced leader. These groups can re-create all the problems that someone is there to get help with."[23]

The other problem with a group of this sort is the difficulty of getting folks to come to it. How on earth would you even sell it to the congregation? "Come Thursday night and tell us about all your sins and traumas. And we'll share ours with you, too!"

I don't think so.

On the other hand, I have no doubt that the church—a group of ordinary believers filled with the Holy Spirit and armed with sacred Scripture—does have the resources to help its people with all kinds of struggles; indeed, we do a disservice to one another if we relegate the solution of all psychological problems to a group of highly trained and often very expensive professionals—some of whom approach such problems from a largely secular perspective.[24]

Perhaps the best I can say is that a small group of three of four people might be a decent venue, if you are able to find several such folks who meet the qualifications for "safe people" laid out above. Even here, I don't think this should be an officially sponsored church function—and in any case, there must be an emphasis on prayer and Scripture rather than just sharing.

Of course, that's starting to sound a bit like your usual midweek Bible study, or maybe an adult Sunday school class. And actually, I have found that this sort of venue provides ample opportunity for transparency—when it is approached in the right manner. Here, you have plenty of structure in place, and if the study-leader or Sunday school teacher will allow sufficient time for discussing the Bible text, and for sharing prayer requests, there should be decent opportunities for openness. It will be especially helpful if the leader asks the right questions, moderates with unconditional love and an absence of judgment, and—as we suggested above—models transparency in applying Scripture to his or her own life.

Again, I'm trying to avoid transparency for its own sake. It's not something that can be artificially drummed up or actively required. It's a lifestyle, a mindset, an attitude; a readiness to humble oneself; to let down defenses; to ask, speak, and listen without the usual screens in place—without any secret agenda, any desire to lift yourself up or put others down. Rather than setting up some sort of designated ministry or venue in which we say, "*Here* you can be yourself," it would be much wiser to see *all* conversation, all fellowship, all personal interaction, as an opportunity to be ourselves—to be real, honest, open, *transparent*.

How about if, instead of setting up a "transparency group," we start by working on our daily conversations with others? Specifically, let's try to get a little less "small talk" and a little more real Christian *sharing* into the way we interact with fellow believers.

"MAKING THE BEST USE OF THE TIME"

In Colossians, Paul writes, "Conduct yourselves wisely toward outsiders, making the best use of the time. Let your speech always be gracious, seasoned with salt . . ." (4:5-6). May I suggest that this should be the case not only when talking with "outsiders" but also with fellow-believers? Should we not "make the most of the time" by gearing our conversation to important spiritual issues? Should we not, even in daily conversation, heed Paul's admonition to "seek the things that are above, where Christ is, seated at the right hand of God"? Should we not fix our minds on "things that are above, not on things that are on earth"? (Col.

3:1-2). And yet . . . don't we usually spend far too much fellowship-time jabbering about various superficial and unimportant "things that are on earth"?

Paul Tournier's excellent book *The Meaning of Persons* has several pages on this unhappy phenomenon; I wish I could quote the entire passage. Hopefully, some excerpts will suffice to convict you as much as the actual text arrested me when I first read it: "Think of what goes to make up most conversations: the exchange of superficial impressions ('What gorgeous weather!'); conventional remarks that do not always come from the heart ('How are you?'); observations whose true intention is self-justification or more or less cleverly to make the most of oneself; flattery; straightforward or veiled criticism."

Tournier is quick to admit that *some* small talk is always necessary—as "a genuine road towards contact, a way of getting to know somebody, a prelude to more profound exchanges. . . . But, let us admit it, it is also often used as a means of avoiding personal contact. It is like a prologue that goes on so long that the play never begins."

Most small talk of this kind is actually a shield that we hide behind. We use jokes, ready-made answers, "patronizing advice," excess erudition, "facile chit-chat," and a host of other superficialities precisely in order to keep from discussing anything deeply personal, spiritually important, or possibly controversial. We talk about the workplace, our domestic routine, school, politics, or such cultural matters as movies, books, sports, and music. Again, these are all good and worthwhile topics—unless that's all you ever discuss! In the end, Tournier concludes that our entire social structure, the so-called "Official System," is "no longer seen only as an annoying obstacle in the way of personal contact, but rather as a grille behind which we shelter our fragile person."[25]

Sisters and brothers, if we want to cultivate transparency, we don't need official small-group venues nearly as much as we need to rethink the social interactions that are already in place. Most of you go to church and stick around afterward to talk with friends; many attend mid-week functions, such as prayer group or Bible study; or perhaps you participate in some sort of service ministry that involves getting together with other Christians to clean, cook, paint, pack boxes, pull weeds, or travel to some disaster-stricken area. All of these are opportunities to draw closer to one another by opening up, asking questions, listening, avoiding judgment, encouraging one another, praying, and sharing helpful Scriptures. These are all opportunities to "set your minds on things that are above, not on things that are on earth."

Try seeing transparency not as ministry, but as a way of life.

OPEN FOR DISCUSSION

1. What do you think of the author's wariness about Christian programs, with their handouts, guidelines, and leader's guides? Do you agree that too much structure can get in the way of the Spirit's work? Or have you sometimes used such a program and found it helpful?

2. Do you agree with the author's insistence that we need to confess specific sins? Describe some arguments in favor of this practice.

3. Hawthorne's *The Scarlet Letter* suggests that if our confessions are too general, it can lead to greater hypocrisy. How might this happen?

4. Reread this guideline for sharing specifics: "The more shameful and personal your sin is, the smaller the audience ought to be for your confession." Do you agree?

5. What are the limits of transparency? Are there some people we should *not* share with? Some contexts in which sharing is unwise? When might others be "overwhelmed" by too much information in a confession?

6. Can authenticity "trump" holiness, as one article suggests? How might that happen, and how do we avoid it?

7. Describe a "safe person"—one who can be trusted with confidences, with whom you'd be willing to share personal sins and struggles.

8. The author expresses hesitation about designating a small-group function solely for the purpose of sharing sins, weakness, hurts, etc. Do you share these scruples? Discuss.

9. Discuss how much of our church conversation consists of "small talk." How and when is small talk necessary? On the other hand, how does it function to shield us from deeper, more personal, or more important conversations? Is this a problem for *you* in your regular interactions with others?

10. How can we work to make our everyday interactions and conversations more transparent?

CHAPTER SEVENTEEN

"The Wounds of a Friend"

Exhorting and Rebuking

While working on this project, I would occasionally come to a chapter and think, "Wow—you could write a whole separate book on this topic alone!" That is certainly the case with our current subject, which involves a tangential but important aspect of transparency: rebuking, challenging, and stimulating fellow-believers to follow Christ more closely.

This is biblical, vital, and—sadly—not very common; which is an excellent reason to devote considerable time to it here. It is not too much to say that if Scripture either commands or forbids something, Christian love requires us not only to obey it ourselves, but also to assist others in obeying, too. In the words of the Westminster Confession of Faith: "In what is commanded to others, we are bound, according to our places and callings, to be helpful to them. . . ."[1]

Fittingly then, the Apostle Paul commands believers to "admonish the idle" and "encourage the faint-hearted" (1 Thess. 5:14); in Colossians, he says, "Let the word of Christ dwell in you richly, teaching and admonishing one another in all wisdom . . ." (3:16); Hebrews commands us to "stir up one another to love and good works, not neglecting to meet together, as is the habit of some, but encouraging one another, and all the more as you see the Day drawing near" (10:24-25); and Jesus says bluntly, "If your brother sins, rebuke him . . ." (Luke 17:3; see also Matt. 18:15).

Various Greek words are used in these verses, but they all have the sense of exhorting, instructing, and admonishing; the verbs in Matthew and Luke can mean "expose," "convict," "reprove," "censure," "warn," or "sternly tell."[2] Equally important, while other such passages address church leaders or those gifted at exhorting (Rom. 12:8, 1 Tim. 4:13), the commands listed above are aimed at all believers—out of an apparent conviction that *every individual Christian* has not only the ability but also the duty to instruct, encourage, and rebuke fellow believers.[3]

The Old Testament book of Leviticus offers a challenging slant on this mandate: "You shall not hate your brother in your heart, but you shall reason frankly with your neighbor, lest you incur guilt because of him" (19:17). Among the possible meanings here is the possibility that if we do not confront fellow-believers, we may wind up with bitter feelings—that is, hate—which could lead to sinful actions toward them.[4] But clearly, one key implication is that if we fail to "reason frankly" with a neighbor, we not only share some guilt for sins he may commit, but have actually perpetrated an act of hatred toward that person—like the parent who "spares the rod" and thereby "hates his son" (Prov. 13:24). Many of us are over-cautious or downright fearful about rebuking others; to those who feel such reticence, Dietrich Bonhoeffer says, "Nothing can be more cruel than the tenderness that consigns another to his sin."[5]

If it is cruel and hateful to avoid confrontation, then overt reproof must be an act of love and kindness. That's why Proverbs famously insists, "Better is open rebuke than hidden love. Faithful are the wounds of a friend; profuse are the kisses of an enemy" (27:5-6; see also 28:23). "The 'wounds' are a metaphor for the painful and plain words that must be spoken in a true friendship in order to heal the beloved and/or to restore a broken relationship." That's commentator Bruce Waltke, who also points out that the insistence on rebuke in Leviticus 19:17 is directly followed by the command, "you shall love your neighbor as yourself . .

." (verse 18); done the right way, rebuke, and exhortation can be acts of other-centered love. By way of contrast, to *hide* love by *not* rebuking—this is often selfish: If we refuse to risk ourselves in the best interests of our neighbor, we may well be succumbing to cowardice, laziness, or both.[6]

The writer of Hebrews affirms the importance of reproof in helping the church steer clear of sin: "But exhort one another every day, as long as it is called 'today,' that none of you may be hardened by the deceitfulness of sin" (3:13). The idea here seems to be that—just as the serpent singled out Eve for temptation, rather than addressing both her and Adam together—we can easily be duped into sinning if we rely solely on our own wisdom, without input from others. And note, too, that the writer is emphatic in commanding this as a consistent and recurring habit: "every day."

The importance of giving and heeding mutual admonition is demonstrated several times in the Old Testament—perhaps most notably with King David and his power-hungry son, Adonijah: for "his father had never at any time displeased him by asking, 'Why have you done thus and so?'" (1 Kings 1:6). Much earlier, the high priest Eli *did* rebuke his sons for their "evil dealings"—warning that "'if someone sins against the Lord, who can intercede for him?' But they would not listen to the voice of the father . . ." (1 Sam. 2:22-25). In these cases, the failure to rebuke—or the failure to listen—resulted in the death of those needing reproof. Likewise, Philip Edgcumbe Hughes laments how the Jewish nation under Moses demonstrably failed to exhort and encourage one another throughout those four long decades of wandering in the desert—with similarly disastrous results: "How different might have been the story of the Israelites in the wilderness if only they had daily fostered among themselves a constant faith in God instead of mutually inciting a spirit of rebellion and unbelief!"[7]

In the words of Larry Crabb:

Christians have only two options when it comes to forming relationships:

either remain comfortably distant from the struggles and sinfulness in one another or open a can of worms. When the first option is selected, church life goes on as usual: warm, polite, enjoyable, orthodox, occasionally disrupted by someone's terrible sin, but generally irrelevant to central parts of people's lives. When the second option is chosen, the group may at times seem more disruptive than helpful. Some members will become dejected, wondering whatever happened to encouragement. Others will be offended and change churches. But when the worms of self-protection and demandingness are let out of the can, when people can get to know each other's hurts and disappointments, when issues that really matter are talked about, then there is the potential for life-changing fellowship.[8]

BUT SCREW YOUR COURAGE TO THE STICKING-PLACE

I have amassed a wide range of passages above in an effort to convict the contemporary church about something it very rarely does. And why do most of us so assiduously avoid an action that is clearly and repeatedly commanded in Scripture? Because it's hard! And scary! Quite simply, we don't want to rock the boat, to risk irritation, anger, or rejection, to be labeled as a busybody, a control freak, or someone who "lords it over others." So you see, this topic really *is* related to transparency—to the aching need we have to be liked and accepted. The fear of man we discussed in Chapter One—this very thing that keeps us from opening up also keeps us from challenging others on their sin.

The 1992 book *Bold Love*, by Dan B. Allender and Tremper Longman III, is an invaluable primer on godly reproof and confrontation. In it, the authors admit that the sort of "bold love" they advocate will unnerve, offend, hurt, and disturb its recipients—but it *is* love, and it will also "compel the one who is loved to deal with the internal disease that is robbing him and others of joy." If we regularly refuse to exercise such love, we are guilty of the same self-protection that keeps us all silent about our own sins; it is a "self-centered commitment to act without courage, compassion, boldness or tenderness for the sake of the other."[9] Ed Welch, whose book *Side by Side* is likewise an excellent resource for drawing others out of sin, goes a step farther by asserting that if we thus "ignore our brothers and sisters, we have sinned against them and we should ask their forgiveness. . . . Most people who have witnessed sin or are even suspicious of it in another don't regret raising such important matters when they are raised well, but they do regret having been silent."[10] To broach such issues may not be especially enjoyable during the actual conversation; Hebrews assures us that "no discipline seems pleasant at the time, but painful. Later on, however, it produces a harvest of righteousness and peace for those who have been trained by it" (12:11, NIV). Here's Bonhoeffer again:

> Why should we be afraid of one another, since both of us have only God to fear? Why should we think that our brother would not understand us, when we understood very well what was meant when somebody spoke God's comfort or God's admonition to us, perhaps in words that were halting or unskilled? Or do we really think there is a single person in this world who does not need either encouragement or admonition? Why, then, has God bestowed the Christian brotherhood on us?[11]

The key, of course, is found in Welch's comment above: "raising such important matters when they are raised well." Just exactly *how* do we broach others' sins in a way that is helpful rather than destructive? How do we avoid the judgment and self-righteousness that would all but assure our concerns going unheard?

Here are a number of important factors that should play into your approach—factors that will hopefully make it both easier for you, and more acceptable to the other person.

A MULTITUDE OF . . . FORBEARANCE

Since "love is patient" and "bears all things" (1 Cor. 13:4, 7), the Scriptures repeatedly tell us to "Let your forbearing spirit be known to all men" (Phil. 4:5, NASB). Whether the person is "idle" or disorderly, faint-hearted or weak, we are to "be patient with them all" (1 Thess. 5:14). This means I will not confront every single sin I see or suspect. Rather, my default setting will be to overlook, to forbear—to deliberately pass over the transgression; often, I may even choose to "cover" a sin or offense that was directed to me personally—for "Good sense makes one slow to anger, and it is his glory to overlook an offense" (Prov. 19:11). This would be a fitting application of Peter's command, "Above all, keep loving one another earnestly, since love covers a multitude of sins" (1 Peter 4:8; see also Proverbs 10:12 and 17:9).[12]

And because love is indeed patient, this sort of forbearance means, at the very least, *waiting*—that is, not jumping on the person the moment any sin emerges. An isolated or occasional sin probably does not need rebuke unless or until it shows signs of becoming a dangerous habit. "Often we lose power to impact a normal sinner for good when we focus on a single offense rather than waiting to see a pattern develop. . . . A wise person resists the temptation to pluck young fruit and, instead, waits for sin to ripen on the vine. He covers over sin until the data of a significant pattern of failure is ripe and irrefutable."[13]

In addition to forbearing, love also "hopes all things" (1 Cor. 13:7). This suggests an effort to think well of other people—to see what is good in them, to give the benefit of the doubt whenever possible. "Covering over sin involves the choice to believe the best in the other. . . . Covering over sin enables all that can be admired in another to surface and flourish." This too should be our default setting. Remembering that one of Satan's nicknames is "the accuser" (Rev. 12:10, NASB), we must avoid a skeptical, devilish spirit of finger-pointing that constantly searches out sin and offense. Biblical love, by contrast, seeks to find, enjoy, and even praise what is good in other people; it even works to trust in their growing capacity to see and deal with their own sin.[14] A kind-hearted disposition toward the other will not only overlook most of their sins, but will also seek to see Christ emerging through their growth and sanctification; and this will help smooth the way for an occasional rebuke or admonition.

That's why Proverbs can insist that the wounds of a *friend* are faithful (27:6). The only basis from which you can approach another person about sin is one of trust, of a loving and well-established friendship. "Confrontation, of any sort, requires a strong bridge to truck the heavy material across the chasm of potential shame and misunderstanding." A relationship of mere acquaintance simply doesn't have the strength to bear that load .[15]

> Meaningful involvement must precede efforts to expose each other's sin. The level of involvement, both past and anticipated, determines the level of exposure. In a local church, I can be involved with only a handful of people at a level that warrants blunt interaction about each other's defensive patterns. No one should appoint himself Minister of Exposure to the entire congregation. When someone tells me I come across as pushy, my ability to receive that input well depends partly on how persuaded I am that the one who's given the input genuinely cares about me.[16]

As regards which relationships will sustain this sort of interaction, age difference can be a factor: "I am told not to harshly rebuke an older person, but to treat him like a parent (1 Timothy 5:1). Age and position should be viewed with respect and treated with dignity even when rebuke is necessary. In general it is best to leave a rebuke up to someone who is an equal of the one who has offended."[17]

And of course, if we desire to respect the other person's dignity, we will keep such conversations private—no matter *what* "age or position" we are addressing! All such rebukes should be strictly one on one—with some notable exceptions that we shall examine later, when we take up Matthew 18:15-17.

WITH PRAYER AND TREMBLING

Our emphasis on patience and forbearance naturally implies that we will not be hasty when confronting others. Do *not* go to the person in anger, and be sure to pray about it beforehand, probably several times; earnestly ask the Lord's help and guidance, and be willing to set it aside if the Spirit seems to be saying, "Not now." And if you're the kind of person who's always eager to confront, that may well disqualify you altogether. At least, that's what Allender and Longman say: "Don't confront if you love to confront." Larry Crabb agrees: "Someone who *enjoys* providing critical feedback is not qualified to do so."[18]

Should you decide to go ahead with it, your patience must also extend to what happens *after* the sin has been broached. Remember what you know so well from your own experience: It takes a long time—sometimes all your life—to change a sin-pattern; even when struggling with all your might, you often fall back into the very things you hate. So do not foolishly expect that your word of rebuke will magically cure the sin at hand. On the contrary: If you courageously insert yourself into the midst of your friend's deepest issues, consider it a commitment to come alongside him or her for the long haul—to pray, to listen, to keep asking and helping, and in particular, to look eagerly for any small thing the Spirit of Christ may be doing as He works to unshackle your friend from what may be a lifelong habit.

You must go to her or him with fear and trembling, always recalling your own weaknesses and sins, even if they may not be in precisely the same area. Indeed, the very best context for such challenges is a relationship in which you yourself have already shared some of your own needs and struggles. That of course is the idea behind Jesus' famous words about judging others too hastily: "Why do you see the speck that is in your brother's eye, but do not notice the log that is in your own eye? Or how can you say to your brother, 'Let me take the speck out of your eye,' when there is the log in your own eye? You hypocrite, first take the log out of your own eye, and then you will see clearly to take the speck out of your brother's eye" (Matt. 7:3-5). If you are not willing to acknowledge and work on your own sins—and to see them as log-sized in comparison with the speck-like sins of others—then you are likewise disqualified from confrontation and rebuke.

Similarly, an openness to your own inadequacy will include the possibility that you are mistaken—that you have misinterpreted what you thought was a sin or sin pattern. Jay Adams is helpful in this area. Though he is addressing a more specific case—one in which we are confronting someone who has specifically sinned against us (Luke 17:3-4)—his words also apply to more general situations involving rebuke or reproof: We go in a tentative manner, and while we will be wary of allowing our friends to defend their sin, we must likewise be willing to hear what they have to say on the matter; we may, after all, have misinterpreted or jumped too quickly to conclusions about what is going on in their lives. Hopefully, in addition to expressing our own concerns, it will also be a time to listen—for *both* reprover and reprovee to listen—and work together on the problem, rather than adopting a sort of one-sided, finger-wagging, parent-child dynamic. "The tentative rebuke provides a fitting prelude to conviction," Crabb writes, "and this may more likely lead to a quick and easier reconciliation than if he had come charging up with his accusations, making no allowances for explanations at all."[19]

FOR THE LOVE OF THE SAVIOR

As a final factor in challenging others, be sure to fix in your mind the ultimate purpose of such challenges. You are not trying to win an argument about whether your brother is sinning. You are not trying to demonstrate your great spiritual discernment, or show how useful you are in God's kingdom, or get other Christians to be the kind of people you think they should be. Rather, you simply want to enable your fellow-believer to love and serve Christ better. *Love is the goal.* Love that is patient, kind, forbearing, and always wants the best for others. If you can constantly remember this, it will help you continue to be patient through any push-back or resistance you may encounter in the process.

And as you persevere through this difficult process, you yourself may also be driven to cling more closely to the Savior.

REPROOF IN ACTION

As I showed with Chapters Fifteen and Sixteen, I feel these tricky waters will be easier to navigate if we can spend some time looking at Scripture passages where it actually occurs—or at least, where it's described in enough detail to give us a clearer notion of what it actually looks like.

Moses demonstrates some of our principles when he rebukes Aaron for the incident of the golden calf in Exodus. Having come down from a face-to-face meeting with God, and finding all Israel worshiping a man-made idol under the apparent leadership of his own brother, Moses asks Aaron, "What did this people do to you that you have brought such a great sin upon them?" (Ex. 32:21). In posing his challenge as a question, Moses allows for the possibility of an explanation of which he is unaware—perhaps that the people somehow forced Aaron into it, as the opening phraseology indicates. At the same time, Moses highlights the depth of the iniquity, together with Aaron's personal role in the matter: "*you* have brought such *great sin* upon them" (my emphasis). All this shows good pastoral care: "Moses was sensitive to the temptation Aaron faced; he acknowledged the pressure he was under. However, he also wanted his brother to take full responsibility for what he had done. This is the right balance. When dealing with sin, spiritual leaders should have compassion for those who have fallen, while at the same time not leaving any room for making excuses."[20]

A similar approach is found in Galatians 6, where the passive verb ("is caught") suggests being overtaken by something, as if to moderate our attitude toward the fellow-believer who sinned. Though we already looked at part of this passage, it is worth studying here in its entirety: "Brothers, if anyone is caught in any transgression, you who are spiritual should restore him in a spirit of gentleness. Keep watch on yourself, lest you too be tempted. Bear one another's burdens, and so fulfill the law of Christ. For if anyone thinks he is something, when he is nothing, he deceives himself. But let each one test his own work, and then his reason to boast will be in himself alone and not in his neighbor. For each will have to bear his own load" (vss. 1-5).

It's quite possible that this passage is closely connected to the previous verse, which rejects conceit, provocation, and envy; suggesting that the Galatians had a problem with these particular sins, one scholar points out that the passage in chapter 6 puts much greater emphasis on the attitude of those "who are spiritual" than on the fallen brother. Since pride, aloofness, and conceit are often far more damaging to the church and the gospel message than overt moral failure, it is imperative that those approaching a fallen brother avoid self-righteousness, and rather recognize that they too are vulnerable to those very same moral failings they seek to correct. While keeping this humble attitude in mind, Galatians 6:1 nonetheless posits a clear Christian duty to help fellow-believers overcome besetting sins—and to do so with "a spirit of gentleness." A fruit of the Spirit in Gal. 5:23, that last quality means "mildness . . . in dealing with people"; the word is elsewhere translated "humility," "meekness," and "consideration." William Hendriksen observes that Jesus himself not only promoted this attitude toward repentant sinners but also exemplified it: "Note how tenderly he dealt with: the sinful woman (Luke 7:36-50), the penitent thief (Luke 23:43), Simon Peter (Luke 22:61; cf. John 21:15-17), the invalid (John 5:14), and the woman taken in adultery (John 8:11)."[21]

"PURGE THE EVIL PERSON"

Those who hesitate to rebuke and correct—who are at least glad to know they can be meek and tentative about it—may be surprised at Paul's attitude in 1 Corinthians 5. In this notable instance, a member of the Corinthian church was guilty of a sin that, according to Paul, "is not tolerated even among the pagans": sexual relations with his father's wife (verse 1). To some, "father's wife" might seem like a polite way of referring to the man's own mother; it was, however, probably a stepmother—though this does not mitigate the scandal, which involved not merely extramarital sex but also incest (cf. Lev. 18:8).[22] Far from being tentative, Paul is both vehement and aggressive in targeting this outrage: "Let him who has done this be removed from among you." Later, he quotes Deuteronomy: "'Purge the evil person from among you'" (5:2, 13; see Deut. 13:5, 17:7).

There are several key differences between this case and some of those covered above. One significant factor is that the matter had become public knowledge; for this reason, Paul sees no need to keep it private or confidential. Even more important, neither the stepson nor the church as a whole was repentant; in fact, quite the opposite seems to be the case. Paul asserts, "You have become arrogant" (5:2, NASB) and "Your boasting is not good" (5:6) —so it appears the church had developed some sort of misplaced ecclesiastical pride in their tolerance for such horrific sin. Thus Paul's comments are addressed less to the individual sinner than to the congregation as a whole: They are the ones censured for boasting—and likewise charged with judging, removing, and purging the sinful brother.

The passage points to the urgent need for reproof and, in cases where there is no repentance, for the more public measure of actually putting someone out of the church—a process involving church discipline, which we shall address in the next section of this chapter. For the moment, we can learn more about rebuke if we examine Paul's whole troubled relationship with this particular church.

To be specific, 2 Corinthians fleshes out the apostle's attitude during reproof and admonition, expounding at length on the pain, distress, and grief he felt in earlier challenging the church so strongly: "I wrote to you out of much affliction and anguish of heart and with many tears, not to cause you pain but to let you know the abundant love that I have for you" (2:4). Furthermore, since both the church and the individual sinner had repented by the time of 2 Corinthians, Paul now rejoices—showing that his motive for confrontation was not harsh or vindictive, but a loving desire for repentance and healing:

> For even if I made you grieve with my letter, I do not regret it—though I did regret it, for I see that that letter grieved you, though only for a while. As it is, I rejoice, not because you were grieved, but because you were grieved into repenting. . . . So although I wrote to you, it was not for the sake of the one who did the wrong, nor for the sake of the one who suffered the wrong, but in order that your earnestness for us might be revealed to you in the sight of God. Therefore we are comforted. (7:8-9, 12-13)

Before saying more about Paul's tender-hearted attitude here, it would be well to admit uncertainty about the subject matter in these later passages from 2 Corinthians. For many centuries, the prevailing interpretation of 2 Corinthians 2 and 7 was that they referred back to the Paul's stern reproof of sexual sin and arrogance in 1 Corinthians 5—as discussed above. In recent decades, however, many commentators have come to believe that the "painful letter" so often cited in 2 Corinthians is *not* in fact 1 Corinthians, but some other missive—now lost—that Paul wrote between these two epistles. The theory: This long-lost letter also had strong words for the church at Corinth—words referring *not* to incest and pride, but to a church-wide rebellion against Paul's teaching; moreover, the breakaway was apparently led by some now-unknown ringleader, and *this* renegade—not the sexually immoral man of 1 Corinthians—is "the one who did the wrong" and later repented, generating Paul's remarks in 2 Corinthians 2 and 7.[23]

Personally, I'm inclined to accept this more recent hypothesis; but even though we don't have space here to work it out in more detail, we can still benefit from what Paul says in these passages. Whether his later remarks refer to 1 Corinthians or to some now-missing letter—whether he is reproving rebelliousness or sexual sin and arrogance—in either case, his tears, anguish, and affliction show that "his intention was not to cause pain but to let them know his love for them. He showed this, not by glossing over a bad situation but by confronting it and demanding (again) that the Corinthians take action. It takes real love to confront a difficult situation rather than side-stepping it." The entire exchange "shows clearly that a loving pastor must sometimes cause sorrow to those he cares for, if they fall into sin." With the help of these passages, it is vital to recognize that issues of sin and rebuke *do* cause heartache, and that church life will not be painless, or free of difficulties and challenges; indeed, the one who confronts will often feel anguish and grief, but—as suggested by Hebrews 12:11—it is nonetheless worthwhile for the sake of peace and purity in the kingdom.[24]

We can thus take note that confronting sin in others will require a willingness to suffer for Christ—not only because of the pain we cause others, but also because, if our attitude is right, the very act of challenging someone should itself cause us grief. Yet if Paul had not fulfilled his painful duty by writing to them in such strong terms, and if they had not responded by repenting, then there would have been grave danger—possibly even spiritual shipwreck—for both the individual(s) involved and the church as a whole. "Accordingly, he was determined, by God's grace, to allow neither concern for their feeling nor unwillingness to give offence to preponderate in such a way as to make him keep silence. . . ."[25]

As we consider applying these truths to our own efforts at confrontation, we might also note the confidence Paul expresses in the eventual response of those he reproved; for in exulting over their swift repentance, he says that even when initially writing to reprove them, "I felt sure of all of you, that my joy would be the joy of you all" (2 Cor. 2:3).

JESUS AND CHURCH DISCIPLINE

No discussion of reproof would be complete without Jesus' vital words on the matter, taken from Luke and Matthew: "Pay attention to yourselves! If your brother sins, rebuke him, and if he repents, forgive him . . ." (Luke 17:3); likewise, "If your brother sins against you, go and tell him his fault, between you and him alone. If he listens to you, you have gained your brother" (Matt. 18:15). Careful readers will note that the context here seems to be narrower than that found in our previous passages—specifically, there appears to have been a personal offense toward the reprover. This is suggested by the phrase "against you" in Matthew and the need for forgiveness in Luke 17; clearly if you are generally admonishing someone because you fear a pastime is becoming idolatrous, or for skipping church twice a month, that person does not need your personal forgiveness.

However, Matthew's "against you" is not found in some of the oldest manuscripts; for this reason, it is probably not part of the original text. Furthermore, the Greek verb for "sins" in Matthew is of a very general nature—and thus, Christ's command probably *does* include more general rebukes, rather than being limited only to some sort of interpersonal conflict.[26]

Even more significant, the passage in Matthew follows admonitions about not causing children to sin (18:5-6) and about going after lost sheep (18:10-14); so the mandate for reproof occurs in a broader context of watchfulness over others' sins: Like the owner of the wayward lamb, we must all make it our business to watch over the welfare of others in the flock.[27] The sentiment here is perhaps echoed at the very end of James's letter: "My brothers, if anyone among you wanders from the truth and someone brings him back, let him know that whoever brings back a sinner from his wandering will save his soul from death and will cover a multitude of sins" (5:19-20). We cannot disregard these key principles, either for our own sake or for that of the church.

Indeed, the broader church context becomes a major issue in Matthew 18, as Jesus addresses a question not covered in any of the other passages on rebuke: What happens if you challenge someone, and she or he refuses to consider what you have said? Let's repeat the previous verse along with the rest of Christ's instructions here:

> If your brother sins against you, go and tell him his fault, between you and him alone. If he listens to you, you have gained your brother. But if he does not listen, take one

> or two others along with you, that every charge may be established by the evidence of two or three witnesses. If he refuses to listen to them, tell it to the church. And if he refuses to listen even to the church, let him be to you as a Gentile and a tax collector. (vss. 15-17)

In the initial confrontation, the emphasis is on privacy—"between you and him alone." After that, if the brother refuses to listen to one-on-one exhortation, then Jesus mandates a progressively broader awareness of the sin, starting with a couple of "witnesses"—probably to aid in exhortation and, if necessary, to confirm later on that the offender did indeed remain intractable. These additional voices may also be helpful if you and the "reprovee" disagree on whether the matter is actually a sin—or on how serious it is. And if the person has been thus confronted yet still will not repent—if she or he is determined to persist in what is clearly a sin—then the matter should then be taken "to the church." This may mean that at first, we initially involve leaders or elders in the local body, as representatives of "the church"; and then, if necessary due to continuing refusal, the entire congregation should be made aware of ongoing unrepentance in the face of more and more widespread admonition. Finally, as a last resort, if the person still won't respond with repentance when held accountable before the entire congregation, he or she is to be treated as an unbeliever, as a "Gentile or a tax-collector"—which is generally taken to mean that the offender is to be put out of the church: excommunicated.[28] It would perhaps be well to add here that while this final step sounds very drastic to a culture that generally resists any sort of judgment or discipline, the extreme nature of excommunication is designed not merely to curtail sin and scandal in the church but ultimately to show the sinner the dire gravity of his sin, thereby leading to repentance and restoration (see, for instance, 1 Cor. 5:5).

This is an *extremely* abbreviated summary of what can be a long, difficult, complicated process—one that is sometimes referred to as "church discipline." This sort of careful accountability—sometimes leading to public censure and even expulsion—goes against the grain of our free-wheeling culture; but it is clearly and succinctly *commanded* by Christ himself, and I wish I had space here to lay out the details of what this looks like and how to go about it. That would be especially desirable because, as counselor Jay Adams points out, the failure to exercise proper church discipline has resulted in countless broken homes, wrecked relationships, and churches "torn by schismatic and factious persons who have been allowed to wreak havoc"—not to mention dishonor to Christ in allowing scandalous sin to flourish unchecked in his precious body.[29]

Indeed, since a primer on church discipline is well beyond the bounds of this book, I can do no better than urge every reader to study Adams's slim but invaluable *Handbook of Church Discipline* (Zondervan, 1986). Because discipline involving the entire church requires precision, delicacy, and discernment, I'm not wild about extracting bits and pieces, lest I leave something out, or mislead you by oversimplifying a complex process; you really should read Adams's entire volume—particularly if you are or church leader, and also if your church lacks any mechanism for implementing Christ's commands in Matthew 18. Nonetheless, it might be well to make a few observations in the context of transparency and mutual reproof.

WISDOM FROM ADAMS

To begin with, Adams makes the eye-opening assertion that even in the early private stage, when reproof is simply "one on one," the reprover cannot make an unconditional vow of confidentiality. While the passage certainly allows a qualified promise of privacy (e.g., "I shall never involve others unless God requires me to do so") Adams points out that vowing never to tell anyone else would preclude us from later involving witnesses, church leaders, and/or the congregation—as required by Christ in the case of continued refusal.[30]

He also observes helpfully that, as Jesus' words clearly indicate, church members are not herein disciplined for the actual specific sins

("They threw me out because I lost my temper!"); rather, discipline is necessitated because of their refusal to listen, to at least consider whether they are in the wrong and begin addressing the sin—or in the case of personal offense, to begin working toward resolution. And in any case, the second stage of discipline, in which two or three others are called in, may be designed to engender forethought about how serious the matter really is. The knowledge that the reprover must involve others if his attempt fails—this may encourage him to drop the issue entirely; he may perhaps decide that not even a private one-on-one approach is warranted—and thus to heed Proverbs 19:11, making it "his glory to overlook an offense."[31]

Perhaps most significant for the issue of transparency, Adams also confirms what we said earlier: Even this longer admonition of involving other parties—this too may extend beyond cases in which one person has sinned against another. One-on-one offenses certainly seem to be the overall context of the passage (see, for instance, Peter's follow-up question, "Lord, how often will my brother sin against me, and I forgive him?"—Matt. 18:21); yet surely we would not wish to restrict discipline and excommunication only to cases where one member had personally sinned against another. Might we not sometimes have to confront, challenge, and perhaps even expel members for refusing to repent of substance abuse, absence from church, or premarital sex—issues that would not have arisen from a specific offense directed at one individual? Galatians 6:1 certainly seems to give warrant for general reproof—as indicated by the phrase "caught in *any* transgression" (my emphasis); and commentator William Hendriksen takes this a step farther: Although Jesus may be speaking about personal offense in Matthew 18, nonetheless, "the underlying requirement of showing love and the forgiving spirit toward all makes it reasonable to state that whenever the interests of the Church demand or even allow it, the rule of Matthew 18:15 should also be applied to public sins."

Hendriksen insists that "the interests of the Church" is a vital qualifier; general reproof for idolatry or bad habits should be kept private, one on one, and not advanced to the other more serious levels unless the sins are becoming public and beginning to endanger the unity of the body—or the truth of the gospel. This was the case, for instance, when Paul had to publicly rebuke Peter for compromising with legalism at Antioch—for falsely upholding the necessity of circumcision and for separating himself from Gentile believers (see Gal. 2:11-14).[32] That was a grave public sin undermining the whole concept of salvation apart from works. Most sins will never require this sort of public confrontation.

SO WHY DON'T WE . . . ?

Despite the difficulty and complexity of these remarks, the real question about Matthew 18 is a simple one: If Jesus so plainly insists on reproof, why don't we do it more often? And why do we have so much trouble making these rebukes a private matter, as Christ so plainly insists ("between you and him alone")? The sad fact is that if we ever talk about someone else's sins, we usually do exactly the opposite: We will discuss it with any number of other people—perhaps even going so far as to ask, "Do you think I should say something to him about it?" And the actual sinner would be the *last* person we speak to, rather than the very first, as our Savior commands. Could it not be possible that speaking a gentle word of reproof or admonition—or at least broaching the matter with a question—might serve as an antidote for slander and gossip, giving others the chance to defend themselves, and helping to defuse any anger or irritation we may have for a perceived slight or sin?

Let's say we could actually get into the habit of approaching others one-on-one regarding issues that seem to threaten their sanctification, their relationship with Christ, or the overall health of the church; if we did this more often, might it not cut down on the amount of more serious discipline at a higher level, involving perhaps public censure and excommunication? Seeing Matthew 18 as a series of carefully sequenced steps, Adams points out that many churches are forced to skip right to the most drastic stage, because no one was willing to confront the person one-on-one at an earlier step—that the courage to do so might actually resolve many potentially damaging and divisive sins.[33] We hesitate to approach others on their sins because we fear a break in the relationship; but I ask you: Which is really scarier? A temporary rift between two people which can hopefully be talked out in private, or an overt scandal in which one person has to be publicly scolded and perhaps even removed from church membership?

I should point out that those who've been thus formally excommunicated are certainly still welcome in church—though they are to be treated as unbelievers (see Matt. 18:17 and 1 Cor. 5:11; this is why, for instance, they are traditionally forbidden from enjoying the Lord's Supper[34]). Nonetheless, most who undergo this process have already left the church anyway, and others leave thereafter. And in addition to the pain of losing such precious sisters and brothers, perhaps because we did not intercede early enough, these individual departures from the flock sometimes result in even wider division if the offender has gotten some members "on his side" and winds up pulling them out of the church along with him.

The longer I go on serving as a church elder, the more amazed I am at the wisdom and succinctness of the process Christ describes in Matthew 18—a process of rebuke hinted at in such other passages as Leviticus 19:17-18, Proverbs 27:5-6, Galatians 6:1, Hebrews 3:13, and James 5:19-20. Such a clear mandate is one we would do well to heed, no matter how risky or frightening it may seem.

MANHATTAN MELODRAMA

I'd like to conclude this somewhat painful chapter with some salutary illustrations on the way this process works—showing that in spite of the sometimes negative emotions, it can yield much fruit in the lives of both reproved and reprover.

When my wife and I first met in 1983, it took us quite a while to realize we were falling in love. Initially, it was a matter of walking her safely back home after our Wednesday evening Bible study in lower

Manhattan; then it was a deepening friendship, and then . . . well, it seemed we were headed for something more serious.

One evening on a dinner-date, I mustered up the courage to ask how she felt about me, and where she thought the relationship was headed. Her catchy reply—"Hmm. That's a heavy one"—was not exactly what I had hoped for. Proceeding carefully, she pointed out that she was somewhat concerned about our very different lifestyles.

"What!" I shouted in horror; "how could you *not* want to spend the rest of your life with such a fine specimen of manhood! Are you crazy?"

I'm kidding—that is not what I said. In fact, I didn't say much of anything—except to quietly ask her what she meant. The ensuing conversation caused me to write these things to a friend:

"Mona is a medical student with two and a half years to go. She lives alone, stays home mostly, she is quiet, hard-working, humble and godly. I, on the other hand, am a would-be visionary with perhaps half a dozen years to live. I go out constantly, my life is filled with chaos, laziness, worldliness and vanity. She wondered was it wise for her to start a relationship with such a fellow. We talked for a long time about my lifestyle."

Her comments were ones I had heard before, without paying too much attention. This time, I listened in somewhat stunned silence as my hopes of a smooth transition to engagement were dashed against the fortress of my future wife's admirable common sense. Later that evening, after the shock began to wear off and I realized that my lax approach to sanctification was threatening this precious relationship, I decided I had better get serious about these areas that should have worried me as much as they did her.

I can't say the turnaround was instantaneous; in fact, even now I am still working on several of those problematic issues. But it *was* a hearty wake-up call—a genuine turning point in my life with Christ. Not only did this gentle reproof serve to fuel a more serious attitude toward sanctification, but also, it showed me that this lovely young woman really did care for me; otherwise, rather than seeking to help me become the man she was looking for, she would simply have written me off. (Indeed, this is precisely what we do when we fail to reprove a friend: We write him or her off as a hopeless case.)

At the same time, I dare say the admonition may have shown *her* that she cared as well. Thus, what seemed on the surface to threaten the relationship eventually brought us closer together—because each had entered an area of openness and vulnerability: me in facing my sins, and she in confessing how she really felt. Had she not taken this godly approach, we might not now being enjoying our 33rd year of wedded bliss.

THREE LITTLE WOMEN

Fans of classic literature may find this scenario vaguely familiar. It's pretty much what happens between Amy and Laurence in Louisa May Alcott's beloved novel *Little Women*, first published in 1869. During a European vacation, the upwardly mobile Amy—who is starting to show some interest in a young suitor named Fred Vaughan—reproves her old friend Laurence for a lazy and careless lifestyle that seems to be sapping his great potential. Result: Laurence turns himself around, young Vaughan is dismissed from the narrative, and the two future spouses begin to realize how much they care for each other.

It's not much of a stretch to see the same overall movement in an even more famous literary romance—the one between Elizabeth Bennet and Fitzwilliam Darcy in *Pride and Prejudice*, by Jane Austen. Citing his "arrogance," his "deceit," and his "selfish disdain for the feelings of others," Lizzie rebukes Mr. Darcy in the strongest possible terms: "I had not known you a month before I felt that you were the last man in the world whom I could ever be prevailed on to marry."[35] Darcy takes these rebukes to heart and swiftly overhauls his demeanor—while both of them slowly realize that they are, after all, perfectly suited to one another. Result: Another happy ending of wedded bliss.

The reconciliation of the future Mr. and Mrs. Darcy, of course, occupies nearly the entire second half of Austen's 1813 masterpiece. But the process doesn't take nearly so long in Thornton Wilder's *Our Town*, a play in which the two lovers—George and Emily—don't realize they're anything more than long-time next-door neighbors until Emily works up the gumption to confront George about how stuck-up he's getting. At that point, they both come to see what they mean to each other, with George expressing particular gratitude that he has a friend who cares enough to challenge him about "that fault in my character."[36] In a few more minutes of stage time, the two of them are married.

* * * * * * * * *

Naturally, not all such admonitions or rebukes are going to result in glorious matrimony; but if they're done right—with equal vulnerability on both sides—they can and should lead to greater closeness, greater sanctification, and greater glory for God, the creator and provider of friends who can meet each other in such honesty and openness.

OPEN FOR DISCUSSION

1. Proverbs 27:5-6 indicates that challenging others on sin is an act of love, while Leviticus 19:17 suggests that failure to rebuke a fellow-believer is tantamount to hatred. Discuss this a bit.

2. Why might we need others to confront us on our sins, instead of just trying to identify and deal with them ourselves?

3. Have you ever had a friend confront or admonish you on sin? What was that like?

4. Have you ever confronted someone on a sin? What made you decide to do it? Are you willing to describe the experience? On the other hand, have you ever decided *not* to rebuke someone and then later regretted it?

5. What does it mean to "cover a multitude of sins"?

6. How do you know when it is time to stop "covering" and actually go to the person? That is, when does a sin become serious enough for confrontation?

7. When one *does* confront, how should it be done? Re-read Galatians 6:1-5; what does this passage tell us about helping others with their sins? What other factors are important in going to someone about sin?

8. Describe the step-by-step process of church discipline as laid out in Matthew 18:15-17.

9. Why is church discipline necessary?

10. Has your church ever had to institute church discipline? What was it like?

11. If your church *doesn't* have a process for discipline according in Matthew 18, consider having a few folks read *Handbook of Church Discipline* by Jay Adams.

12. According to Adams, Matthew 18:15-17 requires that we *not* promise unconditional confidentiality when discussing sin with others. What do you think about this? How can we promise privacy while not vitiating the other steps in Matthew 18?

13. Are we sometimes guilty of gossiping about others instead of confronting them privately, one on one, as in Matthew 18?

CHAPTER EIGHTEEN

"You Yourselves Are Full of Goodness"

Affirming and Praising

How many times have you been to a funeral where the person who died was extolled in the warmest possible terms? If you're like me, you've heard various deeds and character traits repeatedly highlighted by those who knew her or him—with the oft-heard refrain, "He was a good man," or "She will be missed."

Now can you tell me why we wait till *after* death to say these things? Wouldn't it be infinitely better to articulate such praises directly to the person while he or she was still alive? Why do we squander so many wasted opportunities to affirm, encourage, cherish, and appreciate? If we feel strongly enough to say it once the person is dead—to say it even weeping for the loss—why is it so hard to express it face to face?

Frankly, I'm not sure why; but I can tell you that it doesn't seem much easier than the rebukes and admonitions we discussed in the previous chapter.

When I'm alone, I frequently think about how much I appreciate a certain gift or action in someone else, and how great it would be to tell the person. Often, I actually prepare the compliment ahead of time, knowing exactly what I want to praise, and how I want to express it. Yet when the opportunity arises, so often I either let it pass, or don't manage to say exactly what I planned. I get nervous! Which seems absurd, since the recipient is almost certain to love it. In ways that I can't quite pin down, it feels uncomfortably raw or naked to come out with something like, "You are a really good teacher," or "I really appreciate how hard you work as a parent." The somewhat mundane stuff—"Nice shot!", "That's a great tie," "I like what you did with this room"—is certainly easier; but deeper, more significant praises can be very awkward.

It may be that we're afraid the other person won't accept the compliment graciously. In my own experience, I've known cases where the person honestly thought I was kidding.

Perhaps more likely, such a situation requires utter sincerity: There is no room for the sort of jocular sarcasm, the cynical, world-weary, unflappable "cool" we discussed in Chapter Four; to pay someone a sincere compliment, you really do have to drop the mask and bare your soul.

But perhaps the main reason for this difficulty is that Satan detests such interactions—and he will work with all his diabolical might to prevent them. He is the accuser of the brethren (Rev. 10:12, NASB; see also Zech. 3:1). As such, he delights to point the finger, to make us feel guilty, to separate us from God and one another, to convince us that we must keep on wearing our masks because no one could possibly love us as we really are. Few things thwart these purposes so swiftly as unabashed love, grace, and appreciation between people.

So: If Satan so desperately wants to stop us from doing a certain thing, ought we not to work all the harder to make it happen—to help defeat his benighted, shameful kingdom of fear, accusation, camouflage, and guilt?

Scripture certainly provides ample mandate to so do.

We have already cited Hebrews 10, which famously commands us to "stir up one another to love and good works, . . . encouraging one another, and all the more as you see the Day drawing near" (vss. 24-25). To this we might add 1 Thessalonians 5:11: "Therefore encourage one another and build one another up, just as you are doing"—and just as Paul is doing with that statement.

Indeed, since Paul wrote the latter of these injunctions, it's not surprising to find him modeling this in many of his epistles. Frequently, his encouragement is directed to an entire congregation—as in Romans 15: "I myself am satisfied about you, my brothers, that you yourselves are full of goodness, filled with all knowledge and able to instruct one another" (verse 14). Linguistically, Paul emphasizes his compliment with two reflexive pronouns ("I myself," "your yourselves") and with the perfect tense, which indicates a continued state of confidence in their goodness. As one commentator puts it, "There are to be no doubts about his warm approval of the Roman church"—for "full of goodness" does not speak of some occasional virtuous actions but rather of a plentiful supply: "The Romans were outstandingly good."[1]

Similarly, Paul's praise often appears as thanks for what God is doing in the church at hand—such as, for example, his beloved flock at Thessalonica:

> We give thanks to God always for all of you, constantly mentioning you in our prayers, remembering before our God and Father your work of faith and labor of love and steadfastness of hope in our Lord Jesus Christ. . . . For what thanksgiving can we return to God for you, for all the joy that we feel for your sake before our God. . . . We ought always to give thanks to God for you, brothers, as is right, because your faith is growing abundantly, and the love of every one of you for one another is increasing. Therefore we ourselves boast about you in the churches of God for your steadfastness and faith in all your persecutions and in the

> afflictions that you are enduring. (1 Thess. 1:2-3, 3:9; 2 Thess. 1:3-4)

Note well the language of superlatives ("always," "all," "constantly," "abundantly," "every one of you") and the specificity of Paul's gratitude for their work and perseverance. And really, what nicer thing could you say to others than that you thank God for the faith, hope, and love he is working in their lives?

Note, too, the way Paul boasts about his flock—as we often do about the achievements of our own children, and as he himself does again in 2 Corinthians 7-9. Though he warmly commends the Macedonian churches in this passage ("their extreme poverty . . . overflowed in a wealth of generosity," 8:2), the brunt of his praise is reserved for the church at Corinth. Citing their "longing," their "zeal," and their "eagerness," Paul thrice says he *boasted* about this congregation, insisting, "I rejoice, because I have perfect confidence in you" (7:11, 14, 16; see also 8:24 and 9:3). Paul also avers that the Corinthians "excel in everything—in faith, in speech, in knowledge, in all earnestness, and in our love for you" (some manuscripts have "your love for us") (8:7).

Those are remarkable words about a church whose sins had included divisiveness, incest, prostitution, lawsuits, and drunkenness during the Lord's Supper—not to mention a long history of rejecting Paul's authority. His warm praise for such a troubled church touches once again on a topic we have often covered in this book—working to see the best in others despite their sins and failures. "Don't let the unattractive features of someone's life blind you to the good," writes Ed Welch. "All of us can see the good in our friends. Scripture, however, authorizes us to see the good and enjoy it in all people, even when most of us are not always so good. This will encourage others, increase our affection for them, and make it much easier to talk about things that are hard." Welch also insists that such affirmation makes it easier to challenge folks on sin—that it is actually a prerequisite for rebuke and confrontation.[2] Thus, Paul begins his often-aggressive and hard-hitting Corinthian correspondence on a note of warmth, love, and encouragement—one that is laced with his characteristic superlatives:

"I give thanks to my God always for you because of the grace of God that was given you in Christ Jesus, that in every way you were enriched in him in all speech and all knowledge—even as the testimony about Christ was confirmed among you—so that you are not lacking in any spiritual gift . . ." (1 Cor. 1:4-7).

PRAISING INDIVIDUALS, TOO

In addition to encouraging words for churches and congregations, Paul often targets specific Christians for appreciative kudos—the more noteworthy because all these passages appear in letters intended to be read aloud; and thus Paul's praises are public in nature, warmly affirming individual disciples before large groups of fellow-believers. The epistle to Philemon, for example, is addressed not only to its titular recipient but also to Apphia, Archippus, and "the church in your house." To this considerable group, Paul says the following about Philemon himself: "I thank my God always when I remember you in my prayers, because I hear of your love and of the faith that you have toward the Lord Jesus and all the saints. . . . For I have derived much joy and comfort from your love, my brother, because the hearts of the saints have been refreshed through you." Having asked Philemon to accept back his runaway slave, Paul then warmly remarks, "Confident of your obedience, I write to you, knowing that you will do even more than I say" (4-5, 7, 21). Again, Paul points to specific character traits and actions while expressing perfect confidence in Philemon's future compliance and generosity—all while knowing that Philemon is likely to hear these effusions read aloud before the congregation.

Similarly, in 2 Corinthians, Paul also praises his beloved co-worker Titus, who was with him in Macedonia and may well have been present during the composition of the letter that speaks so warmly of him. Paul cites Titus's "earnest care" for the Corinthians: "being himself very earnest he is going to you of his own accord." At the same time, Paul praises some unnamed brother "who is famous among all the churches for his preaching of the gospel"—"whom we have often tested and found earnest in many matters, but who is now more earnest than ever because of his great confidence in you" (8:16-22). Since both Titus and this unidentified preacher were the ones carrying 2 Corinthians to that church, they were probably privy to these praises and actually present when the missive was read aloud to this flock.

But surely the most notable of Paul's encouragement toward individuals can be found in the final chapter of Romans, where the apostle greets no less than 27 Christians by name, often specifying deeds, or character, or both. Mary and Persis, for example, "worked hard" for the church and for the Lord. Prisca and Aquila "risked their necks for my life," thus receiving gratitude not only from Paul but also, "all the churches of the Gentiles give thanks as well." Phoebe "has been a patron of many and of myself as well"; Apelles is "approved in Christ"; and Rufus is said to be "chosen in the Lord" (vss. 1-15). This last phrase must mean more than just "elected for salvation"—since the words in that sense would apply to everyone in the passage; so it must refer to "some eminence belonging to Rufus" and is better translated as "choice." With the word "beloved" recurring four times (vss. 5, 8, 9, and 12), the entire passage shows "the warmth of affection with which the apostle regarded his fellow workers."[3] Though this list of ancient and often challenging names is the sort of Bible passage many folks skip over, it's part of inspired Scripture and is in some ways the logical end-point for all the theology and instruction Paul laid out earlier in this rich missive.

We overlook such passages—and such praises—at our peril.

AND DON'T FORGET YOUR SPOUSE!

Nowhere in the Bible will you find more effusive praises directed from one human to another than in Song of Solomon. These passages are so long and lavish that I can't even quote them all; hopefully, a few plangent excerpts will give you an idea of how these two feel about each other.

Throughout the book, the lovers refer to one another with such extravagant terms as "beautiful," "beloved," "radiant," "sweet," "lovely," "awesome," "better than wine." In two extensive passages, the man specifically praises the woman from head to toe: her hair, her eyes, her nose, her teeth, her cheeks, her lips ("your mouth is lovely . . . like the best wine"), her breath ("like apples"), her neck, her breasts, her belly, her navel, her thighs ("the work of a master hand"), her feet, and her overall figure, or "stature" (4:1-5, 7:1-9). Many of these bodily features are ones that worry women constantly, as they compare themselves to others and suspect that they'll never measure up to some impossible ideal of feminine beauty. The husband's profuse praises seem calculated to allay such concerns—to assure her of what virtually every woman would love to hear: "You are altogether beautiful, my love; there is no flaw in you" (4:7).

The self-conscious concern many women struggle with is hinted at in chapter 1 of the Song, where the woman reflects on her "very dark" complexion with a certain timidity: "Do not gaze at me because I am dark, because the sun has looked upon me" (vss. 5-6).[4] This tanned skin would not have been the cultural ideal at that time, marking her as somewhat lower-class—a worker in the fields (see 1:6), as opposed to the higher-ranking woman who could afford to pamper herself indoors. Yet immediately after this expression of self-doubt, the man responds first by insisting that she is the "most beautiful among women," then by twice repeating, "Behold, you are beautiful." She then instantly turns this phraseology back on him, replying, "Behold, you are beautiful, my beloved, truly delightful" (vss. 8-16).

In fact, passages extolling feminine beauty—like those cited above—are common in ancient Middle Eastern love poetry; but it is much rarer to find writings in which a woman lavishes praise on her man.[5] Yet this is exactly what the loving lady does at length in chapter 5. Like the man's profuse and detailed compliments, hers also are *person-specific*, indicating that she loves *him* in particular, for who he actually is: his complexion, his head, his hair ("black as a raven"), his eyes, his cheeks, his lips, his mouth ("most sweet"), his arms ("rods of gold, set with jewels"), his legs, his body, and his overall "appearance"; he is indeed "altogether desirable" (vss. 10-16).

Brothers and sisters, I challenge you to ask yourselves whether you often—or ever—speak to your spouse this way. My sense is that in many marriages—even Christian marriages—the husband and wife spend far too much time picking at each other, quarreling, one-upping, and struggling to win arguments, with each spouse trying to look good at the expense of the other. This is not the Biblical model for relationships; it is not the model for marriage, and it is certainly not the model presented to us in Song of Solomon.

"None of us can ever receive too much affirmation from others of the reality that we are beautiful and beloved," writes Iain Provan in his commentary on the Song. "No husband and no wife can ever offer the spouse too much affirmation of this kind, in the midst of the intimacy of lovemaking, or be too frank in their language in doing so." He continues:

> Whether in our ordinary relationships or specifically in our marriages, we cannot engage in enough affirmation of the unique worth and beauty of those whom we love. It is itself a major way in which healing comes to our lives . . . as we seek to recover from the influence of a world that depersonalizes and degrades. The effects of this world on us may initially be so great that we feel deeply embarrassed about affirming our lovers in such direct ways, and we may be reluctant to do so. Many of us have suffered such emotional damage that we have learned to keep all emotion tightly bottled up inside us where (we falsely believe) it can do no damage. We avoid words that might uncork the bottle and spurn them when others use them toward us. We become terrified of direct verbal intercourse, and sexual intercourse thus becomes a silent, awkward affair that does not minister to our emotional and spiritual needs as well as our physical needs. We deprive ourselves of a great gift—the gift of affirming words that might, in the context of a

> loving and trusting relationship, bring deep healing to our lives.[6]

Provan of course is specifically addressing spouses, and I believe virtually all of us married folk have serious work to do in the area of praise—of building each other up rather than tearing each other down. As Provan so wisely indicates, some of this affirmation would likely refer to physical qualities, and it should probably occur—at least sometimes—in the context of sexual intimacy.

At the same time, I believe with equal fervor that we need more conscious efforts along these lines even in "ordinary relationships"—as Provan himself suggests in his opening sentence above. Like spouses struggling with intimacy, we often feel awkward or uncomfortable with such heart-felt praises; it makes us vulnerable, naked, *transparent*—and the more specific and substantial the comments may be, the more exposed we will feel. But if we can move courageously out into this somewhat uncharted territory, perhaps we can begin to import into our friendships—into the church, into fellowship, even into relationships with coworkers and schoolmates—some of the precious intimacy that makes life so rich, that helps us feel connected, worthwhile, cared about.

There's no reason such delightful affection and closeness should be restricted to romance and marriage alone.

BEFORE THE FUNERAL

I started this chapter by asking why we wait till someone has died before publicly gushing about how much we appreciate her or him; I wanted us all to think about saying some of these things while the loved one is still with us—and I have two stories along these lines that should make a challenging conclusion.

One involves Mitch Albom's best-selling memoir *Tuesdays with Morrie*, which concerns the author's real-life friendship with a former college prof who has ALS (better known as Lou Gehrig's disease). Since

Morrie knows he hasn't long to live, he decides he wants to have his own funeral *before* he's dead—so he can hear what people have to say about him while he's still alive. Morrie tells Albom that the idea came to him at memorial services for a co-worker:

> His funeral was so sad. . . . All these people saying all these wonderful things about him, and Irv never got to hear any of it. I said, "That's not for me! Somebody's got something nice to say about me, I wanna hear it right now!" So I made some calls, I chose a date, and we had a Living Funeral. . . . It was very successful. Everybody paid tribute to me. I kept thinking, "Boy, Morrie would have liked this." And I did![7]

I too found this such a great idea that I did it myself for both my parents. I had considerable incentive for this, because I got to see my father play Morrie twice on stage. He was an accomplished amateur thespian with a life-long passion for community theater, and it was not easy to watch him slowly deteriorate and then pass on in two different theatrical productions of Albom's tale. But it did encourage me to sit down one day and tell him exactly what I planned to say at his funeral; and shortly thereafter, I wrote out my mom's eulogy as well—and gifted it to her. Perhaps this seems morbid in a culture that wants to pretend death is always far away—but I wanted them to know how I felt *now*, rather than waiting till it was too late. Now that my father is gone, I sure am glad I did it.

On a somewhat different note, I have a beloved friend who lost her husband at a young age after 25 years of marriage. He had a massive heart attack and died without regaining consciousness, leaving behind a grieving widow and high-school-age son. A humble Catholic with a Protestant work ethic, devoted to his wife and family, he spent his whole life laboring in a dreary blue-collar job and keeping up his tiny, aging home—yet I never heard one word of complaint from him. A good man, surely—though as far as I can recall, no one (including me), ever told him so. And now it was too late.

The funeral was especially difficult because he was so young and his death was so entirely unexpected. As the viewing came to an end and the funeral-home workers prepared to call in the pall-bearers, his devastated wife stood beside the the closing coffin for a final farewell; and I happened to hear her say plaintively, "I had so much more to tell you!"

That is one of the most heart-breaking statements I've ever heard. But my dear sisters and brothers, her painful words reflect exactly how you and I are going to feel if we don't take time to tell our loved ones how much we appreciate them.

Do it now, and do it often.

OPEN FOR DISCUSSION

1. Is it hard to give deep and significant praise to others? If so, why? And why is it easier at a funeral?

2. Have you ever given praise or appreciation to someone when it seemed particularly needed or appreciated? If so, describe this.

3. Has anyone ever done this for *you*? Can you describe this experience?

4. In his letters, Paul often "boasts" about other believers—as quoted in several passages above. What does this mean? Why is such boasting OK?

5. Do you think spouses spend enough time praising and encouraging, or do they "pick at" and "one-up" each other? If so, why is this the case? If you are married, how would you describe your own marriage in this area?

6. Do you have any friends who are especially good at praise and encouragement? If so, describe them.

7. Bible commentator Iain Provan says, "None of us can ever receive too much affirmation from others of the reality that we are beautiful and beloved." Is Provan overstating this case? If not, why do you think we need this affirmation so badly?

8. Think of someone you love and appreciate, and make a specific resolution right now to tell him or her about it.

CHAPTER NINETEEN

"A Spirit of Gentleness"

Reacting to Transparency

Time and again, when I would tell friends what my new book was about, they'd ask if I planned to discuss the *judgmental* attitude found in many churches—how the fear of condemnation is a major factor impeding transparency in the modern evangelical world. To put it simply, people hesitate to open up because they're sure others in the church will judge them. Indeed, according to the 2007 bestseller *unChristian*, "Nearly nine out of ten young outsiders (87 percent) said that the term *judgmental* accurately describes present-day Christianity."[1] That's why I started my book with a chapter on the fear of rejection, and that's why I'm going to finish by counseling against any whiff of reproach or condemnation if you are ever blessed to have someone share with you.

Clearly, if we want people to be transparent about some of their deepest sins, fears, and failures, we must be prepared to respond to such disclosures without judgment. Our attitude must mirror that of God the Father working through his son: For in Him we find "no condemnation" (Rom. 8:1); we are "blameless and beyond reproach"—

for "he who believes in Him is not judged" (Col. 1:22 and John 3:18, NASB).

But embracing and embodying God's grace toward sinners is just one of several key responses when others finally bite the bullet and open up. Those crucial factors will be the subject of this final chapter: biblical responses to transparency—including how we react to others who confront us about our sins.

JUDGE NOT . . .

Jesus' famous command, "Judge not, that you be not judged," suggests that the best thing we can do to avoid judgment when someone shares is simply to remember our own sins: They may be different from what's being shared—but at the same time, they may be even worse; for Christ goes on to ask, "Why do you see the speck that is in your brother's eye, but do not notice the log that is in your own eye?" (Matt. 7:1-3).

This forbearing attitude, generated by mindfulness of our own sin, is also articulated in a passage we have examined elsewhere—Galatians 6:1-3: "Brothers, if anyone is caught in any transgression, you who are spiritual should restore him in a spirit of gentleness. Keep watch on yourself, lest you too be tempted. Bear one another's burdens, and so fulfill the law of Christ. For if anyone thinks he is something, when he is nothing, he deceives himself." When dealing with the sins of others, Paul plainly challenges us to remember that we could easily fall into the same transgression, and that we are not to assume a superior air when in fact we are all "nothing" before Christ.

Again, the whole attitude is nicely summed up in Ephesians: "Be kind to one another, tenderhearted, forgiving one another, as God in Christ forgave you" (4:32). If someone shares with me a sin or a struggle, I may not literally have to forgive the person, since that sin was very likely not against me personally; but my attitude should still be one of forgiveness: a readiness never to hold the sin against that person, not to let it taint the relationship, and—like God himself—never to reproach him or her.

Most thesauruses list "blame" as a synonym for "reproach," and this is what we must avoid. Shame researcher Brene Brown points out that it can be difficult to listen well when someone shares, because we want to believe that we are immune from such unhappy experiences—so we insulate ourselves by assigning blame to the sharer; our secret thought—probably also apparent in our demeanor—is, "I'd never do something that stupid!" After all, if we come alongside them in their weakness or pain, that might suggest it could happen to us too.[2] But both Paul and Jesus seem to be saying, "Of course it could! And perhaps in some ways, it already has. If you think otherwise, you are deceiving yourself."

This becomes doubly important when what's being shared is not sin so much as some sort of shame, sadness, trauma, or affliction. In these cases especially, let us not be like Job's so-called friends, who energetically insisted that the poor man's suffering must surely have been caused by some sin he'd committed: He must somehow be responsible for what happened in his life! Since his friends weren't suffering, the sanctimonious implication seems to be that they themselves wisely managed to avoid what Job is going through—and in repeatedly attempting to blame him for it, they become what Job calls "miserable comforters" (16:2).

In a similar way, let us not try to assure the sharer that "it's all for the best"—or ask what God is trying to teach her or him through the difficulty. Such responses are hurtful, condescending, and unsympathetic. These alleged reassurances suggest that the suffering is "a solvable riddle," while also managing to imply—once again—that the person is to blame, since he or she apparently needs to be taught a lesson.[3]

As a final adjunct in the area of judgment, let me caution you against reacting to transparency with horror, shock, or excess disappointment ("How could you let this happen?!")—all of which will, of course, merely confirm and exacerbate the hesitant sharer's embarrassment.[4] Again, a deep and abiding knowledge of one's own sin and weakness will go far in curbing this kind of unhelpful reaction. It's hard to be repulsed by the sin in others when you've already explored the ghastly depths of your own.

MATCHING SIN FOR SIN

While it can be important to acknowledge that we ourselves are no better than the one who's confessing, Ed Welch warns us not to respond by immediately sharing that we have struggled in this area too. "Though our goal might be to make someone feel less alone or embarrassed by their confession, commiserating doesn't help. It shifts the conversation away from what is most important," directing attention to the hearer, rather than keeping it focused on an all-out battle with sin—a focus that would be better served by asking, for example, "What can I do to help?"[5]

Sometimes, we take this unhelpful response of "matching sin for sin" and carry it one step further: We try to "one up" the other person with an even worse sin of our own: "That's nothing; just wait till you hear what I did!" Again, this refocuses the conversation on the hearer rather than the listener, and it does not give enough attention to what is being shared. Neither does any response that begins with "at least": "At least you didn't do this other thing that would have been even worse!" As Brown puts it, "*At least* is not a good lead-in for an empathic response." It can be more about our own discomfort than that of the sharer; and in any case, "'At leasting' someone is equivalent to shutting her down."[6]

JUST LISTEN

Many of these errors fall into the category of "lousy listening." To some degree, they shortchange the other person by trying to downplay the seriousness of what has been shared. You must not do this. If your friend has, perhaps after much fear and trembling, finally come to you with a burden or sin, it may seem kind and merciful to respond with something like, "It really isn't that bad," or "I'm sure everything will be fine." But this is condescending and unhelpful. Of course, there may be some cases in which there is genuine false guilt for something that is not actually a sin, and in these cases you may eventually want to go to Scripture and try to set your friend free; but even then, you must first *listen* and make absolutely certain that you understand—that you are not about to erect a stumbling-block by urging her or him to disregard something that is truly a sin (see Romans 14, especially vss. 13-14).

We also unwisely downplay the problem if we look for someone else to blame rather than actually hearing the brother's confession ("Just wait till I let so-and-so have it for putting you in that position!").[7]

And finally, we are probably not listening too well if we immediately want to jump in and fix the issue. Surely we will wish to help him or her avoid these sins in the future; but even in that case, it would be best to let the sister or brother propose their own ways in which you might help, rather than piling on advice that, again, unhelpfully shifts the emphasis from sharer to hearer.

"The people who have helped me most," writes Paul Tournier, "are not those who have answered my confessions with advice, exhortation or doctrine, but rather those who have listened to me in silence. . . . If we answer with advice, exhortation or theories, we are putting ourselves in a position of superiority, not equality. We are concerning ourselves with ideas, and not with the person. . . ." The moment this advice-giving persona appears, "with its systems of thought and its claims to possess and express truth, our sincerest efforts to help others will finish by crushing and repressing them instead of liberating them."[8]

Larry Crabb reflects similarly on one experience of sharing personal weakness with a group of people: "My most intense fear was that someone would try to *help* me. Instead, I longed for my friends to enter my world, to be intrigued with what God was doing in my life, to ask questions, to honor my place in the journey, and to do it all with no agenda. I didn't want them to offer what our therapy-mad culture thinks is helpful: to look for pathology that can be treated; to find something wrong that can be fixed."

Crabb goes on to point out that this impulse to instantly fix things is actually very selfish, and it reflects a widespread cultural problem: We are intensely bothered when something is flawed and imperfect—even though such circumstances are the very ones in which we learn to depend on God:

> We're a community of fixers. We can't stand to see a problem we can't do something about. We're not *curious about the journey.* We're committed to making things better, to feeling more comfortable. . . . It is not our habit to wait on a hidden God to somehow work out a masterful plan to bring glory to Himself. We prefer a different version of waiting. We follow biblical principles or seek counseling to get our kids straightened out, to make our emotions more pleasant, to cause our relationships to be more satisfying. What we really want is a better life.[9]

WHAT TO *DO* . . .

So far, we've concerned ourselves with a lot of DON'Ts in responding to transparency; and this is accurate. For while there are many pitfalls—habitual errors that probably keep our friends from being transparent with us—in the end there is not a lot you have to consciously *do* on the receiving end of openness. A few simple items include willingness to pray with the person, along with a commitment to listen and pray again in the future—and to help hold the person accountable, if that is something she or he wants.

Perhaps most important, be ready to forcefully remind and reassure this struggling person about the boundless forgiveness we have in Christ. Indeed, this gospel reassurance is the principal goal of confession to others—"to provide a special reminder to particularly acute and scrupulous consciences of the great, general truth of the Gospel. . . . The purpose of confession is not for the one confessing to bare his soul and become more authentic. It is to allow the one hearing the confession to press the words of the gospel promise on the penitent and thus free them from the torments that their own sins brought in their wake."[10]

To this end, it would be well to have several Scripture texts ready to hand—perhaps even memorized—in order to emphasize the fullness of our redemption and of the Father's eternal favor. Some of my favorites along these lines include Colossians 1:22; 1 John 1:9; Psalm 103:3 and 12; Isaiah 43:25 and 44:22; 1 Thess. 5:23-24; Romans 8:1; and John 3:17-18.

Of course, a resolution not to gossip will be crucial as well. In a different context, Jesus instructs us to keep the matter "between you and him alone" when confronting someone else about sin, and this provides a mandate for privacy in most such discussions. Yet those instructions from Christ, found in Matthew 18:15-17, also require us to go to others if the sinner is unwilling to work on the problem. And so—as we saw in Chapter Seventeen—we cannot make an unconditional promise of confidentiality when discussing others' sins. Such a vow would preclude bringing in others in the case of an emergency or a truly unrepentant sinner. Of course, if the person weren't repentant, she or he would probably not be opening up to you in the first place; thus, very few cases of sharing will ever lead to this course of action. But some might!

For instance, if you rashly vowed confidentiality, and the person then told you he was contemplating suicide, you would be compelled to break your promise. For this reason, counseling expert Jay Adams urges that if we are asked to preserve absolute secrecy, we respond along these lines: "I am glad to keep confidence in the way that the Bible instructs me. That means, of course, that I shall never involve others unless God requires me to do so."[11] Should the person ask exactly what this means, you would insist that such cases are rare; that others would not be called in unless it involved unrepentant sin, or grave danger to the church body or the person himself; in any case, it would initially be only "one or two others," in keeping with Matthew 18:16. (And furthermore, those one or two other trusted believers might well be chosen with help from the person who has opened up.)

Along these same lines, Ed Welch's *Side by Side* points out that sometimes we need help in our helping. Reasserting his overall thesis before proceeding, Welch writes, "We started all this by recounting how we need one another's help when we have troubles. That neediness now extends to how we need one another's help *when we help*. Since we do not have all human gifts, abilities, and experience in ourselves, we usually need cohelpers." He goes on to cite an example in which a young woman confides that she has been cutting herself; since "you can't be certain about the dangers, . . . you let her know that the two of you will enlarge the number of people who know"—and that one of them will be her mother.

"Problems *are* complex," he concludes. "Even relatively simple matters, such as child discipline, can be complex. As a counselor, I am always getting help from other pastors and counselors; and helping someone in the context of a group, in which all of us will pray for and help the one in need, is ideal."

Perhaps the best advice in Welch's book on how to respond to sharing would come much earlier in the process. He suggests that our immediate reaction must be gratitude and appreciation—a recognition of the person's courage in coming forward, and of the Spirit's role in prompting such an action: "When someone discloses sin, first, we see the good. Voluntary confession is evidence of spiritual power and deserves our admiration." We are to thank such people for sharing, and to point out that while they may feel guilt and shame at the moment, nonetheless the very act of opening up shows great faith—and proves that God is working in their lives.[12]

I can think of no better way to close this section on responding to transparency than by quoting Paul Tournier's remarks on what makes a good confessor. Beginning with the reflection that true transparency "is a rare and difficult thing," he then goes on to assert that so much of it depends on the listener:

> There are those who pull down the barriers and make the way smooth; there are those who force the doors and enter our territory like invaders; there are those who barricade us in, shut us in upon ourselves, dig ditches and throw up walls around us; there are those who set us out of tune and listen only to our false notes; there are those for whom we always remain strangers, speaking an unknown tongue. And when it is our turn to listen, which of these are we for the other person's sincerity? That should make us think of God, who is not only One who says: "Listen to Me!" but also One who says: "I am listening to you."[13]

REACTING TO REBUKE

Of course, response to someone sharing sin is not the only type of reaction we should be discussing here. Perhaps even more important is how we respond when a fellow believer confronts us about sin, challenging us to holier living and a closer walk with Christ. (How to engage in such challenges is discussed at length in Chapter Seventeen.)

Let's be honest. For most of us, the knee-jerk reaction to admonition or rebuke is likely to be negative: discouragement, irritation, offense, anger, or defensiveness. Needless to say, these responses are to be avoided.

In the first place, try to keep in mind that it probably wasn't easy for the person to broach this issue to you. True, there may be an occasional bull-in-a-china-shop of the sort Tournier describes above; as we saw in Chapter Seventeen, these types of people, who *enjoy* confrontation and are always eager to charge into someone else's spiritual life—these people are thereby disqualified from interpersonal rebuke. But for those doing it right, the process is one of great fear and trembling, with the confronter spending much time in prayer and reflection, trying to work up the fortitude to say something, and the wisdom to say it appropriately. To come to you on the matter, despite such anguish and reluctance, is actually an act of great love, and it must be seen that way—no matter how you may feel about the rebuke itself. Just think: If the person had decided to go easy on you and say nothing, that may in the long run have resulted in far more pain and damage than a few words of reproof or admonition.

If, instead of gratitude for a loving rebuke, you respond in outrage or offense—mightn't that suggest that you know very well the person is right? If she or he were wrong, the accusation wouldn't sting half so much—but if right, the reprover may have hit on something about which you've been deceiving yourself, something that really needed to be uncovered. And honestly, don't we have to admit that whoever rebukes us really doesn't know the half of it, anyway? As Charles Spurgeon famously said, "If any man thinks ill of you, do not be angry with him, for you are far worse than he thinks you to be."[14] "Whoever is truly humbled," writes Barbara Duguid, "will not become easily angered when criticism comes his way, whether justified or unjustified. He knows that the real truth of his depravity is far deeper than anyone can see, and he will not quibble with those who point out his wrongs or falsely accuse him."[15]

Why are you so easily upset when someone criticizes you? Didn't you start out your Christian life by admitting your own utter unrighteousness and your concomitant need for Christ? Do you not confess to God, day after day, a mind-boggling array of sins and transgressions—and now you are upset because a brother or sister has challenged you on one area of concern? As A. W. Tozer asks: Are you actually annoyed because someone is saying about you the very things you always say about yourself in the privacy of personal prayer-time? "Only yesterday you were telling God that you were nothing, a mere worm in the dust. Where is your consistency? Come on, humble yourself, and cease to care what men think."[16]

Tozer goes so far as to insist that we utterly disregard the source of the rebuke, because we probably *need* the feedback, even if we don't like the person who gave it or the way it was phrased. "When reproved, pay no attention to the source. Do not ask whether it is a friend or an enemy that reproves you. An enemy is often of greater value to you than a friend because he is not influenced by sympathy."[17]

Indeed, the biggest problem with an angry or defensive response is one hinted at in this quote and several others above: This sort of reaction may cut off something God himself wants us to hear.

> God will channel truth through others to critique us. . . . Others will talk tough to us. Listen carefully. It could be God at work admonishing us. . . . If our ego armor bristles defensively, it may be an indication that we have not been allowing God to call attention to our faults and failures. When God is consistently evaluating my life I am not nearly as threatened by others who do the same to me. If I am supersensitive to criticism and terribly threatened by evaluation, it could be a good indication that I am not listening to everything God wants to tell me about myself.[18]

As Christians committed to serve and follow Christ with ever-increasing zeal and blamelessness, should we not seek every opportunity to root out our unseen sins, to "strive for . . . the holiness without which no one will see the Lord" (Heb. 12:14)? "We should always be open to an 'audit' from the ones we care about. If we are truly serious about growing, we want to know if we are unknowingly doing something wrong (Ps. 139:23-24). Hidden sins and problems are destructive to us, and if we long to grow, we would want them exposed and healed"—even if it takes a loving but somewhat painful rebuke to bring them out.[19]

Indeed, such warnings and indictments must be seen as *good* things, as signs of hope—of God's love for us. "For the Lord disciplines the one he loves, and chastises every son whom he receives" (Heb. 12:6). And why should not this discipline and chastisement come to us in the form of rebukes from a caring friend? The Lord knows that this can be painful, but it is also proof of our sonship—"for what son is there whom his father does not discipline? . . . For the moment all discipline seems painful rather than pleasant, but later it yields the peaceful fruit of righteousness to those who have been trained by it" (Heb. 12:7-11).

So I say again, if we respond with improper hauteur and indignation, we may miss God's good purposes in chastising us; in fact, this very response suggests we stand in need of the humility that rebuke can bring. Indeed, Andrew Murray, in his fine little book on humility, urges this trait as a precious spiritual treasure, without which "there can be no reaping of Heaven." For this reason, we must eagerly pursue every possible opportunity to develop it—even criticism from others. "Accept every humiliation, look upon every fellow-man who tries or vexes you, as a means of grace to humble you." Every reproof and rebuke, whether just or unjust, whether from a friend or an enemy, can and should be seen as an opportunity to demonstrate that Jesus matters more to us than anything else in the world—including the opinions of other people.[20]

RESPONSES IN SCRIPTURE

Proverbs 9 confirms this right and beneficial response to rebuke, asserting that if you "reprove a wise man, . . . he will love you. Give instruction a to a wise man, and he will be still wiser; teach a righteous man, and he will increase in learning." On the other hand, a strongly negative response indicates that one is by nature a "scoffer" and does not even deserve the charitable act of admonition—for "whoever corrects a scoffer gets himself abuse, and he who reproves a wicked man incurs injury. Do not reprove a scoffer, or he will hate you . . ." (vss. 7-9).

While the Bible offers a few instances of wise and proper acceptance of rebuke, it offers far more instances of people refusing to listen—often to their detriment and destruction.

There's Cain, for instance, who was warned by God himself to "do well"—to resist (or "rule over") the temptation that was "crouching at the door." In refusing to heed this stern advice, Cain became both a murderer and an outcast (Gen. 4:6-12). Much later, Jesus warned Peter that the apostle would thrice deny his beloved Lord. Peter refused to believe this ("If I must die with you, I will not deny you"); and perhaps precisely through this overconfidence, he went on to commit the very sin he'd been warned about—after which "he broke down and wept" (Mark 14:30-31, 66-72). And then there's this cutting condemnation in Ecclesiastes: "Better was a poor and wise youth than an old and foolish king who no longer knew how to take advice"—for this youth eventually "was to stand in the king's place" (4:13-15). As Tozer puts it, the old king had apparently been in power so long, "the idea that there was anyone wise enough or good enough to reprove him would not so much enter his mind." He was a lost man, and "God had left him to his fatal conceit."[21]

More generally, this little episode is perfectly emblematic of Israel's repeated refusal to heed God's admonition throughout the Old Testament—admonition that began with Moses' lengthy warning against sin in Deuteronomy, continued through Joshua and Judges, and culminated in the much later exile of both Samaria and Judah, with the long subjugation of God's people to a series of oppressive pagan regimes. Conducted by a long line of forthright and intrepid prophets whose words now comprise much of the Old Testament, these rebukes, together with Israel's stubborn determination not to listen, seem to reach their apex under the preaching ministries of Isaiah and Jeremiah, as exemplified in this passage where the nation has been punished so often, there's no place left for a chastising blow: "Alas, sinful nation. . . . They have abandoned the Lord. . . . They have turned away from Him. Where will you be stricken again, as you continue in your rebellion? The whole head is sick and the whole heart is faint. From the sole of the foot even to the head there is nothing sound in it, only bruises, welts and raw wounds . . ." (Isa. 1:4-6, NASB).

"A state of heart that rejected admonition was characteristic of Israel at various periods in her history," writes Tozer, "and these periods were invariably followed by judgment." He goes on to point out that Israel's hard-hearted resistance to teaching and rebuke persisted into the time of Christ, who "found them chuck full of that arrogant self-confidence that would not accept reproof." And Tozer then bracingly applies this to the modern-day church, insisting that we take heed to criticisms and rebuke leveled at us—for "churches and Christian organizations have shown a tendency to fall into the same error that destroyed Israel: inability to receive admonition." Urging openness to rebuke not only for individuals but also for the larger Christian body, Tozer writes, "Don't defend your church or your organization against criticism. If the criticism is false it can do no harm. if it is true you need to hear it and do something about it."[22]

A BIBLICAL FEW WHO WERE WILLING TO LISTEN

Fortunately for those of us who want to do better, Scripture offers a handful of cases in which rebuke was wisely heeded—perhaps the simplest being David's response to Nathan's challenge regarding adultery with Bathsheba and the subsequent murder of her husband. Faced with Nathan's stinging words, David responds bluntly, "I have sinned against the Lord" (2 Sam. 12:13). (Of course there is more of David's contrite response in Psalm 51, but we have dealt with that in Chapter Fifteen). Not quite as prompt but nonetheless similar is the case of Balaam, who was foolishly aiding Israel's pagan enemies and had to be rebuked—first by a donkey, and then by the angel of the Lord. Though he initially resisted, striking and threatening to kill the beast, yet eventually God opened his eyes, and "he saw the angel of the Lord standing in the way." At that point, Balaam bowed down and repented: "I have sinned," he admitted. "Now therefore, if it is evil in your sight I will turn back" (Num. 22:27-34).

Even more illustrative is Israel's response to censure from Ezra, when he sought to remedy the sin they'd committed by intermarrying with pagans. Ezra's initial "rebuke" is unusual: a lengthy public prayer of confession, together with such gestures of public grief as tearing his robe and plucking hair from his beard and scalp (9:1-15). Convicted in this unorthodox but effective way, "the people wept bitterly," and one leader spoke for them: "We have broken faith with our God and have married foreign women . . ."—after which they made plans to right the wrong: "let us make a covenant with our God to put away all these wives" (10:1-3). Later, they are confronted more directly by Ezra: "You have broken faith and married foreign women, and so increased the guilt of Israel. Now then make confession to the Lord, the God of your fathers and do his will. Separate yourself from the peoples of the land and from the foreign wives." To this, their corporate response is terse and contrite: "It is so; we must do as you have said" (10:10-12). And they then proceed to institute the necessary reforms with great care and precision. (See 10:16-44; for a somewhat different method of rebuke, try Nehemiah 13—especially verses 25-27.)

Perhaps the most vigorous response in Scripture to rebuke occurs after the Apostle Paul had sent the Corinthian church a letter worded so strongly that it caused pain to both the writer and the recipients (2 Cor. 2:3-4, 7:8-9). As discussed earlier in Chapter Seventeen, we are not sure of the exact reason for this rebuke—but in any case, the Corinthian response was apparently swift and decisive: They punished the offender and in every other way sought to redress what had apparently become a public scandal—and the person involved repented of his sin and offense as well (2 Cor. 2:6-7). Paul compliments this exemplary response in no uncertain terms:

> I rejoice, not because you were grieved, but because you were grieved into repenting. . . . For see what earnestness this godly grief has produced in you, but also what eagerness to clear yourselves, what indignation, what fear, what longing, what zeal, what punishment! At every point you have proved yourselves innocent in the matter. So although

> I wrote to you, it was not for the sake of the one who did the wrong, nor for the sake of the one who suffered the wrong, but in order that your earnestness for us might be revealed to you in the sight of God. Therefore we are comforted. (2 Cor. 7:9-13)

In this striking passage, we see that a proper, godly, earnest response is a great comfort to the rebuker; perhaps even more important, it also brings encouragement and reassurance to the one being rebuked—for it reveals a heart for God and a desire to do right by his word and his people.

And according to Dietrich Bonhoeffer, one final benefit of such a right response is that we ourselves then become better able to reprove and admonish others:

> The more we learn to allow others to speak the Word to us, to accept humbly and gratefully even severe reproaches and admonitions, the more free and objective will we be in speaking ourselves. The person whose touchiness and vanity make him spurn a brother's earnest censure cannot speak the truth in humility to others; he is afraid of being rebuffed and of feeling that he has been aggrieved. The touchy person will always become a flatterer and very soon he will come to despise and slander his brother.[23]

* * * * * * * * *

Hearing reproof is difficult; but never hearing it at all is worse. With so many dangers inherent in the lack of counsel—either in not heeding it or not getting it in the first place; and with so many benefits to this mutual aid that is clearly commanded by Christ himself, we must train ourselves to welcome it as an act of love sent by our heavenly father—who always wishes to draw us closer to himself and to his precious Son.

OPEN FOR DISCUSSION

1. Does the modern church have a problem with judging others, and if so, how does this impede transparency? How might we fix or address this problem? How might you fix or address it in yourself, individually?

2. Besides judging, what are some other responses to avoid when a person shares with you?

3. Can you recall specific times when a friend opened up about struggles or sins? What was your reaction?

4. Discuss whether and when it might be necessary to bring in other "co-helpers" when someone is sharing a sin-struggle. Doesn't this violate confidentiality?

5. Why do we react so negatively when someone rebukes or criticizes us? The author posits that an immediate response of anger or offense merely suggests that somewhere deep inside, we know the rebuke is correct and justly deserved; what do you think about this suggestion?

6. A. W. Tozer insists that we should listen to criticism no matter what the source is. Do you agree? Why might this be useful or necessary?

7. The author discusses several examples reproof in the Bible. Can you think of others? In these cases, was the rebuke heeded or ignored, and what happened afterward?

8. Dietrich Bonhoeffer suggests that if we properly and regularly receive rebuke rather than rejecting it, this will in turn make us better at offering such reproof to others. Do you agree? Explain.

CONCLUSION

"Fully Known"

The Situation As It Could Be

In 1971, John Lennon famously asked us to "imagine there's no heaven." As we finish our study on transparency, I ask you to imagine something quite different—pretty much the opposite, in fact.

Imagine frank openness and vulnerability founded on the certainty of God's love. Imagine caring more about him and his promises than you care about yourself. Imagine that because of this, you are finally able to drop the act and be yourself.

Imagine not worrying nearly so much about what people think of you.

Imagine leaving behind the feeling that you have to do everything perfectly—and the conscious or unconscious jockeying you do to lift yourself up by putting others down. Imagine loving the good in others just as much as—or even more than—you love it in yourself.

Imagine accepting responsibility for your failures and sins.

Imagine climbing out from under the wounds and scars you still carry around from insults and ostracism when you were younger. Imagine a willingness to be uncool, a life in which you never feel as though you have to measure up to people in the movies or on TV—or on those glossy magazines in the grocery check-out line.

Imagine heeding the Apostle Paul's command not to think more highly of yourself than you ought, but to think "with sober judgment" (Rom. 12:3).

Imagine the church—the body of Christ—functioning with the sort of perfect interdependence pictured in 1 Corinthians 12, where even weakness is "indispensable," and no one tries to say, "I have no need of you"; imagine a place in which, "if one member suffers, all suffer together; if one member is honored, all rejoice together" (vss. 21-26).

Imagine the sort of intimacy and connection you could find if everyone felt free to admit who they really were.

Imagine being naked and unashamed.

Imagine the similar peace of mind you could achieve if only you could give up the never-ending rat race for worldly success.

Imagine being yourself, because you have nothing left to prove.

Imagine embracing your weakness as a pathway to the strength and faithfulness of God. Imagine that even your own sinfulness is part of that pathway—that God allows us to go on struggling with sin so that we must cling to his righteousness rather than wearily manufacturing our own.

Imagine, then, resting in Christ rather than continually tormenting yourself because you don't measure up.

Imagine really believing—fully, deeply, and all the time—that you are wholly forgiven for your sins; imagine believing—fully, deeply, and all the time—that Christ loves you with the lavish and personal devotion a husband showers on his bride; the kind of passion seen between the loving lovers in Song of Solomon.

Imagine being like Moses, David, Peter, and Paul; but please remember that this will mean telling others openly about your sins, just as they did. Imagine following the lead of other Bible characters by likewise opening up about your weaknesses, your griefs, your frustrations, and—yes, this too—your joys and passions.

Imagine a savior who is himself transparent; and imagine knowing a heavenly father who is virtually infinite in his loving desire to reveal himself to man.

Imagine a beloved friend—or two or three, or a small group of friends—with whom you could really be yourself; with whom you could share your sins and struggles; who would also tell you of theirs; and who can all hold one another accountable as sinners struggling toward Christ.

Imagine the body of Christ growing ever stronger, holier, and more unified in this manner.

Imagine a life without fear.

Imagine a church in which the leaders are the most transparent people. Imagine a church where you know very well that everyone else is struggling just as much as you are. Where you don't have to put on a face when you go in. Where you needn't leave your wounds, your transgressions, and your shame at the door—and then, with the same old exhaustion and loneliness, pick them back up again when you leave.

Imagine this as a place where we have finally learned to encourage one another all the time—to rebuke, admonish, challenge, stimulate; and to thank and praise others as well, freely expressing gratitude and appreciation for the gifts of Christ we see manifested in one another.

Imagine, too, being able to receive such feedback with grace and wisdom, hearing in it the voice of God as he ever works to draw us to himself.

* * * * * * * * *

Hopefully, we shall not always have to imagine such a place.

Not only will we try to work more and more transparency into our marriages, our friendships, our families, and especially our churches; but also, we look forward to a life of utter transparency in heaven—openness before God and before one another. Nothing hidden. No reproach, no judgment, no darkness, no secrets. A return to the Garden of Eden—naked and unashamed.

For God shall know us as we truly are; and we shall know him; and in this knowledge, love will be perfected once and for all:

"Love bears all things, believes all things, hopes all things, endures all things. Love never ends. . . . For now we see in a mirror dimly, but then face to face. Now I know in part; then I shall know fully, even as I have been fully known" (1 Cor. 13:7, 12).

OPEN FOR FINAL DISCUSSION

1. The author has tried to make a strong case for transparency as something vital in relationships and church. Was this convincing to you? If so, what did you find most persuasive? If not—what kind of doubt or uncertainty remains? Were there parts of the book you didn't agree with?

2. Which parts of the book were most helpful?

3. Which were most challenging?

4. Which parts hit closest to home—that is, you felt like you could really relate to the point being made?

5. Do you feel as though your own relationships and your own church do (or do not) have some degree of transparency? Where do you see transparency in your family and/or your friendships? Where do you see it in the life of your church?

6. Are there specific steps you could take to make yourself more transparent?

7. Are there steps that might make your church more transparent?

8. Do you know any people, families, groups, or churches that seem especially transparent? How have they achieved this, and how can you get some of this into your own life?

ACKNOWLEDGMENTS

This book has truly been an exercise in weakness and transparency—constant proof of the very things I was writing down. Nearly every morning, as I sat staring at my computer screen, I would think to myself, "I can't do this! I don't have the focus, the wisdom, or the energy to take all these jumbled notes and turn them into something smooth, pleasing, helpful, and biblical." And then I would pray, with the desperate sense of clinging to my laptop, as though it were about to tilt sideways and dump my entire writing project into the abyss of my own incompetence.

But our weakness is God's strength, and always by the end of the session, I had something down that manifested the goodness and wisdom of a faithful heavenly father. I'm convinced that if I had not started every morning this way—with a frank acknowledgment of my needs—neither I nor the project would have emerged intact at the other end of the writing process.

Of course, there are many others I need to thank in addition to the great friend who walked me through the valley of the shadow of inadequacy—starting with the authors whose shoulders I stood on. As I mentioned in the intro, when I began this project as a series of Sunday school classes, I could find no single book that addressed the subject of Christian transparency. Hence, I was compelled to cast a wide net for passages and chapters from a huge array of authors who touched on the topic without addressing it at length. Chief among these were Brene Brown, Ed Welch, Larry Crabb, and Dietrich Bonhoeffer. *TrueFaced*, by Bill Thrall, Bruce McNicol, and John Lynch, offers much wisdom on unresolved sin in our lives, and Paul Tournier's *The Meaning of Persons* is an endlessly insightful classic that should be read by every thoughtful Christian.

Many of these authors and titles—along with others—were recommended by well-read friends who had heard what I was writing about. These friends include Dave Rising, Beth Hoppes, Wayne Brauning, Tim and Linda Bryant, Alicia Carner, Peter Krol, and Steve and Diane Ippolito. I'm also indebted to Dr. Peter Keely; his weekly counseling sessions—though they addressed personal issues of my own—helped undergird a lot of the thinking here. Thanks especially to friends who read and commented on the manuscript, including David Brauning, Len Richards, Paul Browne, Dave Rising, Peter Krol, Tim Bryant, and my lovely wife, Mona Chang. Their careful work saved me from many embarrassing errors while also encouraging me to expand, rewrite, trim, or clarify several key points.

I am especially grateful to the adult Sunday school classes at New Life and Omega Orthodox Presbyterian churches in Williamsport, Pa. Their input, feedback, and insights during thoughtful Sunday morning discussions were invaluable as I developed the outline and filled in details for the final version you are holding in your hands.

For sundry precious advice on marketing, layout, format, and other 21st-century facts of life (about which I was sadly ignorant), I particularly thank Cassie Blair, Janeen Ippolito, Bryce Johle, Curt Musheno, Vida Saylor, and Robin Van Auken. And kudos to Patrick McGuire Newman for the excellent cover design!

And further gratitude goes to my wife, who once again served as sole bread-winner in our household while I was finishing this project; also to the Loyalsock Township School Board for granting me yet another semester of unpaid leave so I could focus entirely on writing.

And last but not least, I am forever in the debt of my wife, my children, my parents, my extended family, my students, my employers, my church, and my many friends—all of whom continue to love me despite my sins and weaknesses, my vanity and short temper, my idolatry, my worldliness, my seemingly unkillable narcissism, and occasional outright stupidity. Together, these people taught me to embrace transparency, showing that it is a doorway not to rejection, but rather to community, intimacy, authenticity, and peace of mind.

END NOTES

INTRODUCTION: The Situation As It Is

1. Dietrich Bonhoeffer, *Life Together*, trans. John W. Doberstein (Harper, 1954), 110.

2. Bill Thrall, Bruce McNicol, and John Lynch, *TrueFaced: Trust God and Others with Who You Really Are: Experience Edition* (NavPress, 2004), 22, 134, 145.

3. Barbara Duguid, *Extravagant Grace: God's Glory Displayed in Our Weakness* (P&R, 2013), 26.

4. Henry Cloud, *When Your World Makes No Sense: Four Critical Decisions That Can Bring Hope and Direction into Your Life* (Nelson, 1990), 38.

5. J. Grant Howard, *The Trauma of Transparency: A Biblical Approach to Inter-Personal Communication* (Multnomah, 1979), 137.

CHAPTER ONE: Worrying About What Others Think

1. Edward T. Welch, *When People Are Big and God Is Small: Overcoming Peer Pressure, Codependency and the Fear of Man* (P&R, 1997), 182, 237.

2. Donald Miller, *Scary Close: Dropping the Act and Finding* True *Intimacy* (Nelson, 2014), 5.

3. Welch, *When People Are Big*, 16; Brene Brown, *Daring Greatly: How the Courage To Be Vulnerable Transforms the Way We Live, Love, Parent, and Lead* (Gotham-Penguin, 2012), 125.

4. Brene Brown, *I Thought It Was Just Me (but It Isn't): Making the Journey from "What Will People Think?" to "I Am Enough"* (Gotham-Penguin, 2007), 229.

5. Material in this and the previous paragraph is nicely covered in Welch, *When People Are Big*, 42-44.

6. Edward T. Welch, *Shame Interrupted: How God Lifts the Pain of Worthlessness and Rejection* (New Growth, 2012), 272.

7. Welch, *Shame*, 278.

8. Ibid., 277.

9. Wayne A. Mack, *Your Family God's Way: Developing and Sustaining Relationships in the Home* (P&R, 1991), 86.

10. Welch, *When People Are Big*, 135.

11. Ibid., 40.

12. Welch, *Shame*, 209, 278.

13. Ibid., 48.

CHAPTER TWO: Perfectionism

1. *Merriam-Webster's Collegiate Dictionary*, 11th Edition (Merriam-Webster, 2004).

2. Brene Brown, *The Gifts of Imperfection: Let Go of Who You Think You're Supposed To Be and Embrace Who You Are* (Hazelden, 2010), 56, 24.

3. William Hendriksen, *Exposition of Philippians* (Baker, 1962), 161; *ESV Study Bible* (Crossway, 2008), 2285.

4. *ESV Study Bible*, 2430.

5. Brown, *Gifts*, 57.

6. Ibid., 56.

7. Brene Brown, *I Thought It Was Just Me (but It Isn't): Making the Journey from "What Will People Think?" to "I Am Enough"* (Gotham-Penguin, 2007), 147.

8. Robert L. Thomas, ed., *New American Standard Exhaustive Concordance of the Bible*, with Hebrew -Aramaic and Greek Dictionaries (Holman, 1981) 1687.

9. R. T. France, *The Gospel According to Matthew: An Introduction and Commentary* (Inter-Varsity, 1985), 129; see also William Hendriksen, *Exposition of the Gospel According to Matthew* (Baker, 1973), 317.

10. Reinier Schippers, *telos*, in *The New International Dictionary of New Testament Theology*, ed. Colin Brown (Zondervan, 1971), vol. 2, 59-65.

11. J. Grant Howard, *The Trauma of Transparency: A Biblical Approach to Inter-Personal Communication* (Portland: Multnomah, 1979), 41.

CHAPTER THREE: Rivalry and Blame-Shifting

1. Leon Morris, *Luke: An Introduction and Commentary* (Inter-Varsity, 1988), 290.

2. Dietrich Bonhoeffer, *Life Together*, trans. John W. Doberstein (Harper, 1954), 90-91.

3. Timothy Keller, *The Freedom of Self-Forgetfulness: The Path to True Christian Joy* (10Publishing, 2012), 35.

4. J. Grant Howard, *The Trauma of Transparency: A Biblical Approach to Inter-Personal Communication* (Multnomah, 1979), 26, 30.

5. Philip Graham Ryken, *Exodus: Saved for God's Glory* (Crossway, 2005), 1002-3; the quote that begins "when he reaches . . . " is Brevard Childs, quoted in Ryken, 1003.

6. Edward T. Welch, *When People Are Big and God Is Small: Overcoming Peer Pressure, Codependency and the Fear of Man* (P&R, 1997), 74.

7. Phillips Brooks, quoted in Ryken, *Exodus*, 1005.

CHAPTER FOUR: School and Cool

1. Cathy Guisewite, *The Collected Cathy: A 2-in-1 Volume Including: Another Saturday Night of Wild Abandon and A Mouthful of Breath Mints and No One to Kiss* (Andrews and McMeel, 1982), 89.

2. The 85% figure is from Brene Brown, *Daring Greatly: How the Courage To Be Vulnerable Transforms the Way We Live, Love, Parent, and Lead* (Gotham-Penguin, 2012), 189-90; the rest of the quoted material here is taken from Brown's *I Thought It Was Just Me (but It Isn't): Making the Journey from "What Will People Think?" to "I Am Enough"* (Gotham-Penguin, 2007), xxiv, 246.

3. Brene Brown, *The Gifts of Imperfection: Let Go of Who You Think You're Supposed To Be and Embrace Who You Are* (Hazelden, 2010), 2.

4. Ibid., 121; and Brown, *Daring*, 167-70.

5. Brown, *Daring*, 138.

6. Brown, *Just Me*, 175; and Brown, *Daring*, 26.

7. Brown, *Just Me*, 204-5; and Brown, *Gifts*, 84. For a telling encomium on living in the realm of the ordinary, see also Michael Horton's *Ordinary: Sustainable Faith in a Radical, Restless World* (Zondervan, 2014).

8. Barbara Duguid, *Extravagant Grace: God's Glory Displayed in Our Weakness* (P&R, 2013), 75.

9. Dwight L. Carlson, *Why Do Christians Shoot Their Wounded? Helping (Not Hurting) Those with Emotional Difficulties* (IVP, 1994), 134.

CHAPTER FIVE: Self-Preservation

1. *Merriam-Webster's Collegiate Dictionary,* 11th Edition (Merriam-Webster, 2004).

2. J. D. Douglass, ed., *New Bible Dictionary*, 2nd ed. (Inter-Varsity, 1982), 966.

3. Edward T. Welch, *Side by Side: Walking with Others in Wisdom and Love* (Crossway, 2015), 15.

4. Paul David Tripp, "In Need of Help," *Wednesday's Word*, 21 August 2013, http://www.paultripp.com/wednesdays-word/posts/in-need-of-help-devo (accessed 7 Sept. 2016).

5. Welch, *Side by Side*, 60.

6. Henry Cloud and John Townsend, *Safe People: How to Find Relationships That Are Good for You and Avoid Those That Aren't* (Zondervan, 1995), 128-29.

7. Tripp, "In Need."

8. Lauren Slater, "The Trouble with Self-Esteem," 3 Feb. 2003, *New York Times Magazine*, http://www.nytimes.com/2002/02/03/magazine/the-trouble-with-self-esteem.html?pagewanted=all (accessed 15 August 2016). Information from this piece is used throughout the current chapter.

9. *The Confession of Faith and Catechisms: The Westminster Confession of Faith and Catechisms as Adopted by the Orthodox Presbyterian Church*, with Proof Texts (The Committee on Christian Education of the OPC, 2005), 26-28.

10. C. S. Lewis, *Mere Christianity* (Macmillan, 1978), 114.

CHAPTER SIX: Sanctification

1. Nathaniel Hawthorne, *The Scarlet Letter* (Signet, 2009), 205-6.

2. John Powell, *Why Am I Afraid To Tell You Whom I Am? Insights on Self-Awareness, Personal Growth and Interpersonal Communication* (Argus, 1969), 80, 5-9.

3. Paul Tournier, *The Meaning of Persons*, trans. Edwin Hudson (Harper, 1957), 68-69, 98.

4. J. Grant Howard, *The Trauma of Transparency: A Biblical Approach to Inter-Personal Communication* (Multnomah, 1979), 219.

5. Richard Baxter, *A Christian Directory: The Practical Works of Richard Baxter* (Soli Deo Gloria, 1990), 896.

6. Dietrich Bonhoeffer, *Life Together*, trans. John W. Doberstein (Harper, 1954), 116-17.

7. Edward T. Welch, *Shame Interrupted: How God Lifts the Pain of Worthlessness and Rejection* (New Growth, 2012), 18, 209.

8. Brene Brown, *The Gifts of Imperfection: Let Go of Who You Think You're Supposed To Be and Embrace Who You Are* (Hazelden, 2010), 9-10.

9. Bonhoeffer, *Life Together*, 112.

10. Bill Thrall, Bruce McNicol, and John Lynch, *TrueFaced: Trust God and Others with Who You Really Are: Experience Edition* (NavPress, 2004), 106.

CHAPTER SEVEN: One Body

1. Quoted in Wayne A. Mack, *Your Family God's Way: Developing and Sustaining Relationships in the Home* (P&R, 1991), 134.

2. Henry Cloud and John Townsend, *Safe People: How to Find Relationships That Are Good for You and Avoid Those That Aren't* (Zondervan, 1995), 170-72.

3. Larry Crabb, *Becoming a True Spiritual Community: A Profound Vision of What the Church Can Be* (Nelson, 1999), 32-33.

4. Ibid., 46-48, 179.

5. Larry Crabb, *Inside Out* (NavPress, 2007), 109.

6. Welch, *Side by Side*, 15.

7. Donald Miller, *Scary Close: Dropping the Act and Finding* True *Intimacy* (Nelson, 2014), 158.

8. Bill Thrall, Bruce McNicol, and John Lynch, *TrueFaced: Trust God and Others with Who You Really Are: Experience Edition* (NavPress, 2004), 95.

9. Larry Crabb, *Real Church: Does It Exist? Can I Find It?* (Nelson, 2009), 60.

10. Thrall, McNicol,and Lynch, *TrueFaced*, 96.

CHAPTER EIGHT: Real Intimacy

1. Arthur W. Pink, quoted in Wayne A. Mack, *Your Family God's Way: Developing and Sustaining Relationships in the Home* (P&R, 1991), 136.

2. Brene Brown, *Daring Greatly: How the Courage To Be Vulnerable Transforms the Way We Live, Love, Parent, and Lead* (Gotham-Penguin, 2012), 34,104.

3. Bill Thrall, Bruce McNicol, and John Lynch, *TrueFaced: Trust God and Others with Who You Really Are: Experience Edition* (NavPress, 2004), 87, 30.

4. Material in this paragraph and the previous one is taken from Henry Cloud and John Townsend, *Safe People: How to Find Relationships That Are Good for You and Avoid Those That Aren't* (Zondervan, 1995), 28-29, 36.

5. Paul Tournier, *The Meaning of Persons*, trans. Edwin Hudson (Harper, 1957), 158.

6. Larry Crabb, *Real Church: Does It Exist? Can I Find It?* (Nelson, 2009), 60, 66, 61; Crabb also inspired the following sentence about worshiping with those we know best—see Crabb, *Becoming a True Spiritual Community: A Profound Vision of What the Church Can Be* (Nelson, 1999), xiv.

7. Cloud and Townsend, *Safe People*, 36.

CHAPTER NINE: The Virtue of Weakness

1. *ESV Study Bible* (Crossway, 2008), 2238.

2. Ibid.

3. Philip Edgcumbe Hughes, *The Second Epistle to the Corinthians: The English Text with Introduction, Exposition and Notes* (Eerdmans, 1962), 451.

4. Charles Hodge, *A Commentary on 1 & 2 Corinthians* (Banner of Truth, 2000), 665.

5. Donald Miller, *Scary Close: Dropping the Act and Finding* True *Intimacy* (Nelson, 2014), 45; Henry Cloud and John Townsend, *Safe People: How to Find Relationships That Are Good for You and Avoid Those That Aren't* (Zondervan, 1995), 67; Bill Thrall, Bruce McNicol, and John Lynch, *TrueFaced: Trust God and Others with Who You Really Are: Experience Edition* (NavPress, 2004), 113. The last of these four quotes is from Edward T. Welch, *Side by Side: Walking with Others in Wisdom and Love* (Crossway, 2015), 12, 45, 151.

6. Barbara Duguid, *Extravagant Grace: God's Glory Displayed in Our Weakness* (P&R, 2013), 30-32.

7. Ibid., 144.

8. Edward T. Welch, *Shame Interrupted: How God Lifts the Pain of Worthlessness and Rejection* (New Growth, 2012), 33.

CHAPTER TEN: Rest and Reassurance

1. Brene Brown, *Daring Greatly: How the Courage To Be Vulnerable Transforms the Way We Live, Love, Parent, and Lead* (Gotham-Penguin, 2012), 82.

2. Wayne A. Mack, *Your Family God's Way: Developing and Sustaining Relationships in the Home* (P&R, 1991), 81.

3. Brene Brown, *I Thought It Was Just Me (but It Isn't): Making the Journey from "What Will People Think?" to "I Am Enough"* (Gotham-Penguin, 2007), 107.

4. Lynn Hirschberg, "Who Can Justify Her Love?", *Vanity Fair* 4 April 1991, at *UltraMadonna.com* http://www.ultramadonna.com/en/articles/17/who_can_justify_her_love/view/3#ixzz4J0j4M00 (accessed 1 Sept. 2016).

5. A. W. Tozer, *The Pursuit of God* (Christian, 1948), 112-16.

6. Henry Cloud and John Townsend, *Safe People: How to Find Relationships That Are Good for You and Avoid Those That Aren't* (Zondervan, 1995), 50; Dietrich Bonhoeffer, *Life Together*, trans. John W. Doberstein (Harper, 1954), 116-17.

CHAPTER ELEVEN: Believing the Gospel

1. *The Confession of Faith and Catechisms: The Westminster Confession of Faith and Catechisms as Adopted by the Orthodox Presbyterian Church*, with Proof Texts (The Committee on Christian Education of the OPC, 2005), 26-28.

2. Stephen J. Cole, "Lesson 39: Who Is This Wretched Man? (Romans 7:14-25, Overview)," 2001, *Bible.org*, https://bible.org/seriespage/lesson-39-who-wretched-man-romans-714-25-overview (accessed 4 Oct. 2016).

3. *The Reformation Study Bible*, ed. R. C. Sproul (Ligonier, 2005), 1042; *ESV Study Bible* (Crossway, 2008), 1755.

4. Dietrich Bonhoeffer, *Life Together*, trans. John W. Doberstein (Harper, 1954), 97.

5. Donald Guthrie, *The Letter to the Hebrews: An Introduction and Commentary* (Inter-Varsity, 1999), 118.

6. Philip Edgcumbe Hughes, *A Commentary on the Epistle to the Hebrews* (Eerdmans, 1987), 166-68.

7. J. Grant Howard, *The Trauma of Transparency: A Biblical Approach to Inter-Personal Communication* (Multnomah, 1979), 105.

8. Edward T. Welch, *Side by Side: Walking with Others in Wisdom and Love* (Crossway, 2015), 46-47.

9. Paul Tournier, *The Meaning of Persons*, trans. Edwin Hudson (Harper, 1957), 164.

10. Bill Thrall, Bruce McNicol, and John Lynch, *TrueFaced: Trust God and Others with Who You Really Are: Experience Edition* (NavPress, 2004), 99.

11. Iain M. Duguid, *The Song of Songs: An Introduction and Commentary* (Downers Grove: Inter-Varsity, 2015), 93.

12. R. C. Sproul, "The Practice of Love," in *Developing Christian Character* (audio series, Ligonier Ministries, 2016).

13. *Reformation Study Bible*, 1822; Dick Lucas and Christopher Green, *The Message of 2 Peter & Jude: The Promise of His Coming* (Inter-Varsity, 1995), 99.

14. Edward T. Welch, *When People Are Big and God Is Small: Overcoming Peer Pressure, Codependency and the Fear of Man* (P&R, 1997), 151.

15. Philip Edgcumbe Hughes, *The Second Epistle to the Corinthians: The English Text with Introduction, Exposition and Notes* (Eerdmans, 1962), 214.

16. Peter Scazzero, with Warren Bird, *The Emotionally Healthy Church: A Strategy for Discipleship That Actually Changes Lives,* Updated and Expanded Edition (Zondervan, 2010), 85.

CHAPTER TWELVE: Dying to Self

1. John Nolland, *The Gospel of Matthew: A Commentary on the Greek Text* (Eerdmans, 2005), 691; *The Reformation Study Bible*, ed. R. C. Sproul (Ligonier, 2005), 1388.

2. Steve Brown, *Hidden Agendas: Dropping the Masks That Keep Us Apart* (New Growth, 2016), 82.

3. Both this quote and the previous one are from Dietrich Bonhoeffer, *Life Together*, trans. John W. Doberstein (Harper, 1954), 95-96, 114.

4. David E. Garland, *1 Corinthians* (Baker, 2003), 128.

5. Timothy Keller, *The Freedom of Self-Forgetfulness: The Path to True Christian Joy* (10Publishing, 2012), 25-28.

6. Gordon D. Fee, *The First Epistle to the Corinthians* (Eerdmans, 1987), 161.

7. Edward T. Welch, *Shame Interrupted: How God Lifts the Pain of Worthlessness and Rejection* (New Growth, 2012), 275.

8. Andrew Murray, *Humility* (N.p.: Fig, 2012), 46.

9. Jack Miller et al., *Sonship: A Sixteen Tape Set* (World Harvest Mission, 1997).

10. Edward T. Welch, *What Do You Think of Me? Why Do I Care?: Answers to the Big Questions of Life* (New Growth, 2011), 131-32.

CHAPTER THIRTEEN: Accepting Limitations

1. Peter Scazzero, with Warren Bird, *The Emotionally Healthy Church: A Strategy for Discipleship That Actually Changes Lives,* Updated and Expanded Edition (Zondervan, 2010), 145.

2. Ibid., 157.

3. Ibid., 143.

4. Ibid., 153.

5. Ibid., 145.

6. Dwight L. Carlson, *Why Do Christians Shoot Their Wounded? Helping (Not Hurting) Those with Emotional Difficulties* (IVP, 1994), 143-44.

7. Scazzero, *Emotionally Healthy Church*, 149-50.

8. Ibid., 156-57.

9. Edward T. Welch, *Shame Interrupted: How God Lifts the Pain of Worthlessness and Rejection* (New Growth, 2012), 265.

10. Scazzero, *Emotionally Healthy Church*, 152.

CHAPTER FOURTEEN: Seeing Transparency in Scripture

1. Douglas J. Moo, *The Letter of James: An Introduction and Commentary* (Inter-Varsity, 1985), 182; Joseph B. Mayor, *The Epistle of James* (Kregel, 1990), 545-46.

2. Bruce K. Waltke, *The Book of Proverbs: Chapters 15-31* (Eerdmans, 2005), 417.

3. "Acts 19," *Cambridge Bible for Schools and Colleges, BibleHub.com,* http://biblehub.com/commentaries/cambridge/acts/19.htm (accessed 10 August 2015); F. F. Bruce, *The Book of Acts,* revised edition (Eerdmans, 1988), 369.

4. Brene Brown, *The Gifts of Imperfection: Let Go of Who You Think You're Supposed To Be and Embrace Who You Are* (Hazelden, 2010), 8-9.

5. Iain Provan, *Ecclesiastes, Song of Songs* (Zondervan, 2001), 72.

6. Michael A. Eaton, *Ecclesiastes: An Introduction and Commentary* (Inter-Varsity, 1983), 67-68.

7. Provan, *Ecclesiastes*, 83.

8. *ESV Study Bible* (Crossway, 2008), 36.

9. Ibid., 1889; see also *New American Standard Bible: Study Edition* (Holman-Lippincott, 1975), 983-84, and Robert H. Stein, *Mark* (Baker, 2008), 1-5.

10. R. Alan Cole, *The Gospel According to Mark: An Introduction and Commentary* (Inter-Varsity, 1989), 308.

11. Stein, *Mark*, 691-92.

12. *ESV Study Bible*, 1031; Marvin E. Tate, *Psalms 51-100* (Dallas: Word, 1990), 274.

13. *ESV Study Bible*, 1066.

14. Ibid., 1038.

15. J. Todd Billings, "Lament: Self-Indulgent Whining, or Faithful Complaints? [Part 1]," February 2015, *Reformation 21*, http://www.reformation21.org/articles/lament-selfindulgent-whining-or-faithful-complaints.php (accessed 26 Mar. 2015).

16. *The Reformation Study Bible*, ed. R. C. Sproul (Ligonier, 2005), 1311; F. F. Bruce, *Habakkuk*, in *The Minor Prophets: An Exegetical Exposition and Commentary* (vol. 2: Obadiah, Jonah, Micah, Nahum, Habakkuk), ed. Thomas Edward McComiskey (Baker, 1993), 835.

17. J. A. Thompson, *The Book of Jeremiah* (Eerdmans, 1980), 459.

18. R. K. Harrison, *Jeremiah and Lamentations: An Introduction and Commentary* (Inter-Varsity, 1973), 114.

19. Thompson, *Jeremiah*, 458.

20. Francis I. Andersen, *Job: An Introduction and Commentary* (Inter-Varsity, n.d.), 109.

21. Ibid., 100, 68.

22. Ibid., 108-9; see also *ESV Study Bible*, 895.

23. *ESV Study Bible*, 890-91, 933.

24. Andersen, *Job*, 99, 109, 129; *ESV Study Bible*, 877.

25. *Reformation Study Bible*, 691.

26. Andersen, *Job*, 66.

27. *ESV Study Bible*, 1032; Bruce, *Habakkuk*, 844-45.

CHAPTER FIFTEEN: Looking at Biblical Case Studies

1. "Penitential Psalms," *Wikipedia*, 2 Jan. 2016, https://en.wikipedia.org/wiki/Penitential_Psalms (accessed 3 Oct. 2016).

2. *ESV Study Bible* (Crossway, 2008), 534; see also *New American Standard Bible: Study Edition* (Holman-Lippincott, 1975), 937.

3. Peter C. Craigie, *Psalms 1-50* (Word, 1983), 266-67.

4. Matthew Henry, *Matthew Henry's Commentary on the Whole Bible*, vol. 3: Job to Song of Solomon (McLean: MacDonald, n.d.), 433.

5. Derek Kidner, *Psalms 1-72: An Introduction and Commentary on Books I and II of the Psalms* (Inter-Varsity, 1973), 190-91; *The Reformation Study Bible*, ed. R. C. Sproul (Ligonier, 2005), 782.

6. Kidner, *Psalms*, 155.

7. Ibid., 62.

8. Marvin E. Tate, *Psalms 51-100* (Word, 1990), 127.

9. *ESV Study Bible*, 1012; Kidner, *Psalms*, 224-26.

10. Joseph W. Smith III, *Sex and Violence in the Bible: A Survey of Explicit Content in the Holy Book* (P&R, 2014), 29.

11. Dale Ralph Davis, *2 Samuel: Out of Every Adversity* (2002), 79.

12. David E. Garland, *1 Corinthians* (Baker, 2003), 85.

13. Wayne A. Mack, *Your Family God's Way: Developing and Sustaining Relationships in the Home* (P&R, 1991), 137.

14. *ESV Study Bible*, 2326; see also Denny Burk and Heath Lambert, *Transforming Homosexuality: What the Bible Says About Sexual Orientation and Change* (P&R, 2015), 108-9.

15. Peter Scazzero, with Warren Bird, *The Emotionally Healthy Church: A Strategy for Discipleship That Actually Changes Lives,* Updated and Expanded Edition (Zondervan, 2010), 122.

16. Quoted in Leon Morris, *The Epistle to the Romans* (Eerdmans, 1988), 291.

17. Quoted in Morris, *Romans*, 298.

18. Timothy Keller, *The Freedom of Self-Forgetfulness: The Path to True Christian Joy* (10Publishing, 2012), 30; see also Larry Crabb, *Becoming a True Spiritual Community: A Profound Vision of What the Church Can Be* (Nelson, 1999), 33; see also Brene Brown, *I Thought It Was Just Me (but It Isn't): Making the Journey from "What Will People Think?" to "I Am Enough"* (Gotham-Penguin, 2007), 65.

19. Philip Edgcumbe Hughes, *The Second Epistle to the Corinthians: The English Text with Introduction, Exposition and Notes* (Eerdmans, 1962), 239; Ralph P. Martin, *2 Corinthians* (Nelson, 1986) 185.

20. Robert L. Thomas, ed., *New American Standard Exhaustive Concordance of the Bible*, with Hebrew-Aramaic and Greek Dictionaries (Holman, 1981) 1655.

21. *ESV Study Bible*, 2023; *Reformation Study Bible*, 1512.

22. Robert H. Stein, *Mark* (Baker, 2008), 660; R. Alan Cole, *The Gospel According to Mark: An Introduction and Commentary* (Inter-Varsity, 1989), 296-97.

23. Smith, *Sex and Violence*, 99.

24. I. Howard Marshall, *The Gospel of Luke: A Commentary on the Greek Text* (Eerdmans, 1978), 832; Cole, *Mark*, 296; Dwight L. Carlson, *Why Do Christians Shoot Their Wounded? Helping (Not Hurting) Those with Emotional Difficulties* (IVP, 1994), 44; Scazzero, *Emotionally Healthy Church*, 33.

25. *The Confession of Faith and Catechisms: The Westminster Confession of Faith and Catechisms as Adopted by the Orthodox Presbyterian Church*, with Proof Texts (The Committee on Christian Education of the OPC, 2005), 357-58; James Boice, "How To Know the Will of God," *The Bible Study Hour, Oneplace.com*, n.d., http://www.oneplace.com/ministries/the-bible-study-hour/read/articles/how-to-know-the-will-of-god-11927.html (accessed 6 Oct. 2016).

26. "Chapters and Verses of the Bible," *Wikipedia*, 21 Nov. 2016, https://en.wikipedia.org/wiki/Chapters_and_verses_of_the_Bible (accessed 30 Nov. 2016).

27. David Allan Hubbard, *Hosea: An Introduction and Commentary* (Inter-Varsity, 1989), 192; J. Andrews Dearman, *The Book of Hosea* (Eerdmans, 2010), 289.

28. Dearman, *Hosea*, 287; Edward T. Welch, *When People Are Big and God Is Small: Overcoming Peer Pressure, Codependency and the Fear of Man* (P&R, 1997), 176-77.

29. Edward J. Young, *The Book of Isaiah: The English Text, with Introduction, Exposition, and Notes*, vol. 3 (Eerdmans, 1972), 285.

30. *ESV Study Bible*, 1739; David W. Baker, *Nahum, Habakkuk and Zephaniah: An Introduction and Commentary* (Inter-Varsity, 1988), 118-19.

31. Alec Motyer, *Zephaniah*, in *The Minor Prophets: An Exegetical Exposition and Commentary* (vol. 2: Obadiah, Jonah, Micah, Nahum, Habakkuk), ed. Thomas Edward McComiskey (Baker, 1993), 958.

CHAPTER SIXTEEN: Making It Work

1. Denny Burk and Heath Lambert, *Transforming Homosexuality: What the Bible Says About Sexual Orientation and Change* (P&R, 2015), 95-96.

2. Dietrich Bonhoeffer, *Life Together*, trans. John W. Doberstein (Harper, 1954), 116-17.

3. Nathaniel Hawthorne, *The Scarlet Letter* (Signet, 2009), 135-36, 246.

4. Steve Brown, *Hidden Agendas: Dropping the Masks That Keep Us Apart* (New Growth, 2016), 124.

5. *ESV Study Bible* (Crossway, 2008), 936; Peter C. Craigie, *Psalms 1-50* (Word, 1983), 32-33.

6. Larry Crabb, *Real Church: Does It Exist? Can I Find It?* (Nelson, 2009), 61; Wayne A. Mack, *Your Family God's Way: Developing and Sustaining Relationships in the Home* (P&R, 1991), 45.

7. J. Grant Howard, *The Trauma of Transparency: A Biblical Approach to Inter-Personal Communication* (Portland: Multnomah, 1979), 127.

8. Mack, *Your Family*, 45; Crabb, *Real Church*, 61.

9. Quoted in Carl Trueman, "What Luther Says to This Confessional Age," Oct. 2014, *Reformation21*, http://www.reformation21.org/articles/we-live-in-a-confessional.php (accessed 10 Oct. 2016).

10. Brett McCracken, "Has 'Authenticity' Trumped Holiness?", 26 Jan. 2014, *The Gospel Coalition,* https://www.thegospelcoalition.org/article/has-authenticity-trumped-holiness-2 (accessed 10 Oct. 2016).

11. Ibid.

12. For a hard-hitting elaboration of this truth, see C. S. Lewis, *The Problem of Pain* (Macmillan, 1978), 59-60.

13. Larry Crabb, *Becoming a True Spiritual Community: A Profound Vision of What the Church Can Be* (Nelson, 1999), 31.

14. Bill Thrall, Bruce McNicol, and John Lynch, *TrueFaced: Trust God and Others with Who You Really Are: Experience Edition* (NavPress, 2004), 70.

15. Edward T. Welch, *Side by Side: Walking with Others in Wisdom and Love* (Crossway, 2015), 67, 87-97.

16. Henry Cloud and John Townsend, *Safe People: How to Find Relationships That Are Good for You and Avoid Those That Aren't* (Zondervan, 1995), 145-46, 166.

17. Crabb, *Becoming*, 170-71, 198, 133.

18. Welch, *Side by Side*, 87.

19. Crabb, *Becoming*, 198.

20. Dwight L. Carlson, *Why Do Christians Shoot Their Wounded? Helping (Not Hurting) Those with Emotional Difficulties* (Downers Grove: IVP, 1994), 133.

21. Paul Tournier, *The Meaning of Persons*, trans. Edwin Hudson (Harper, 1957), 158.

22. Brene Brown, *I Thought It Was Just Me (but It Isn't): Making the Journey from "What Will People Think?" to "I Am Enough"* (Gotham-Penguin, 2007), 107.

23. Cloud and Townsend, *Safe People*, 167.

24. Crabb, *Becoming*, 46-48, 177-84.

25. Tournier, *Meaning*, 142-48.

CHAPTER SEVENTEEN: Exhorting and Rebuking

1. *The Confession of Faith and Catechisms: The Westminster Confession of Faith and Catechisms as Adopted by the Orthodox Presbyterian Church*, with Proof Texts (Willow Grove: The Committee on Christian Education of the OPC, 2005), 237.

2. Robert L. Thomas, ed., *New American Standard Exhaustive Concordance of the Bible*, with Hebrew-Aramaic and Greek Dictionaries (Holman, 1981) 1647, 1651-52, 1668, 1672.

3. This has been the widespread testimony of scholars writing on these passages; see Leon Morris, *1 and 2 Thessalonians: An Introduction and Commentary* (Inter-Varsity, 1984), 103-4; Richard N. Longenecker, *Galatians* (Nelson, 1990), 273; Philip Edgcumbe Hughes, *A Commentary on the Epistle to the Hebrews* (Eerdmans, 1987), 147; J. Grant Howard, *The Trauma of Transparency: A Biblical Approach to Inter-Personal Communication* (Multnomah, 1979), 186-87.

4. *ESV Study Bible* (Crossway, 2008), 242.

5. Dietrich Bonhoeffer, *Life Together*, trans. John W. Doberstein (Harper, 1954), 107.

6. Bruce K. Waltke, *The Book of Proverbs: Chapters 15-31* (Eerdmans, 2005), 375.

7. Hughes, *Hebrews*, 147.

8. Larry Crabb, *Inside Out* (NavPress, 2007), 181.

9. Dan B. Allender and Tremper Longman III, *Bold Love* (NavPress, 1992), 208, 58.

10. Edward T. Welch, *Side by Side: Walking with Others in Wisdom and Love* (Crossway, 2015), 135, 148.

11. Bonhoeffer, *Life Together*, 106.

12. Allender and Longman, *Bold Love*, 300; Welch, *Side by Side*, 138.

13. Allender and Longman, *Bold Love*, 301.

14. Ibid., 300.

15. Ibid., 303.

16. Crabb, *Inside Out*, 182-83.

17. Allender and Longman, 303.

18. Ibid., 304; Crabb, *Inside Out*, 183.

19. Jay E. Adams, *Handbook of Church Discipline* (Zondervan, 1986), 50-51.

20. Philip Graham Ryken, *Exodus: Saved for God's Glory* (Crossway, 2005), 1001.

21. Longenecker, *Galatians*, 272-74, 262; Thomas, *New American Standard Concordance*, 1677; William Hendriksen, *Exposition of Galatians* (Baker, 1968), 232-33.

22. Joseph W. Smith III, *Sex and Violence in the Bible: A Survey of Explicit Content in the Holy Book* (P&R, 2014), 84-85.

23. Colin G. Kruse, *The Second Epistle of Paul to the Corinthians: An Introduction and Commentary* (Inter-Varsity, 1999, 17-24; *The Reformation Study Bible*, ed. R. C. Sproul (Orlando: Ligonier, 2005), 1681; *ESV Study Bible*, 2219-20.

24. Kruse, *Corinthians*, 81, 145; *Reformation Study Bible*, 1681.

25. Philip Edgcumbe Hughes, *The Second Epistle to the Corinthians: The English Text with Introduction, Exposition and Notes* (Eerdmans, 1962), 268-70.

26. R. T. France, *The Gospel According to Matthew: An Introduction and Commentary* (Inter-Varsity, 1985), 274; John Nolland, *The Gospel of Matthew: A Commentary on the Greek Text* (Eerdmans, 2005), 744; William Hendriksen, *Exposition of the Gospel According to Matthew* (Baker, 1973), 697-98.

27. Hendriksen, *Matthew*, 697.

28. Adams, *Handbook*, 70, 74; Hendriksen, *Matthew*, 700-701; *Reformation Study Bible*, 1390.

29. Adams, *Handbook*, 8.

30. Ibid., 32, 52.

31. Ibid., 32-33, 54-55; Hendriksen, *Matthew*, 699.

32. Hendriksen, *Matthew*, 698.

33. Adams, *Handbook*, 47.

34. *Confession of Faith and Catechisms*, 144.

35. Jane Austen, *Pride and Prejudice* (Bantam, 1981), 145.

36. Thornton Wilder, *Our Town: A Play in Three Acts* (Perennial, 1998), 71.

CHAPTER EIGHTEEN: Affirming and Praising

1. Leon Morris, *The Epistle to the Romans* (Eerdmans, 1988), 508-9.

2. Edward T. Welch, *Side by Side: Walking with Others in Wisdom and Love* (Crossway, 2015), 88-89, 93.

3. John Murray, *The Epistle to the Romans: The English Text with Introduction, Exposition and Notes* (Eerdmans, 1968), vol. 2, 231; Morris, *Romans*, 531.

4. G. Lloyd Carr, *The Song of Solomon: An Introduction and Commentary* (Inter-Varsity, 1984), 76.

5. Ibid., 139.

6. Iain Provan, *Ecclesiastes, Song of Songs* (Zondervan, 2001), 295, 326-27.

7. Jeffrey Hatcher and Mitch Albom, *Mitch Albom's Tuesdays with Morrie* (Dramatists Play Service), 21.

CHAPTER NINETEEN: Reacting to Transparency

1. David Kinnaman and Gabe Lyons, *unChristian: What a New Generation Really Thinks about Christianity . . . and Why It Matters* (Baker, 2007), 182.

2. Brene Brown, *I Thought It Was Just Me (but It Isn't): Making the Journey from "What Will People Think?" to "I Am Enough"* (Gotham-Penguin, 2007), 147-50.

3. Edward T. Welch, *Side by Side: Walking with Others in Wisdom and Love* (Crossway, 2015), 105.

4. Brene Brown, *The Gifts of Imperfection: Let Go of Who You Think You're Supposed To Be and Embrace Who You Are* (Hazelden, 2010), 10.

5. Welch, *Side by Side*, 147.

6. Brown, *Just Me*, 55; see also Brown, *Gifts*, 10-11.

7. Brown, *Gifts*, 10.

8. Paul Tournier, *The Meaning of Persons*, trans. Edwin Hudson (Harper, 1957), 192.

9. Larry Crabb, *Becoming a True Spiritual Community: A Profound Vision of What the Church Can Be* (Nelson, 1999), 15, 18.

10. Quoted in Carl Trueman, "What Luther Says to This Confessional Age," Oct. 2014, *Reformation21*, http://www.reformation21.org/articles/we-live-in-a-confessional.php (accessed 10 Oct. 2016).

11. Jay E. Adams, *Handbook of Church Discipline* (Zondervan, 1986), 32.

12. Welch, *Side by Side*, 162, 146-47.

13. Tournier, *Meaning of Persons*, 165.

14. "Charles Spurgeon Quotes," *AZQuotes*, http://www.azquotes.com/author/13978-Charles_Spurgeon (accessed 25 Oct. 2016).

15. Barbara Duguid, *Extravagant Grace: God's Glory Displayed in Our Weakness* (P&R, 2013), 215.

16. A. W. Tozer, *The Pursuit of God* (Harrisburg: Christian, 1948), 113.

17. Warren W. Wiersbe, ed., *The Best of A. W. Tozer: 52 Favorite Chapters* (Baker, 1978), 125.

18. J. Grant Howard, *The Trauma of Transparency: A Biblical Approach to Inter-Personal Communication* (Multnomah, 1979), 101-8.

19. Henry Cloud and John Townsend, *Safe People: How to Find Relationships That Are Good for You and Avoid Those That Aren't* (Zondervan, 1995), 35.

20. Andrew Murray, *Humility* (N.p.: Fig, 2012), 2, 41, 46-47.

21. Wiersbe, *Best of Tozer*, 123.

22. Ibid., 123-25.

23. Dietrich Bonhoeffer, *Life Together*, trans. John W. Doberstein (Harper, 1954), 106.

SELECT BIBLIOGRAPHY

Adams, Jay E. *Handbook of Church Discipline.* Zondervan, 1986.

Allender, Dan B., and Tremper Longman III. *Bold Love.* NavPress, 1992.

Billings, J. Todd. "Lament: Self-Indulgent Whining, or Faithful Complaints? [Part 1]." February 2015. *Reformation 21.* 26 Mar. 2015. http://www.reformation21.org/articles/lament-selfindulgent-whining-or-faithful-complaints.php.

Bonhoeffer, Dietrich. *Life Together.* Trans. John W. Doberstein. Harper, 1954.

Brown, Brene. *Daring Greatly: How the Courage To Be Vulnerable Transforms the Way We Live, Love, Parent, and Lead.* Gotham-Penguin, 2012.

---. *The Gifts of Imperfection: Let Go of Who You Think You're Supposed To Be and Embrace Who You Are.* Hazelden, 2010.

---. *I Thought It Was Just Me (but It Isn't): Making the Journey from "What Will People Think?" to "I Am Enough."* Gotham-Penguin, 2007.

Brown, Steve. *Hidden Agendas: Dropping the Masks That Keep Us Apart.* New Growth, 2016.

Burk, Denny, and Heath Lambert. *Transforming Homosexuality: What the Bible Says About Sexual Orientation and Change.* P&R, 2015.

Carlson, Dwight L., M.D. *Why Do Christians Shoot Their Wounded? Helping (Not Hurting) Those with Emotional Difficulties.* IVP, 1994.

Cloud, Henry, and John Townsend. *Safe People: How to Find Relationships That Are Good for You and Avoid Those That Aren't.* Zondervan, 1995.

The Confession of Faith and Catechisms: The Westminster Confession of Faith and Catechisms as Adopted by the Orthodox Presbyterian Church. With Proof Texts. The Committee on Christian Education of the OPC, 2005.

Crabb, Larry. *Becoming a True Spiritual Community: A Profound Vision of What the Church Can Be.* Nelson, 1999.

---. *Inside Out.* NavPress, 2007.

---. *Real Church: Does It Exist? Can I Find It?* Nelson, 2009.

Duguid, Barbara. *Extravagant Grace: God's Glory Displayed in Our Weakness.* P&R, 2013.

ESV Study Bible. Crossway, 2008.

Howard, J. Grant. *The Trauma of Transparency: A Biblical Approach to Inter-Personal Communication.* Multnomah, 1979.

Keller, Timothy. *The Freedom of Self-Forgetfulness: The Path to True Christian Joy.* 10Publishing, a division of 10ofthose.com, 2012.

Kinnaman, David, and Gabe Lyons. *unChristian: What a New Generation Really Thinks about Christianity . . . and Why It Matters.* Baker, 2007.

Lane, Timothy S., and Paul David Tripp. *Relationships: A Mess Worth Making.* New Growth, 2008.

Mack, Wayne A. *Your Family God's Way: Developing and Sustaining Relationships in the Home.* P&R, 1991.

McCracken, Brett. "Has 'Authenticity' Trumped Holiness?" 26 Jan. 2014. *The Gospel Coalition.* 10 Oct. 2016. https://www.thegospelcoalition.org/article/has-authenticity-trumped-holiness-2.

Miller, Donald. *Scary Close: Dropping the Act and Finding* True *Intimacy.* Nelson, 2014.

Miller, Jack, et al. *Sonship: A Sixteen Tape Set.* World Harvest Mission. Jenkintown, 1997.

Miller, Rose Marie. *From Fear to Freedom: Living as Sons and Daughters of God.* Shaw, 1994.

Murray, Andrew. *Humility.* Fig, 2012.

Powell, John. *Why Am I Afraid To Tell You Whom I Am? Insights on Self-Awareness, Personal Growth and Interpersonal Communication.* Argus, 1969.

The Reformation Study Bible. Ed. R. C. Sproul. Ligonier, 2005.

Scazzero, Peter, with Warren Bird. *The Emotionally Healthy Church: A Strategy for Discipleship That Actually Changes Lives.* Updated and Expanded Edition. Zondervan, 2010.

Simmons, Rachel. *Odd Girl Out: The Hidden Culture of Aggression in Girls.* Harvest-Harcourt, 2002.

Slater, Lauren. "The Trouble with Self-Esteem." 3 Feb. 2003. *New York Times Magazine.* 15 Aug. 2016. http://www.nytimes.com/2002/02/03/magazine/the-trouble-with-self-esteem.html?pagewanted=all.

Thomas, Robert L., ed., New *American Standard Exhaustive Concordance of the Bible.* With Hebrew-Aramaic and Greek Dictionaries. Holman, 1981.

Thrall, Bill, Bruce McNicol, and John Lynch. *TrueFaced: Trust God and Others with Who You Really Are: Experience Edition.* NavPress, 2004.

Tournier, Paul. *The Meaning of Persons.* Trans. Edwin Hudson. Harper, 1957.

Tozer, A. W. *The Pursuit of God.* Christian, 1948.

Tripp, Paul David. "In Need of Help." *Wednesday's Word* blog. 21 August 2013. http://www.paultripp.com/wednesdays-word/posts/in-need-of-help-devo.

Trueman, Carl. "What Luther Says to This Confessional Age." Oct. 2014. *Reformation21*. 10 Oct. 2016. http://www.reformation21.org/articles/we-live-in-a-confessional.php.

Welch, Edward T. *Shame Interrupted: How God Lifts the Pain of Worthlessness and Rejection.* New Growth, 2012.

---. *Side by Side: Walking with Others in Wisdom and Love.* Crossway, 2015.

---. *What Do You Think of Me? Why Do I Care?: Answers to the Big Questions of Life.* New Growth, 2011.

---. *When People Are Big and God Is Small: Overcoming Peer Pressure, Codependency and the Fear of Man.* P&R, 1997.

Wiseman, Rosalind. *Masterminds and Wingmen: Helping Out Boys Cope with Schoolyard Power, Locker-Room Tests, Girlfriends, and the New Rules of Boy World.* Harmony, 2013.

---. *Queen Bees and Wannabes: Helping Your Daughter Survive Cliques, Gossip, Boyfriends, an Other Realities of Adolescence.* Three Rivers, 2002.

Yancey, Philip. *Soul Survivor: How My Faith Survived the Church.* Doubleday, 2001.